Digital Literacy for Technical Communication

Digital Literacy for Technical Communication is designed to help technical communicators make better sense of technology's impact on their work, so they can identify new ways to adapt, adjust, and evolve, fulfilling their own professional potential. This collection is comprised of three sections, each designed to explore answers to these questions:

- How has technical communication work changed in response to the current (digital) writing environment?
- What is important, foundational knowledge in our field that all technical communicators need to learn?
- How can we revise past theories or develop new ones to better understand how technology has transformed our work?

Bringing together highly-regarded specialists in digital literacy, this anthology will serve as an indispensible resource for scholars, students, and practitioners. It illuminates technology's impact on their work and prepares them to respond to the constant changes and challenges in the new digital universe.

Rachel Spilka is Associate Professor at the University of Wisconsin-Milwaukee. Her current research interests are in re-examining audience and defining, from the perspective of students, promising strategies for achieving greater diversity in academic programs in the field. Over the past thirty years, she has interspersed academic positions with work in industry, including serving as manager of the Society for Technical Communication (STC) Research Grants Committee and Ken Rainey Excellence in Research Award Committee. Her previous edited volumes *Writing in the Workplace: New Research Perspectives* (Southern Illinois University Press, 1993) and, with Barbara Mirel, *Reshaping Technical Communication: New Directions for the 21st Century* (Erlbaum, 2003) both received the Best Edited Collection Award in Scientific and Technical Communication from the National Council of Teachers of English (NCTE).

Digital Literacy for Technical Communication

21st Century Theory and Practice

Edited by Rachel Spilka

Routledge
Taylor & Francis Group

NEW YORK AND LONDON

First published 2010
by Routledge
270 Madison Ave, New York, NY 10016

Simultaneously published in the UK
by Routledge
2 Park Square, Milton Park, Abingdon, Oxon OX14 4RN

Routledge is an imprint of the Taylor & Francis Group, an informa business

© 2010 Taylor & Francis

Typeset in Sabon by
HWA Text and Data Management, London
Printed and bound in the United States of America on acid-free paper by
Edwards Brothers, Inc

Library of Congress Cataloging in Publication Data
Digital literacy for technical communication: 21st century theory and
practice / edited by Rachel Spilka.
      p. cm.
   Includes index.
   Communication of technical information. 2. Technical writing.
   3. Technical communication. 4. Internet literacy.
   I. Spilka, Rachel, 1953-T10.5.D55 2009
   601´.4–dc22   2009032368

ISBN10: 0-8058-5273-5 (hbk)
ISBN 10: 0-8058-5274-3 (pbk)
ISBN 10: 0-203-86611-8 (ebk)

ISBN 13: 978-0-8058-5273-8 (hbk)
ISBN 13: 978-0-8058-5274-5 (pbk)
ISBN 13: 978-0-203-86611-5 (ebk)

Contents

Foreword

JoAnn T. Hackos

I am the proud new owner of a Kindle, purchased in the first quarter of 2009. After reading about the usability problems of the first version, I waited until the reviews of the second version indicated that user friendliness had significantly improved[1]. As I write this Foreword, I have purchased three books for the device, an autobiography of Alexander Hamilton, a detective mystery, and a scientific text for my husband. I have also downloaded a sample section of a travel book that I'm considering. My initial reasons for the purchase were to reduce the weight of the case I lug through airports and lift to stash in the overhead storage bins; take more books with me than I could easily carry, especially the 4- to 5-pound biographies I enjoy; depart from my professional and personal world of printed books; and extend the experience I started more than 30 years ago with mainframe, desktop, and laptop computers, 15 years ago with the Internet, and most recently with an iPhone.

My literary friends are both aghast and curious. How could I, they ask, abandon a real book, with its familiar heft? Have I not succumbed to the siren song of the digital age, abandoning traditional values? They ask: Does it feel different reading on a small screen? Is the experience the same? Does using an intrusive technology somehow degrade the experience of immersing oneself in a text?

As the authors of this anthology clearly demonstrate, people who need technical information and communicators responsible for developing that information are both faced with a challenging new environment. They need to learn new methods for using technology in the workplace and using technology to deliver and receive information. In only the past 30 years, readers and writers have moved from a predominately print environment to one in which authoring, reading, and communicating take place through digital technologies. As with the introduction of any new technology, we see the familiar patterns outlined by Geoffrey Moore in *Crossing the Chasm* (1991). New technologies are first adopted by the innovators, those who are most adventurous and intrigued by everything different. The innovators and early adopters are followed by the early and late majorities, those who wait until the new technologies are more stable and reliable before accepting them. At the end of the technology adoption life cycle are the laggards, those who argue that traditional methods are best and who find ways to avoid change.

Today, digital technologies for the development of content seem well established among the early and late majorities. Technical communicators were quick to adopt word processing and desktop publishing in the 1980s because the advantages over writing with pen and paper or even with a typewriter were clearly persuasive. More recent introductions of XML authoring are still in the early adopter stage, not quite ready to cross the chasm into the majority. Part of the resistance to computer-mediated structured authoring, like XML and the Darwin Information Typing Architecture (DITA),[2] appears to be based not so much on the technology (which seems simple enough to learn) but on a cultural change that the technology demands and fosters.

The cultural change required of technical communicators is a product of cost-reduction strategies developed in a competitive business environment. Certainly, word processing and desktop publishing were instituted to reduce the costs of authoring, but to technical communicators, they appeared to enhance their ability to create attractive, useful, and unique information. Content management, supported by technologies like XML and content management databases, strives to reduce costs by emphasizing the standardization of content and the interdependencies among closely related content chunks. For an organization and its management to succeed in reducing costs through content management, technical communicators must adhere to standards and work in highly collaborative environments. Whereas once technical communicators could work independently, following only those standards that they agreed with, content management technologies now require communicators to work collectively and to submit their work to constant review for compliance with standards.

Communicators are also affected by the changes that technology has made in the delivery of information to users. Early use of digital media meant embedding help text in computer software and adding printable formats first to CD-ROMs and then to Web sites. Now the digital media are much more varied and more unlike traditional print publications. Yet, technical communicators have been slow to adopt newer forms, in part because of political barriers. Technology specialists who are distant from and often antagonistic toward technical communicators often control Web sites that are best supported by topic-based, HTML-formatted content.

When communicators can exert influence on the presentation of Web site content, then it is more likely that hypertext modes of delivery are supported, even encouraged. Hypertext provides a richer environment than the standard PDF format, including links to relevant content, interactive graphics, video, and the possibilities of customization and personalization. Yet, producing rich content requires new skills using multiple media that technical communication organizations, flattened by years of reductions in force, frequently lack.

Social media for content dissemination and collaboration is intriguing to technical communicators, especially those innovative enough to have personal experience with new social-communication environments like Facebook and Twitter. However, information-development management has taken only tentative steps toward using Web 2.0 technologies. A recent survey conducted by The Center for Information-Development Management (CIDM)[3] showed that managers are interested but cautious. They foresee liability problems for content that has not been reviewed by subject-matter experts. They wonder how to encourage knowledgeable users to contribute regularly through blogs and wikis. They are suspicious of innovations that might lead to the demise of their departments.

At the same time, managers acknowledge that expertise among user communities regarding the use of products is often superior to expertise available inside the organization. They know that expert users prefer to communicate with one another through user groups and other resources. They acknowledge that many other groups in the organization are developing content and sending it to external users. As a result, they have begun to take tentative steps in the direction of social media and collaborative content development.

Digital Literacy for Technical Communication provides you with new ways to think about the development of content by providing insights into the challenges of audience analysis, structured authoring, cross-cultural communication, content management, and information design. Here you will gain a better understanding of the nature of your interactions with technology and how those technologies have changed and continue to change the nature of the workplace. You also are asked to consider how your role as a communicator and an information developer is changing significantly enough to be referred to as a "seismic shift."

The authors argue throughout that the roles and responsibilities of technical communicators are changing rapidly—in some cases for the worse. The focus on producing "books" by individual authors working independently is rapidly coming to an end. Authors can no longer expect to work in isolation from others in the organization or from the user community. No threat is implied, though: the new ways of working, supported by new technologies, are liberating as well as challenging.

By the way, I am thinking about purchasing a Kindle for my 91-year-old mother. She uses audio books for the blind but they rarely have the biographies and story types that she prefers. Kindle provides an audio text with an artificial speaking voice that's actually pretty good. With this new technology, I could send her books that she would most enjoy and that we once could read together. Is it possible that someone in the ninth decade of her life can adapt to a new technology if the benefits are sufficient and accessible? We'll see.

Notes

1 For an interesting discussion of possibly profound ways that e-books will change our reading and writing habits, see S. Johnson, April 20, 2009.
2 See http://dita.xml.org for information about DITA.
3 See http://www.infomanagementcenter.com for more information.

References

Center for Information-Development Management (2009). Retrieved from http://www.infomanagementcenter.com.

Johnson, S. (2009, April 20). How the e-book will change the way we read and write. *Wall Street Journal*, p. R1.

Moore, G. (1991). *Crossing the chasm*. New York: HarperBusiness.

Preface

This book is designed to be relevant and useful for technical communication practitioners, students, and educators. The collection's central purpose is to help current and future technical communicators better understand how the nature of their work—and their potential contributions to industry—have changed dramatically in the new digital environment of modern work.

The anthology starts off by describing the transformative impact that digital literacy has had on the field of technical communication and on the work of technical communicators.

The first two chapters both aim to assist both newcomers to the field and veterans in catching up or keeping up with the profound implications that technology has had on technical communication's potential value and contributions to industry.

The next three chapters of this collection suggest that three new areas of knowledge—the rhetoric of technology, information design, and content management—should now constitute fundamental knowledge in the field, or supplement what the field now considers to be core areas of learning. The authors of these chapters summarize these areas of knowledge, but also point to ways that technical communicators might use this new knowledge to alter their own perceptions, and to construct powerful arguments in industry, regarding the nature and status of their work now and in the future.

The final four chapters in this anthology can serve as models to the field in demonstrating the value of adjusting theories in the field to the realities of the new digital environment of our work. Here, authors illustrate new ways to either explore new theoretical directions (in cultural and cross-cultural theories) or update traditional theories (in audience and ethics) to reflect a better understanding of workplace writing in the new digital work environment. Modernizing theories in the field will be important, this collection suggests, for moving technical communicators toward a better understanding of what it means, or what it takes, to contribute to the modern technology-driven workplace.

The Evolution of This Book

The idea for this book emerged from a sense of increasing uneasiness about the ability of practitioners and educators in the field to catch up, keep up, and understand necessary changes in their work resulting from the new pervasiveness of technology in work environments. While some of us embraced the new technology arising in the 1990s and proliferating even more dramatically in the 2000s, others of us found it challenging to grasp all that was new and different, and to determine which new directions we should take for our work to remain vital and significant. As early as 2002, I submitted a proposal for a book that aimed at that time to serve as an overview of central theories influencing the field of technical communication, and that would model strategies for applying or contextualizing those theories to practice. However, despite the merits of this type of volume to the field, at least in the future, I soon realized that the time was not right for such a book. Given the dramatic reversals and changes in the field in recent history and especially in the preceding few years, it became obvious, after careful thought, that any book attempting to canvass past and current theories in the field would have questionable merit for the field— simply because the field was no longer the same.

Dramatic changes had just taken place—and were continuing—in the way technical communicators were doing their work. Technology had assumed such a pervasive presence in the field that had started losing a clear sense of which previous and current theories continued to have validity.

Any examination of theories in the field suddenly demanded that we ask new questions, such as these: which theories still seem relevant and useful to practice—that is, which ones still seem to matter? Conversely, which theories have lost their credibility and their continued value for the field because they have become outdated, and of those, which theories still had potential to regain validity after some revision?

An addendum to the first book proposal was then delivered to the publisher. Instead of a book that would summarize and model contextualization of past theories in the field, what seemed most useful was an anthology that would reexamine, first, changes in the work of technical communicators, due to technology; second, new areas of foundational knowledge for the field; and third, a handful of new (early) attempts to revise influential current and past theories in the field to demonstrate how they might prove relevant and useful toward developing a better understanding of practice in the field.

The Anthology's Purposes For Particular Target Audiences

With these new goals in focus, this anthology is designed to serve professional needs of these three main audience segments:

- Newcomers to the field of technical communication; this group includes both current practitioners now working in industry, and either current or future practitioners who are pursuing degrees, certificates, or just more credentials at the undergraduate or graduate level in academic programs.

- Veterans in academia or in industry who have been in the field of technical communication for some time; this group might have been struggling to keep up or catch up with changes in the field caused by technological advances, but it also includes long-time professionals who are seeking new ideas for increasing the relevance or status of their work. For example, educators in academic programs might be sensing the need to update their programs and curricula, given the dramatic changes in industry. And practitioners in the field might sense the need to update their knowledge and perspectives in order to make more informed decisions regarding their work, now and in the future, in either existing or future jobs.

- Decision makers in academia or in industry, including administrators of academic programs in technical communication and managers of technical communicators; this group of readers might be seeking ideas or guidance for how best to update training or practice due to recent changes in the field.

Shaping the Collection

In 2006, invitations to contribute to this volume were emailed to technical communicators who specialized in particular areas of knowledge that the anthology aimed to cover. Potential contributors were asked to submit abstracts, those abstracts were approved or adjusted further, and then initial drafts were submitted. After receiving substantive feedback on those early drafts, authors revised further, this time, a request to aim the chapters more to the practitioner audience, for example, by adding more concrete examples, or using industry scenarios instead of academic scenarios, or finding other strategies for "grounding" their discussion in practice.

The decision was then made to solicit practitioner input on the next (by now, third) drafts of chapters for these reasons:

- The book's most important contribution will be to provide knowledge and ideas that can help *all* professionals in the field of technical communication adjust to the changes in our field, regardless of whether they are primarily teaching or learning in academia or working in industry. This book needs to have significance and value for both academics and practitioners.

- Although all authors in the anthology have had important industry experience or their work has been enriched by sustained connections with industry, all are right now working in academia. It was therefore important to inform academic perceptions with the realities of practice in work contexts.

I aimed to ensure that each chapter would be reviewed by at least three practitioners. Toward that goal, I used these sources to identify well-qualified practitioners to review the anthology chapters:

- *Personal list* of practitioner contacts.
- *Lists of Fellows, Associate Fellows, and Honorary Fellows* of the Society for Technical Communication (STC), accessed from the STC Web site in summer and fall, 2008
- *Lists of STC managers at specialty interest groups ("SIGDOCs"),* also accessed from the STC Web site during that same time
- *Web sites and blogs* of practitioners with a long-term specialization or publications in particular areas of the field, such as content management and ethics
- *Practitioner contacts* of some contributing authors in the collection, or in one case, practitioner contacts of a professional colleague of a contributing author.

Attempts were also made to ensure diversity of practitioner reviewers; I wanted a broad spectrum of practitioners according to the following criteria:

- *Length of time in their careers*: because this anthology is targeted at newcomers to the field, veterans in the field, and those in-between, chapter reviewers range from those just starting their careers in technical communication to those retired from decades of work in the field.
- *Types of professions*: I also wanted this anthology to reflect perspectives from the computer industry, of course, but also from such wide-ranging professions as medicine/health, travel, publishing, engineering, information science, and small nonprofit agencies advocating for environmental or social causes.
- *Specializations and interests*: I did my best to match practitioners with chapters related to their career specializations—just as one example, I matched practitioners working throughout the world with Thatcher's chapter on cross-cultural approaches to the field.
- *Status as consultants or full-time company employees*: Reviewers include veterans in the field who own their own consulting businesses and company employees who work part- or full-time, either on-site or at a distance from company locations.
- *Size of companies*: I tried for a mixture of technical communicators working at consulting firms, small nonprofits, small or medium-sized businesses, and large corporations.
- *Geographical locations*: Although the anthology focuses on digital literacy, which suggests the growing irrelevance of geographic location, an attempt was made for some diversity in this category. About a third of the practitioner reviewers are from the Midwest, where I work; the others are from other regions of the country or overseas.

I emailed an invitation to each practitioner to review an assigned chapter, and then emailed the latest draft of the assigned chapter to each one who accepted my invitation.

Twelve practitioners participated in three online focus groups; each focus group consisted of four practitioners who were given two to three weeks to read the assigned chapter, and then a week to post comments about their assigned chapter asynchronously; two focus groups chose to continue those discussions into a second week. The other 22 practitioners completed individual reviews of their assigned chapters; they were asked to read the chapter and then provide a written assessment about what they perceived to be strengths and shortcomings of the chapter, along with any revision advice that they might have for the author. As soon as I collected focus group or "traditional" written feedback from practitioners, I forwarded it to the appropriate chapter authors and asked them to consider that practitioner feedback as they revised their chapters further.

When authors submitted third drafts, which they had revised based on practitioner input, I conducted a simultaneous copyedit and comprehensive edit of their latest drafts and asked the authors to revise a final time. Authors in this collection therefore completed four drafts of their chapters.

Acknowledgements

Throughout this project, I have come to realize that it truly "takes a village" to develop an anthology about the tremendous impact of digital literacy— past and future, actual and ideal—on the work that we all do. From the start, this project has been consistently collaborative, reflecting input from at least thirty practitioners in addition to the eleven authors of this collection, and managed first by two co-editors and then by just one.

I'll begin by thanking the practitioner reviewers who contributed their wisdom—and the closest equivalent that we have in the field to "street smarts"—to this collection.

The practitioner reviewers spoke up strongly when, for example, they were struggling to understand concepts or sections, or the "writing was too academic," or the chapter needed to give more examples that practitioners would find meaningful, or even when they would find a chapter "clear, relevant, and interesting."

Each of the following practitioners reviewed a single chapter in this anthology and then either participated in online focus group discussions related to their assigned chapter, or submitted an individual written critique of that chapter. All of them were busy. None of them really found it easy or comfortable to fit the review into their work weeks. But all of them gave their best effort to ensure that this collection would reflect what practitioners experience, consider important, or believe to be "true" in their work. I am grateful for their great honesty and for the true sacrifices they made to ensure that this collection would be oriented to practitioners as much as to academics.

Lori Anschuetz, Mollye Barrett, Kit Brown, Jennifer Burchill, Jassamine Clemente, Dan Charles, Elizabeth Colvin, Ken Cook, Anna Eckmann, Jeannette Eichholz, Marie-Louise Flacke, Patricia Goubil-Gambrell, Mike Hassett, Mike Hughes, Amy Janczy, Nolwenn Kerzreho, Rich Maggiani, Ray Magnan, Mike McCallister, David Owens, Mak Pandit, Jonathan Price, Sam Racine, Mary Elizabeth Raven, Janice (Ginny) Redish, Michelle Schoenecker, Karen Schriver, Bill Swallow, Lisa Tallman, Catherine Lukas-Ter Horst

Another practitioner whom I want to thank is JoAnn Hackos, one of the true leaders in technical communication who consistently has maintained close connections with both the practitioner and academic communities of the field. I am grateful to JoAnn for finding the time in her incredibly busy schedule to write the Foreword for this collection.

The authors of this collection have been truly inspirational to me. I thank all of them, first of all, for negotiating truly challenging writing and revision processes. It is not easy, for example, to summarize vast, sweeping changes in the field and in the work that we do, or to explain key concepts and theories of knowledge that are so new to the field (and explain their potential value to technical communication work) to a diverse audience consisting of novices and veterans, students and professionals, and technical communicators engaged in the broad spectrum of disciplines and work in professional contexts. It was also quite an investment for them to revise three or four times in response to different types of feedback. I also thank this group of authors for their amazing wisdom and insight about what it will take for our field to keep evolving and to remain vital in industry. I have learned a great deal from them and believe that readers will, as well.

I am especially grateful to my colleague at the University of Wisconsin-Milwaukee, Dave Clark. During the first half of this project, Dave functioned as a co-editor of this collection and his vision for revising the anthology's purposes and contents led to a book that I am confident readers will consider relevant and important to the work that they do. Dave's insightful comments on abstracts and early chapter drafts were instrumental in inspiring many authors to reshape chapter contents to match the central purposes of the collection. During the last half of this project, Dave stepped down as co-editor, but his contributions to the quality of this anthology have been many and I thank him for being such a great partner in this effort.

Also of tremendous help were Linda Bathgate and Katherine W. Ghezzi of Routledge. Linda's flexibility throughout this project was greatly appreciated and her patient and positive reviews of different incarnations of the project contributed greatly to the success of this project. Kate's patience with a wide variety of last-minute questions was remarkable and her clear explanations helped ensure smooth progress of work in the final stages of development.

Finally, I am grateful to my daughters, Rahel and Zahara, for their love, and for their tremendous patience and understanding during all stages of this project.

Introduction

Government

Twitter, an increasingly popular social networking site, ... is taking Congress by storm. As of last count, 121 members of Congress are "tweeting." It's the new media answer to long floor speeches, and anyone who's anyone on Capitol Hill seems to be doing it ... Tweeting during Obama's speech was a source of laughs for comedian Stephen Colbert, who joked that even the president was doing it: "OMG, totally addressing Congress. LOL. Mitch McConnell looks like a turtle" ... All comedy aside, lawmakers who embrace new technology understand that the Internet already has drastically changed the political landscape, said Rep. John Culberson, a Republican from Texas who claims to have been the first U.S. politician to chat with constituents through a computer back in 1987. "Whether we like it or not, the electronic information superhighway will force us all to change. It's not survival, it's evolution."

(Marrero, 2009)

Medicine and Health Care

U.S. hospitals have a long way to go to join the digital age. Fewer than 2% have abandoned paper medical charts and completely switched to electronic health records, a new national survey found. Another 8% to 11% of hospitals have basic electronic systems in place where at least one department has converted to digital. The sobering findings come as the Obama administration plans to spend $19 billion to help modernize medical-record keeping systems ... The new numbers come as no surprise. Hospitals and doctors have been slow to make the leap to paperless despite evidence suggesting electronic health records can improve efficiency and help reduce deaths and injuries caused by medical errors ... The most common obstacle to conversion cited by the surveyed hospitals was cost—$20 million for small hospitals to $200 million for large academic centers. About three-quarters of hospitals without a computerized system said lack of capital was a barrier, 44% cited maintenance costs, and 36% cited doctor resistance, according to the survey of 2,952 mostly small and medium U.S. hospitals conducted last year.

(Associated Press, 2009)

Technical Communication

"Adapt or Die: Technical Communicators of the Twenty-First Century."

To succeed and prosper, and to fulfill their potential to truly impact the clarity of message and the understanding between organizations and their customers, technical communicators must move away from their comfort zones and assert themselves. They need to define their own opportunities and then move boldly forward. In short, it's time to adapt or move over.

(Myers, 2009)

"It's Not Survival, It's Evolution"

Over the past decade especially, technology has had a huge impact on industry. As might be expected, different professions are reporting either fast or slow growth of digitalization and seem to vary widely in terms of embracing or resisting technology.

The first two excerpts that begin this Introduction illustrate this disparity: While twittering is making quick inroads in government and gaining rapid acceptance among elected officials, the adjustment to electronic health records for patients has been much slower and more gradual in the health care industry.

In the field of technical communication, everyone is aware that technology has turned our world upside down. Most sites of our work are now high-tech, digitalized environments in which paper products are growing scarce while products of technology proliferate. Over the past few decades, the "digital revolution" has transformed just about every work environment and the way that most of us do our work. It has altered every aspect of our jobs, including how we gather information, think, develop and share ideas, collaborate, analyze, plan, and make decisions; find, use, manipulate, manage, and store information; and develop, evaluate, revise, and complete information products. As several authors point out in this collection, in this field, we have even reached the point of becoming technology and technology has now become us. Simply put, just about every aspect of our work has changed.

But despite the clear penetration of technology in nearly all facets of our work, technical communicators have varied in their receptivity, responsiveness, and willingness to embrace technology and all of the changes that come with it, and some have been slower than others to adjust to the changes. Why is it that some technical communicators are similar to many physicians in being somewhat reluctant to adjust to the digitalization of their work environment, while others resemble elected politicians in embracing new technologies, even to the point of looking for excuses to use them in even the most outrageous of settings?

Of course, it now seems a given that technical communicators have little or no choice but to adapt, and at first, the title, "Adapt or Die," used for an *Intercom* magazine article (Myers, 2009), seems simple, but is it really? Some important complexities underlie those three simple words. For example, is the title mainly meant to deliver a serious warning to technical communicators? Does it imply that (too many) technical communicators have been slow to adapt to the massive changes in the new digital environments of our work, and is it cautioning us to do so, now, or else lose our jobs, or maybe even worse, "die" professionally, with the possible implication that those of us who do not adapt, have no future in this field? Or is the title alarmist mainly to attract more reader attention? Consider how the author ends her article by writing, "in short, it's time to adapt or move over," which implies that the title "Adapt or Die" might just mean that technical communicators have important options to consider; given the pervasiveness of technology in our field, technical communicators need to take stock, now, of what recent changes in their work contexts mean for their work, and then make a decision, for example, to adapt to the changes and become a valuable asset to a work environment, or to continue doing technical communication at a work site that is not (yet) in the mainstream of what is happening now in our field, or to consider switching to related types of jobs that might benefit from the traditional skill set that most technical communicators can offer.

While the first interpretation of the "Adapt or Die" article implies the need for survival, the second implies a need for evolution, and it is this later interpretation—that evolution is necessary for our individual and collective approaches to our work—that gets to the heart of the central purpose of this anthology.

This anthology is not about the *survival* of the field, nor does it have as its central purpose to alarm, scare, warn, or provide ultimatums to readers who are either newcomers or veterans in the practice, study, or teaching of technical communicators. This collection also does not insist that failing to adapt will mean the end of the field, or the end of any chance for us to find vital, meaningful work in our field

The collection, however, does point to the critical need for *evolution*. Throughout this anthology, you will find different descriptions, or stories, about the professional evolution that each one of us has made, already, or needs to make. You will also find in this book both general and particular strategies for adapting to the new realities of technical communication work.

Although this collection resists arguing that it's a matter of professional survival that we all "adapt," every chapter in this anthology urges us to understand the changes brought about during the "digital revolution," and then to use that knowledge to reexamine and revise our practice, our theories, or both. To assist us in this goal, the book begins with histories and descriptions of the "digital revolution" and its impact on our field and on our work; moves next to explanations of basic language and concepts of new foundational knowledge in our field; and then concludes with some early attempts to reexamine and revise our current understanding of the field— that is, our theories—so that we can all begin the process of understanding better the dramatic changes that we have witnessed or are now "living" daily as a result of the "digital revolution."

A pervasive theme that runs throughout this anthology is that the evolution of our field—and our process of adapting to change—calls for a new framework for our work. Mostly due to the profound impact of technology on our field and on our work, many of us are moving away from an era of much self-introspection, characterized by rather narrow definitions of our field, work, and capabilities. In recent years, we have been developing, instead, a new self-perception as team-players, as collaborators who contribute now to larger, team-oriented projects and goals, and who do our work both within and across multiple departments and disciplines, and in some cases, both within and across industry and academia.

Past publications,[2] my own included, often focused on defining technical communication by identifying parameters or boundaries to what we do. Discussions and debates tended to concern what the field could or should accomplish, and whether the field was a field or an emergent profession. A key goal was to legitimate our field by showing how it was distinct from other disciplines and professions. Until recently, we tended to assume a defensive, sometimes even a defiant posture, as though we were daring others to find good reasons for us *not* to be there, become established, or expand. In short, we tended to define ourselves in terms of how we were different from others, and with our efforts to separate and distinguish our work from what others did, we isolated ourselves to some extent, because otherwise (our unarticulated fears suggested), our identity would or might weaken and our field would or might be at risk of disappearing altogether.

Certainly, such a stance would not work well for technical communicators in the modern age of digitalization. Now, numerous other fields are claiming a stake in information and content design, development, and management, just as we are; we do not and should not work in isolation, especially with the goals of other fields being quite consistent with our own. Also, more powerful than any "competition for power" in the sense of "controlling" information design and content management has come, very naturally, a collaborative spirit in industry, one that welcomes or requires the input of talents from a wide variety of specializations and fields. As a result, our field seems most interested now in embracing collaboration opportunities. The new realization seems to be that in order to thrive, the field needs to expand by rejecting traditional boundaries and by joining others in striving for larger, cross-disciplinary goals.

As you will see in numerous chapters of this anthology, one profound outcome of the digital revolution has been a blurring of boundaries in our field and our work. Consider, for example, these recent developments in the field, which all point to the easing up of artificial "fences" between disciplines and to the pursuit of mergers and more opportunities for collaboration:

- More technical communicators are now working in project teams; typically, we are just some of many "players" on cross-functional teams that collaborate mostly through digital media.
- More of us are migrating to jobs with other titles and responsibilities, and increasingly, we are identifying ourselves not as members of any one field, such as technical communication, but rather, as cross- or multi-disciplinary. This is one important reason that membership in the Society for Technical Communication (STC) has decreased dramatically in recent years (see the chapters by Carliner and by Dicks, this volume).
- At the 2007 Annual Conference of the Association of Teachers of Technical Writing (ATTW), one of the most riveting discussions concerned this question: "What if technical communication were to merge into other disciplines and lose its identity as a field?" Many at that session agreed that such a trend had already started to happen.
- The previous Research Grants Committee of the Society for Technical Communication (STC) stipulated in a 2004 RFP that its goal was to award a large grant to a collaborative research team, one that would pool together knowledge and talents across different disciplines or specializations to investigate a large-scale problem of the field.
- In some major academic programs in the field, technical communication programs have assumed a new secondary status within revised or broader disciplinary identities. For example, the previously titled "Department of Technical Communication" at the University of Washington recently became just one of many instructional options within a larger and newly titled, "Department of Human Centered Design and Engineering" (HCDE). As Spyridakis (2009) explains, "The field is changing ... Given where the computing world is going, our field is much broader than simply writing and editing. The new name reflects that broader focus."

Today, for technical communicators, what seems most critical and meaningful is how we can contribute to social, team, or collaborative efforts toward the greater good of large-scale projects likely to involve digital communication within and across companies. Our work is also more likely than before to be international in scope. Instead of our previous focus (and struggle) to legitimate ourselves by separating ourselves from others, the unmistakable trend now is to identify how we can contribute to social or corporate efforts beyond our own current goals and contexts. This anthology therefore urges technical communicator to replace one of our field's previous important questions—"who are we?"—with different questions, such as these:

- How can we adapt, adjust, and contribute?
- How can we make a difference, not by isolating ourselves or distinguishing ourselves from others, but rather, through collaborative efforts?
- How can we help toward goals that are larger in scope than those we have worked on in the past?
- How can we contribute to the social good with our unique perspective, knowledge, and strategies?
- How can we join others in "adding value" and in making a difference?
- How can we show how we matter in the context of the larger social environment of our work and how can we help in broad, even global ways?

This anthology represents early attempts to investigate these critical questions as we seek a more accurate understanding of useful strategies we might use to adapt to the changes, and as we continue to identify ways to move forward with our work, even during stressful economic times, with greater confidence and resolve to add value to larger social spheres, in ways that truly matter.

In the following sections, I will explain the decision to use the term "digital literacy" in the title of this collection, and will then describe, more specifically, the structure and uses of this anthology.

Deciding on the Term "Digital Literacy"

During the evolution of this project, it was quite a challenge to choose a term that might best describe what we do now in the modern workplace in response to the digital metamorphosis of our field. The term "digital literacy" is a relatively new concept in the field, and there is no agreement in the literature about whether this—or any other term—is most accurate in describing what now constitutes the goal of effective writing and communication in digital environments.

Because most technical communicators work with information in an attempt to fulfill goals somehow related to writing, reading, and communication in general, I decided early in this project that the word "literacy" would be appropriate to describe what professionals in the field focus on and hope to achieve in their work. "Literacy" has many different definitions and many associate it with reading and writing, but as Wysocki and Johnson-Eilola point out (1999), it is a slippery term that takes some effort to "unpack" and truly understand. Because we do much more than read and write in our work, a definition of "workplace literacy" that works well for the purposes of this book would need to encompass the compilation of activities associated with the reciprocal relationship of theory (understanding, analysis) and practice (information development, management, evaluation, revision, production, delivery) related to writing and communication that takes place within and across professional contexts for professional purposes.

Many terms have emerged that all, in one way or the other, refer to the recent "digital revolution" of workplace literacy, including these:

- computer literacy
- cyberliteracy
- Internet literacy
- information literacy
- technological literacy
- electronic literacy
- digital literacy

Any of these terms could have been used in the title of this volume. However, I did dismiss the first four choices right away. The first three terms—computer literacy, cyberliteracy, and Internet literacy—are arguably too narrow in scope, as this anthology aims more broadly to cover any type of literacy affected by technology of all types and its discussions are not restricted to computers or cyberspace. "Information literacy" is strong in reflecting the breadth of our work and our goals, but this term could refer to traditional print media and does not necessarily refer to technology or to digital forms of communication.

Any one of the final three terms would have been good choices for the book's title. "Technological literacy" refers broadly to literacy impacted by technology, and would be a fitting way to describe the broad nature of literacy as discussed in this volume. Kastman-Breuch defines "technological literacy" as "scholarship that addresses the ability to use technology; the ability to read, write, and communicate using technology; and the ability to think critically about technology" (2002, p. 269). Such a definition works well to capture the nature and purpose of this anthology. "Electronic literacy" and "digital literacy" are also broad enough in scope for the purposes of this anthology and refer aptly to current work of technical communicators.

I chose "digital literacy," instead of "technological literacy," simply because the word "digital" refers a bit more directly to the rise of computer technology, and in our field, the introduction of computer technology, more than anything else, led to the paradigm shift that has transformed our work so remarkably over the past thirty years or so. I also consider Selfe and Hawisher's 2002 definition of "digital literacy" useful: they define it as "the practices involved in reading, writing, and exchanging information in online environments as well as the values associated with such practices—social, cultural, political, educational" (p. 232).

For this anthology, I define "digital literacy" in a way that combines Selfe and Hawisher's definition of "digital literacy" and Kastman-Breuch's definition of "technological literacy," but in the case of the latter, with more focus on the "digital" nature of literacy and on both scholarship and applications of scholarship on practice in the field. Digital literacy, then, is defined in this volume in this way:

> Theory and practice that focus on use of digital technology, including the ability to read, write, and communicate using digital technology, the ability to think critically about digital technology, and consideration of social, cultural, political, and educational values associated with those activities.

Note that Glister (1997) argues that the most important ability in digital literacy is thinking critically, or making educated judgments about what we find online. This anthology, as a whole, can be viewed as an effort to do just that.

Complicating the issue, of course, is whether it is fair to refer to "literacy" in the singular. Our work in technical communication typically takes place in complex, multiple social environments, as Selfe and Hawisher (2002) observed in their study of electronic literacy in the field; from their study results, they concluded that workplace literacy "exists within a complex cultural ecology of social, historical, and economic effects." Other scholars have proposed that not just one literacy, but multiple literacies—or seen in a slightly different way, multiple layers of literacy—exist in work contexts (see Nagelhaut, 1989; Selber, 2004; Slattery, 2007; Cargile-Cook, 2002; Kastman-Breuch, 2002). As Selber argues, no one term can cover the multiple literacy practices involved in creating digital texts and multi-modal designs.

Several technical communication specialists have proposed theoretical frameworks for describing, or integrating what it is that we do in the field. Cargile-Cook (2002), for example, calls for a framework consisting of six layered literacies (basic, rhetorical, social, technological, ethical, critical), while Nagelhaut (1989) calls for four (rhetorical, visual, information, computer). Kastman-Breuch (2002) advocates that we use a multiple perspective framework of technological literacy—a collective adoption of issues that avoids favoring one issue of technological literacy over another. In this volume, the term "digital literacy" is used as a plural or collective term that refers to multiple literacies and even to multiple layers of literacy, in the spirit of this important, recent scholarship.

Let's turn next to a description of the book's structure and target users.

Anthology Structure and Target Users

As we have seen, the central purpose of this anthology is to assist technical communicators in adapting to the new focus on technology and digital literacy in their work and work environments. More specifically, this collection is designed to explore answers to these questions:

- How has technical communication work changed in response to the now, mostly digital writing environment?
- What is important, new foundational knowledge in our field that all technical communicators need to learn?
- How can we revise past theories (that is, explanations, perspectives, and thoughts about "best practices") or develop new ones in technical communication to understand better how technology has transformed our work?

This anthology has three Parts, each one corresponding with one of these three questions.

Part I: Transformations in Our Work

The first Part is designed to answer the first of the three questions: how has technical communication work changed in response to the now, mostly digital writing environment?

Many of us struggle to keep up with the constant changes that alter, daily, what it means to be digitally literate within and across modern work contexts. How many of us fully understand all new types of technology that have sprung up in recent years? How many of us have kept up with all or even most changes in industry, such as the fragmentation of content and information; new composing processes at work sites; and new styles of management? And what impact have such changes had on what is valued or not valued about the work that we do? Do the changes mean that we need to abandon skills that we have worked so hard to acquire and to set aside strategies that have worked for us in the past, but that have become outmoded? Has the time arrived that we now need to work especially hard to acquire new skills and to develop and try out new strategies?

We now need to negotiate a complex, often global world of intersections and interrelationships, multiple goals and constraints, and new ways of creating, disseminating, storing, and retrieving information and of managing knowledge and content. To help readers grasp a fuller sense of this challenge, and to catch up with changes in our work and work environments, especially those caused by technology and the "digital revolution," Part I aims to provide readers with a useful historical context for the dramatic transformation of our field since around the 1970s.

Two chapters in this part provide overviews of the field during essentially the same time frame; although they focus on different developments, each chapter tells the story of our field's recent evolution in a unique way, and together, they reveal how the field—and subsequently the work that technical communicators do—has become increasingly more complicated and challenging.

When first envisioning the structure of this anthology, I initially assumed that just one overview chapter would suffice to canvas the dramatic changes in our field over the past three or four decades. However, quite soon, I saw value in having two specialists in technical communication "tell the story" in their own, unique way.

Saul Carliner starts us off with his chapter, "Computers and Technical Communication in the 21st Century." After describing how technology changed the jobs and job titles of technical communicators in a major organization in the computer industry, Carliner provides a broader history of the development of technology and its impact on the work that we do. He describes, for example, how our field has changed between the early years of mainframes and mini-computers, during an era when technical communicators were called "writers, editors, and illustrators," up to recent times, characterized by many technical communicators working on software for managing computer networks, qualifying for jobs by earning degrees in computer science or usability, and focusing on the design of large databases and overseeing content management systems and the creation and publication of user-created content.

While Carliner focuses mostly on an overview of changes in technology and the computer industry, R. Stanley Dicks' chapter, "The Effects of Digital Literacy on the Nature of Technical Communication Work," surveys changes in the economy, management, and methodologies that together, created what Dicks calls "a seismic shift" that dramatically altered the nature of technical communication work. In particular, Dicks describes the impact on our work, first, of large macro-economic changes "fuelled primarily by the transition from the industrial age to the information age and a perhaps larger transition from industrial age management capitalism to a post-capitalist society," also known as the transition to "the support economy" (p. 52). He then describes how our work has changed dramatically due to new management principles and practices (including value added; reengineering; outsourcing, downsizing, and rightsizing; globalization; and flattening); and from new methodologies (such as single sourcing, agile development methods, scrum, distributed work, and Web 2.0 and transparency). Dicks also analyzes implications for education and training due to the new focus on symbolic-analytic work among technical communicators.

Everyone in the field needs to know how our new universe of technical communication evolved and what it looks like today. Historic knowledge, coupled with an understanding of probable or inevitable future developments, can help us re-position ourselves to navigate modern contexts and invent effective new strategies for the next era of work in our careers. Given this broad purpose, Part I is especially designed to help technical communicators in the following categories:

- Maybe you are very new to the field of technical communication. Newcomers to the field, especially, need to understand the recent history of technical communication, which has been altered remarkably by the impact of technology. You might be in a bachelor's, masters, or doctoral degree program or working toward a certificate or concentration in technical communication or a related field. Or, you might have been trained in another field, but you're thinking about trying for a technical communication job in industry. Or, perhaps you have just been hired in a technical communication job, and need a "crash course" about what the field has been going through during the past few decades.
- Part I could also be of considerable use and relevance to practitioners who have been in the field awhile. Recent changes in our field due to the "digital revolution" have been so remarkably pervasive and volatile that even those of us who have been in the field for some time have found it challenging to keep up—or to catch up—with all that is new and different in our work. You might be a practitioner who has encountered technology to some extent in your work, but feel, even so, a bit "left behind" or "not quite caught up" in terms of keeping up with all of the changes. Maybe you pretend to grasp all that has happened due to technology, but to be honest, you do not yet fully or adequately grasp the extent to which technology and its impact might mean to your job or career, now and in the future. Even veterans in the field would benefit from reading recent histories of our field, maybe primarily to inform your own practice, or to provide solid advice and guidance to others you might be mentoring in the field.
- Or maybe you are an educator who understands that your students need sufficient preparation in writing with or about technology, but who does not yet understand fully the digital revolution in technical communication—or its impact on specific writing and communication practice—well enough to teach it to others. If so, similar to the practitioners just described, you might be seeking an opportunity to catch up or keep up with the field.

Part II: New Foundational Knowledge For Our Field

Part II answers the second question, "What is important, new foundational knowledge in our field that all technical communicators need to learn?

Most academic programs in technical communication continue to require students to complete "core coursework" in skill areas that Dicks describes in Part I as "commodity work." As Dicks explains, technical communicators are now doing "commodity work" less often, or not at all, so now our greatest need is to prepare students for "symbolic-analytic work" that they soon will be expected to do handle competently. Unfortunately, academia has been slow to keep up with changes in the field brought about by technological advances. Even a brief glimpse at any random three or four academic programs in our field will expose outdated courses and curricula. With a handful or so of notable exceptions, academia has fallen behind in updating its courses and curriculum to keep pace with industry changes.

The chapters in Part II provide overviews of three areas of knowledge that, arguably, constitute the most important new foundational knowledge in our field: the rhetoric of technology, information design, and content management. All three chapters of Part II aim to prepare readers to understand and then apply this knowledge to contribute in valuable ways to the important, new "symbolic-analytic" work of technical communication.

First, in "Shaped and Shaping Tools: The Rhetorical Nature of Technical Communication Technologies," Dave Clark shows how understanding "the rhetoric of technology" can help us understand better the relationship of technology and our work in technical communication. While defining "the rhetoric of technology," Clark argues that such work is not as coherent and fixed as "the rhetoric of science," but it does have coherence in addressing "specific concerns of technical communicators" and is useful in challenging "conventional understandings of writing technologies," which Clark points out is "an incredibly important task in a field that is constantly expected to learn and use new tools like content management systems" (p. 87). Clark describes four approaches or theories that technical communicators have found most useful in understanding the rhetoric of technology: classical rhetorical approaches, technology transfer theories, genre theory, and activity theory. As Clark points out, any or all four of these approaches can help us analyze the unique rhetoric—or meaning, value, and relevance—of tools and technologies that we use in our own work and that both shape and are shaped by the way we do our work.

Next, in "Information Design: From Authoring Text to Architecting Virtual Space," Michael J. Salvo and Paula Rosinski provide useful explanations of key terms and applications related to information design. They begin by arguing that technical communicators are uniquely qualified to manage information design in work contexts, because of our history of applying effective design principles, our proven understanding of genre and innovation in work contexts, and our contribution already to ensuring a contextual orientation to design. Salvo and Rosinski then provide what they call a "lexicon" of "emerging language" in information design. By helping us understand new concepts related to information design in industry—including granularity, homogeneity and heterogeneity, mapping, signposting, metadata and taxonomies, tag clouds (and folksonomies), pattern language, ambience, and findability—this chapter will assist us in handling the important "symbolic-analytic" work of doing and managing information design in work contexts.

Next, in his chapter, "Content Management: Beyond Single-Sourcing," William Hart-Davidson argues that our unique backgrounds, experience, qualifications, and skill set position us well to understand and then coordinate content management efforts, and that such work can elevate our status in industry. Hart-Davidson begins by presenting what he calls "a broader, more nuanced view of CM and CMS than is typically found in the technical communication literature." Content management, Hart-Davidson argues, goes beyond single sourcing, and technical communicators are well qualified to take the lead with CM work. According to Hart-Davidson, "Technical communicators can and should orchestrate, coordinate, and negotiate CM. But for this to happen, they will need to take on increasingly varied organizational roles and responsibilities." He then presents a framework that "articulates these roles and responsibilities," one that technical communicators can use in their own organizations to persuade management to give them the opportunity to assume a leadership role in CM efforts (pp. 129–130).

All three of these Part II chapters target educators, students, and practitioners:

- Together, chapters in this Part present a strong message to academia: if you are an educator or program administrator wishing to prepare students sufficiently well to compete for and handle today's technical communication jobs, you will need—soon—to provide instruction in this new foundational knowledge, or even better, to require that students take courses in these areas of instruction. Of course, depending on resources, this instruction may need to be integrated into existing courses, although it would be ideal for new required core courses to develop that would provide students with thorough instruction in these new areas of knowledge.
- Students in academic programs are another key audience for Part II. Whether you are taking courses or seminars in theory and practice now, or simply want to learn about new foundational knowledge in the field, you would benefit greatly from becoming familiar with all three chapters in this Part.
- Practitioners in the field might find themselves at the stage of their career when they need or want to learn the fundamentals of new foundational knowledge in the field. Maybe you are in this category, and want to learn and then apply that knowledge intelligently and effectively either to your own approaches to doing work, or to discussions going on at your work site about how best to move forward with innovations in technology, information delivery, and content management.
- Both educators and practitioners might also find Part II useful toward the goal of contributing soon to cutting edge research and scholarship in the field. If you are in this category, learning more about new foundational knowledge in the field might inspire you to ask the kinds of questions that could lead to research that the field absolutely needs,

right now, toward a greater understanding of what it takes to write and communicate effectively in a now digital environment. If you currently lack sufficient knowledge and background to do this, you would benefit from reading the three chapters in this Part of the anthology.

Part III: New Directions in Cultural, Cross-Cultural, Audience, and Ethical Perspectives

Part III addresses the third main question of this anthology: How can we revise past theories (that is, explanations, perspectives, and thoughts about "best practices") or develop new ones in technical communication to understand better how technology has transformed our work?

Given the recent, dramatic "seismic shift" in our work, our field needs to address questions like these, and soon: Which theories remain relevant and useful to technical communicators? Which theories are no longer of much value in explaining or leading to improvements in the work that we do? Which theories need radical change to adapt to all of the changes? And which new theories do we need to develop next in order to reach a better understanding of both shortcomings and "best practices" of our work?

Current theories in our field may or may not be adequate to reflect recent change in industry due to the "digital revolution"—systematic analysis about this is in very early stages in our field. It is quite possible that new theories will need to be conceived and developed to help us make sense of the rich complexities of workplace writing in this new age of technology in work contexts, but without analyzing current practice and theory in work contexts, we don't yet quite know if this is true.

This anthology assumes the following about theories in general:

- not all theories are relevant or useful for practice;
- all theories have flaws;
- all theories need continual testing;
- all theories, though, have potential relevance and benefits for practice.

This collection also assumes that at this stage in our field's history, our theories have not kept pace with practice. An important hypothesis of this anthology is that the theories of our field, including those that we have described in our publications and have taught in academic programs, have become flawed in the sense that they probably do not adequately describe or explain practice in the present. During the upcoming decade, some of the most challenging work in our field will involve questioning existing theories and deciding whether to update them, or just abandon them in order to develop new theories that are more accurate and successful in making sense of modern practice in our field.

Part III presents four attempts at an early, systematic analysis of whether past or current theories related to cultural, cross-cultural, audience, and ethics remain relevant and useful to our field.

Bernadette Longo, in her chapter "Human+Machine Culture: Where We Work," critiques current theoretical models and assumptions that promote the concepts of a "universal audience" or "an all-inclusive community" in digital environments. To Longo, it is illogical to assume that either concept could even be possible. According to Longo, the goal many aspire to achieve, of forming of "an all-inclusive community through the use of computer technologies," is "not achievable or even desirable." Longo points out how "The idea of community has been especially attractive to people who advocate building communities through virtual, online groups or social networks," but current theories for this utopian ideal are flawed. First, "these virtual communities encourage simulated social interactions that lead to simulated human connections;" also, incorporating the idea of community into activity theory "seeks to confine the idea of community to a component that can be isolated in an organizational research setting." Instead, Longo advocates that we study "the idea of community ... within its cultural context in order to come to an understanding of why people make the decisions they do in a given circumstance" (p. 148).

In the next chapter, "Understanding Digital Literacy Across Cultures," Barry Thatcher argues that "a weakness of much research and practice on digital literacy is that it fails to provide a global or cross-cultural framework for understanding how digital media function outside the United States or many Western European countries." Thatcher points out how "digital media simply do not fit all communicative and cultural traditions the same way" and that current theories are inadequate, as they "generally presuppose a broad framework of U.S. cultural values and organizational behavior" that may or may not be applicable to digital media situated in communication and rhetorical situations in other cultures. The practical goal of this chapter, Thatcher notes, is to address "ethnocentrism with the practical goal of helping technical communicators adapt their approaches for cross-cultural contexts." To help us achieve that goal, Thatcher provides what he calls "a global framework for understanding how digital literacies relate to communicative traditions both in U.S. contexts and around the globe." He also demonstrates how we can adapt our digital literacies for cross-cultural contexts by "using five strategies that are common in U.S. technical communication practice" (pp. 170–171).

The third chapter in Part III is Ann M. Blakeslee's "Addressing Audiences in a Digital Age." Similar to Longo and Thatcher, Blakeslee argues that current theories, in this case, of audience, are inadequate to describe current practice. According to Blakeslee, "as a field we have not yet addressed this shift to digital documents in our examinations of audience with digital texts." To describe this need, Blakeslee reports findings from five case studies that she conducted of technical communicators considering how they research and think about audiences while working on typical digital projects. Blakeslee's data points to flaws in a current notion that digital communicators now address a "universal audience" and therefore can use a "generic one-size-fits-all approach to digital audiences." What Blakeslee found, instead, is that in digital environments, "writers are continuing to view audiences in very particular ways" and to "rely on a framework of problem solving and contextualization to analyze and address their digital audiences" (p. 200). Blakeslee advocates that the field identify "best practices" for addressing digital audiences that combine problem solving and contextualization. To help us toward that goal, she concludes her chapter with practical suggestions and provides, as well (in appendixes), two lists of important research topics and questions pertaining to audiences of digital documents, which can guide upcoming research on writing for audiences in digital environments.

The fourth chapter in Part III is "Beyond Ethical Frames of Technical Relations: Digital Being in the Workplace World," by Steven B. Katz and Vicki W. Rhodes. As Katz and Rhodes point out, "Organizations seldom consider their relationship to technology as ethical frames of reference" and "Professionals often view and use technology to communicate as if it were value-free." The authors ask, "... how often do you or your organization evaluate the way you think about, interact through, and exist with technological advances?" According to the authors, current ethical theories and practices are not yet adequate to help technical communicators handle the impact of the "digital revolution" on our work and work sites. To address this need, Katz and Rhodes call for us to "both acknowledge and actively engage in multiple ethical frames of technical relations." They define ethical frames as "a set of philosophical assumptions, ideological perceptions, and normative values underlying and/or guiding how people relate to and exist with technology." After identifying and describing five known ethical frames that define human–machine relations, the authors suggest, through a case study, a sixth, new ethical frame that can reveal how "technical relations are embedded and enacted, and through which people, procedures, media, and machines for all intents and purposes digitally become one and the same." With this sixth frame, the authors propose, technical communicators "can more fully reveal the complex, dynamic interrelations between humans and technologies, and help professional workplaces better adapt to them to improve business as well as the relationships that result" (pp. 230–232).

Together, these four chapters in Part III will likely be most useful to readers in these situations:

- You might be a veteran, maybe even a leader in the field of technical communication, and have seen, already, changes in practice due to what some call the "digital revolution," but you are less sure about how to theorize or make sense of changes in ways that can help you guide the field toward a sense of "best practices" for technical communication.
- You might also be someone (a newcomer, or someone who has been in the field for some time) who wants to understand better the "why" behind the "what" and "how" in our field—that is, you might be interested in whether past and current theories in the field are adequate in reflecting

or explaining changes in practice in work contexts, or in exploring new theoretical directions toward a more accurate understanding of altered practice in our field.

In closing, the aim of this anthology is to help you make better sense of technology's impact on your work. It might prove especially useful for those readers who are seeking new ideas, suggestions, and guidance for how best to navigate the new digital universe of our field. Ideally, in some of these pages, you will discover new ways to adapt, adjust, and evolve so that you will move closer to fulfilling your own potential in the new digital universe.

Note

1 See, for example, Spilka, 2002; Mirel and Spilka, 2002; Kynell-Hunt and Savage, 2003, 2004.

References

Associated Press (2009). Hospitals lag in digital age: Few adopt electronic records, study finds. *Milwaukee Journal Sentinel*, March 27.

Cargile-Cook, K. (2002). Layered literacies: A theoretical frame for technical communication pedagogy. *Technical Communication Quarterly* 11.1: 5–29.

Glister, P. (1997). *Digital literacy.* New York: John Wiley and Sons.

Kastman-Breuch, L. (2002). Thinking critically about technology literacy: Developing a framework to guide computer pedagogy in technical communication. *Technical Communication Quarterly* 11.3: 267–88.

Kynell-Hunt, T. and Savage, G. J. (2003). *Power and legitimacy in technical communication: The historical and contemporary struggle for professional status.* Vol I. Amityville, NY: Baywood Publishing.

Kynell-Hunt, T. and Savage, G. J. (2004). *Power and legitimacy in technical communication: Strategies for professional status.* Vol II. Amityville, NY: Baywood Publishing.

Marrero, D. (2009). Twitter gets loyal users in Congress. *Milwaukee Journal Sentinel*, April 8.

Mirel, B. and Spilka, R. (Eds.) (2002). *Reshaping technical communication: New directions and challenges for the 21st century.* Mahwah, NJ: Lawrence Erlbaum.

Myers, E. M. (2009). Adapt or die: Technical communicators of the twenty-first century. *Intercom*, March, 2009.

Nagelhout, E. (1999). Pre-professional practices in the technical writing classroom: Promoting multiple practices through research. *Technical Communication Quarterly* 8.3: 285–300.

Selber, S. A. (2004). *Multiliteracies for a digital age.* Carbondale, IL: Southern Illinois University Press.

Selfe, C. L. and Hawisher, G. E. (2002). A historical look at electronic literacy: Implications for the education of technical communicators. *Journal of Business and Technical Communication* 16.3: 231–76.

Slattery, S. (2007). Undistributing work through writing: How technical writers manage texts in complex information environments. *Technical Communication Quarterly* 16.3: 311–326.

Spilka, R. (2002). Becoming a profession. In B. Mirel and R. Spilka (Eds.), *Reshaping technical communication: New directions and challenges for the 21st century* (pp. 97–109). Mahwah, NJ: Lawrence Erlbaum.

Spyridakis, J. (2009). Quoted in H. Hickey, Technical communication adopts new name: Department of Human Centered Design and Engineering. *University Week*, University of Washington, January 29. Retrieved April 15, 2009 from: http://uwnews.org/uweek/article.aspx?id=46689

Wysocki, A. and Johnson-Eilola, J. (1999). Blinded by the letter: Why are we using literacy as a metaphor for everything else? In G. E. Hawisher and C. Selfe (Eds.), *Passions, Pedagogies, and 21st Century Technologies*. Logan, UT: Utah State University Press.

Part I
Transformations in Our Work

1 Computers and Technical Communication in the 21st Century

Saul Carliner

This chapter describes the impact of digital technology on technical communicators. It starts by describing how technology changed the jobs and job titles of technical communicators in one organization. Then it provides a broad history of the development of technology for technical communication and covers, as well, implications of the technologies on the work of technical communicators.

Note that this history has an admittedly personal dimension to it, and like all histories, this one reflects a particular point of view. It focuses on the role of the technical writer documenting software and similar high-technology products; that's my background in this field and what I have experienced and know best. But such an emphasis has validity and value, especially if we consider demographics of the field of technical communication, which suggest that my experience represents that of the majority of technical communicators. According to my recollections of the membership demographics of the Society for Technical Communication (STC), the world's largest professional organization for technical communicators between the 1980s and 2000s, when I was an officer of the organization and regularly received reports about our membership numbers, writers/editors accounted for well over 50% of the membership, and nearly 60% of the membership was employed in the high-technology sector, including computer hardware and software and telecommunications. The membership numbers I would receive later in the decade were similar to those in a survey I conducted in 1985 for my research methods course at the University of Minnesota of people attending the International Technical Communication Conference (as STC's annual conference was once called). It's true that technical communicators working in certain sub-segments of the field, like those writing military specifications and those working in scientific communication, most likely experienced a history that differs from the one described here. But although my general focus is on the technical writer working in the high-technology field, I also cover the effect of technology on people serving other roles in the development of technical communication products. Overall, the aim of this chapter is to provide a history that all readers of this collection will find useful, as they contemplate the impact of technology on their past, current, and future work in the field.

How Technology Affected Technical Communication in One Organization

One way to gain insight into ways that digital technology has changed the work of technical communicators over the years is to follow changes in technology and a corresponding change in job titles and responsibilities at one of the largest employers for technical communicators. The changes experienced within this computer manufacturer mirror those experienced by many other technical communicators, including those working for other organizations in the same industry, or in other industries, such as defense, government, medical devices, and hospitality. Table 1.1 (p. 24) summarizes the transition that I will be describing in this part regarding technical communicators' jobs in this organization between the late 1970s and now.

Consider, first, the responsibilities of technical communicators at that company in the late 1970s (Davis, 1989). At that time, its primary products were mainframe and mini-computers serving large numbers of users and housed in large, specially cooled spaces. The primary difference between a mainframe and mini-computer was the number of users they could serve: mini-computers served only a few to several hundred users; mainframes served several hundred to several thousand users. The company manufactured computer hardware and developed nearly all of the software that ran on these computers. These systems were sold in low to moderate volumes to customers who would provide weeks of training to the staff that programmed and operated them. In turn, the computer manufacturer provided extensive on-site technical support and assistance, including the time-consuming tasks of setting up and customizing these systems.

In this environment, the primary job of technical communicators was to document the functions and features of these systems, kind of like a technical version of taking minutes at a meeting. The job titles of technical communicators—writer, editor, or illustrator—reflected their role in the production of technical content. These jobs were considered professional (that is, in practical terms, under the regulations of the United States and other jurisdictions, these workers were not eligible for overtime pay). Production was handled by a separate class of workers, called production assistants, who were considered para-professionals (that is, the job was classified under U.S. labor regulations as nonprofessional, so workers were eligible for overtime pay). The main qualification for the job of a technical writer in this environment was experience supporting and servicing products that were the subject of documentation. These workers developed competency in writing through training and on-the-job mentoring.

The primary task of these technical writers was to edit product specifications and make them usable as reference materials by technically astute users, who already received in-depth training and had easy access to this manufacturer's technical support staff should issues arise that the documentation did not address. In a few instances, people were hired with formal training in technical writing, but during the 1970s, this employer typically emphasized technical knowledge over writing skill. Field experience with the product was also sought from editors and illustrators, though they, too, could expect to receive specialized training in those areas. Writers prepared their manuscripts by either marking up in handwriting earlier versions of published materials or typing extensive new or revised passages (either themselves or with the assistance of a typing pool). The production staff then retyped the content and prepared the materials either on a compositor (a special typewriter that prepares content for offset printing) or with an emerging class of software known as automated text processing systems. Nearly all of the material was published in printed form, though the first help systems appeared during this time. These systems were considered experimental in nature and supplemental to the user experience. (An all-too familiar help screen advised, "Help not available," reinforcing the role of Help as a supplemental resource.)

The business climate in general, and the environment for technical communication in particular, changed considerably by the mid-1980s with the growth in number of types and customers for the company's minicomputers and, more significantly, with the introduction of the company's best-selling personal computer. Although the mainframe computer remained popular, the other products not only provided significant revenue, but also served different markets and, in turn, changed the nature of technical communication. Mini and personal computers were sold in large volumes to customers who had little or no computer experience. The organizations purchasing these computers invested the least amount needed to train their staffs in managing computer operations—and designated only a few key staff members to such roles.

With such large numbers of customers to serve, the company changed its approach to technical support. It provided only essential support and shifted responsibilities like setting up and customizing computers and troubleshooting computer problems to its increasingly novice users. Customers who needed more support had to pay for it through service contracts or on an as-needed basis.

In addition, although the company continued to develop software that ran on these computers, the increasingly specialized use of computers ultimately brought about an increasing number of software applications that were developed by third parties (that is, by other companies), and called third-party software to address these market niches. Some of these market niches were highly specialized, such as membership organizations, medical and dental offices, tax preparation, and the petroleum industry. Other market niches focused on specialized uses of computers, such as forecasting, creating and managing databases, and creating, managing, and preparing

Table 1.1 Transitions in the technical communication job at a large employer of technical communicators

	Late 1970s	Mid- to Late 1980s	Late-1990s to Early 2000s	Early 2000s to Now
Primary product	Large systems sold in moderate to low volumes to people who would provide generous training to the staff that operate them and be provided with generous support from the company.	Mid-range systems and, eventually, PCs, which were sold in high volumes to people who would have to set up and operate them themselves. Operating systems, database software, and similar products.	PCs and other high volume, low-cost systems. High-end software, especially for commercial use. Customized materials for clients for whom the company was designing implementations	Software for managing networks of computers, and the information on them. Also, services for planning, installing, customizing, and managing such networks for customers.
Title	Writer, editor, illustrator.	Information developer (applies to all job classifications)	Tier 1: Software engineer (or similar title), responsible for design and interface responsibilities. Tier 2: Technical writer, responsible for implementing the designs.	Tier 1: Software engineer (or similar title), responsible for design and interface responsibilities. Tier 2: Technical writer, responsible for implementing the designs.
Qualifications for the job	Usually, field experience with technical expertise (would be taught the writing skills). Occasionally, university-trained writers (would be taught the technology).	Communication of technical content to target audience(s). Usually university education in technical communication (university degrees became a requirement). Occasionally hired people with technical expertise and converted them into technical writers, especially during periods of redeployment.	Tier 1 jobs: Degrees in computer science, usability, or related degrees, or job experience. Tier 2 jobs: Wordsmithing experience and writing or communication degrees.	Tier 1 jobs: Degrees in computer science or usability, or related degrees, or job experience. Tier 2 jobs: Wordsmithing experience and writing or communication degrees. Experience with content management software.

Primary job responsibility	Wordsmithing the technical specifications so that they would be useful as reference documentation by trained personnel.	Preparing information for use by target user	Preparing information for the target user	Designing large databases of technical content and providing that content. Overseeing the creation and publication of user-created content.
Primary means of production	Typewriters and compositors, then highly specialized automated text processing systems.	Automated text processing systems using markup languages that resembled HTML.	Web-based authoring systems, desktop publishing systems like Interleaf. Except for complex coding, handled by the author.	Content management systems that operate under DITA.

information for publication, an area then known as word processing and desktop publishing.

Both the change in markets for computers and the rise of word processing and desktop publishing led to profound changes in the work of technical communicators in this organization. The primary responsibility of technical communicators shifted from documenting the functions and features of products for use by highly trained, well-supported computer professionals, to explaining how to perform key tasks with the systems to computer novices and others who (the company assumed) would develop, at best, limited expertise with computers. To address this changing need, the company replaced its specialty-based job classes of technical writer, technical editor, and technical illustrator with a single job title: information developer (Davis, 1989). Information developers were supposed to serve as advocates for computer users and to supply their versatile base of skills (writing, editing, and illustration) to explain products, services, and their uses to users. In response to this new mandate, information developers experimented with new modes of simplified and user-centered communication, such as task-oriented writing, wordless instructions, and online help systems (which became increasingly common each year of the decade). Adding to the challenge, this U.S.-based company grew substantially outside of its home country, and increasingly needed to translate and localize its systems and their documentation. As a broader response to less sophisticated users working in a widening range of contexts, these information developers tried to influence the design of the systems so that they would pose fewer barriers to users, and to assess the overall usability of systems shipped to market. In essence, these information developers saw themselves as the user advocates.

Although product and technical expertise continued to be highly valued, because the new job emphasized synthesizing information in context and using a variety of communication skills to create technical content, the preferred job candidate for information development positions had a university degree in technical communication or a similar field. The company occasionally hired experienced people with product and technical skills and then retrained them as information developers, but this happened during difficult economic periods and was primarily an effort to maintain employment opportunities for these redeployed workers, not to bring technical skills into the information development group. All information development jobs were classified as professional, except for those in probationary (entry-level) positions.

At this time, the rise of word processing and automated publishing also affected the way that information developers prepared content. Increasingly, information developers prepared their own material for production, entering it in text processing systems themselves rather than marking up drafts and typing insert pages for others to retype. Furthermore, the text processing system used in this company involved a complex text markup language. In such systems, information developers use tags to indicate different parts of the text, like <p> to indicate a paragraph and <h3> to indicate a third-level heading. These systems contrasted with the popular PC-based word processing and desktop publishing used elsewhere at the time. The PC-based systems did not involve tags. Instead, they let users see the text exactly as it would be printed (called What-You-See-Is-What-You-Get, or WYSIWYG) systems. In contrast, at the company, text processing software worked on a mainframe computer, sometimes with the use of PCs that emulated mainframe terminals; the PCs would be connected to the mainframe computer and the image on the screen would then appear like that of a mainframe terminal rather than that of a PC screen. This use of a text-processing system reflected the company's significant investment in these mainframe-based publishing systems. Although the company continued to maintain a production staff (whose job titles did not change during this period), its size dwindled as technical communicators increasingly handled many production tasks themselves.

By the late 1990s, the shift from mainframe computers to PCs was complete, and the Internet had emerged as the primary means of communicating online. The market for mainframe and mini-computers had changed significantly by this time. Although demand still existed, customers increasingly used these mainframes to manage large networks of PCs. Similarly, although the company still manufactured PC hardware, it had long ceded the PC software market to other companies. The hardware market had become increasingly competitive and price-sensitive. That is, customers now assumed that, for the most part, product quality did not vary among brands, so they chose their PCs based on price; not surprisingly, consumers tended to prefer the lowest priced computer.

To survive in this environment, the company increasingly moved to providing specialized services to customers. For most customers, "receiving services" meant that the company would provide all of the computer equipment and software needed in the organization, and then, for an additional fee, would manage that network of hardware and software, as well as write and manage specialized software needed within the organization (this software was called customized applications, because it was intended for use only within one organization).

The job of the technical communicator underwent another round of profound changes in this period. In addition to working within product development groups to prepare materials for users, technical communicators worked at client sites to document these installations and customized applications. Even among those who worked in product development groups, the technical communicators tended to work within two broad categories of assignments. Some became designers of the experiences that users would have with the systems. These technical communicators determined what support users needed throughout their experience with the systems and then designed interactions with the computer that facilitated this experience; that is, these communicators designed the screens, prompts, and forms with which users interacted in the application software, wrote accompanying text. These technical communicators also designed Web sites that provided additional user support, and wrote some materials used there, and assessed the user experience using a variety of techniques such as rapid prototyping and usability testing. The other group of technical communicators primarily followed the direction of this first group using plans established by the first group, prepared content for publication in print, or online, or both.

Recognizing this stratification of work, the company replaced its job classification of information developer with two new job titles. The first group of technical communicators was given the title of "software engineer" and classified in a professional position. The second group was given the title of "technical writer" and classified in a para-professional position. Regardless of how technical communicators were classified, or whether they were called software engineers or technical writers, all prepared their own content for publication using Web publishing software and complex content management systems. A separate group of specialized workers who had programming training and strong computer science backgrounds set up and maintained these publishing systems, though they rarely prepared content for publication.

The technical communication job at this company continues to evolve in the first decade of the twenty-first century. In terms of products, the company continues its move away from manufacturing hardware (it even sold its PC manufacturing operations) and toward developing enterprise-wide software, which manages large networks of computers and information on them. The company receives an ever-larger share of its revenues from installing, customizing, and managing computer networks for customers. Still, within the two-tiered framework for the work of technical communicators introduced during the previous decade, technical communicators play one of two roles: designers who create interactions between users and the software, and documenters who provide instructions to users on how to most effectively use the software. Although it continues to publish some content in print, the company publishes most content online, some on public Web sites, some in password-protected locations. Much information is published as individual topics; that is, as a series of one-screen discussions of a subject, rather than as complete manuals. Users typically find topics by searching the database, following well-identified links, or by being directed to a specific Web page by a cross-reference from another Web page or by a person.

As a result of these changes, the company now approaches its information as a database of content, rather than as a library. Publishing a database carries different requirements than publishing books or even online help. Some of the difference affects the design and writing of technical content. Designers of these databases focus on the architecture—or structure—of the database, so different users can easily find information of interest to them. They also focus on ensuring consistency of formats across the database to prevent users from encountering structural inconsistencies in otherwise similar articles, terminology, or technical content. These decisions are encapsulated in templates, which are like fill-in-the-blank forms in which writers create content.

Some differences of preparing databases of content involve the technology for publishing it. The company has championed the Darwin Information Typing Architecture (DITA), a standard that defines how technical content is identified when it is created. DITA facilitates the use of templates in producing content for publication and ultimately for users searching for published content.

Using databases to publish content also lets the company welcome contributions from people outside the technical communication department, including those who work for the company in technical and marketing capacities and customers who have developed expertise with the products and services and who have a first-hand user's perspective. In many instances, these contributors follow templates established by communication professionals.

In this environment, the job of the technical communicator continues along its two tracks of development, with one focused on the design and programming of information databases and the other focused on providing content for these databases. As one of the managers of this company observed, "Our people are becoming information programmers."

Five Phases in the Development of Technology for Technical Communication

Over the past 30 years, technology has affected technical communication in profound ways. Although technical communicators in different organizations followed their own paths in adopting and integrating technology, most were affected by two overarching trends. The first trend is the increasing role of computers in the production process. Computers went from playing no role in the production process to being the primary means of publishing content. The second trend is the increasing move of content to online, from a time when organizations published nearly everything in print to now, when organizations publish nearly all content online (even if the content is published in a format in which users are actually expected to print it, such as PDF files).

The example also illustrates that the changes did not happen overnight. Rather, they happened gradually, in phases. A review of the changes brought about by technology suggests that they occurred in five phases, starting when production tasks were automated, and continuing through the late 2000s, a time in which nearly all content is published online, and organizations actively seek to add contributions from users and developers through the use of social computing (Web 2.0). The following parts describe each of these phases.

Phase One: Automation of Production Tasks (1970s and Early 1980s)

The first phase in the development of technology for technical communication was characterized by the automation of various production tasks, occurring between the late 1970s and mid-1980s.

A significant shift in printing from hot to cold type had occurred a decade earlier (Arnston, 1998). Hot type refers to a process for setting type for printing, in which highly skilled typographers prepare a printing plate, character-by-character, from a manuscript. Because it required completely retyping (so to speak) the text, hot type processes required additional proofreading. Correcting errors was costly. Cold type allowed people to make printing plates by shooting a photograph of an original. Then printers could make corrections more simply by pasting replacement text over the error.

Not surprisingly, typing was the first and most significant production task that was automated, a change that reduced labor and the number of errors. Initially the typewriter, developed in the nineteenth century, primarily offered type-once services. Corrections, additions, and other changes required the complete retyping of content. In fact, one person I know who wrote a dissertation during the days when only typing was offered, commented to me that she paid her typist $US 1.00 a page and would ask herself whether each change was worth another dollar. By the mid-1970s, correcting capabilities were added to typewriters (Beattie and Rahenkamp, 1981). The most basic included a correction ribbon, which allowed a typist to type over a mistake and then correct it. This worked with small changes only, however, and encouraged surface-level and small scale revision. The more elaborate (and expensive) solution involved the addition of document storage capabilities to the typewriter. The document could be saved on something resembling a diskette (an extremely fragile, small, thin disk suitable for recording data) in function, though it was considerably larger in size. If corrections or additions were needed, a typist could insert the disk back into the storage device, type the changes, and produce a corrected document, without retyping the entire document (Beattie and Rahenkamp, 1981).

Meanwhile, computers were not yet suitable for typing, because they had no display screen on which users could see what they typed. With the advent of display screens for computers in the 1970s, entry of data for computers moved from punch cards to keyboards and screens and, soon after, to software—known then as *text processing* systems—for entering, storing, changing, and printing text (Gillette, 1983).

Because computers used character interfaces, these early text processors were not capable of producing What-You-See-Is-What-You-Get (WYSIWYG) type. Instead, users needed to instruct computers how to format the printouts of the content they typed. They did so using various codes to indicate how the content should appear. For example, the early word processor SCRIBE, used at Carnegie-Mellon University (Reid, 1981), had tags like .p to indicate the beginning of a paragraph. Other tags indicated different levels of headings and the use of emphasis type (such as bold and italic). Other text processing systems used similar tags.

For the most part, the systems printed output on dot-matrix printers, but the output was not suitable for publishing (indeed, many people felt it wasn't even suitable for reading in draft form as the text was light and hard to see). As a result, additional systems were developed that could print material in a way that was suitable for publishing purposes. Such material is called camera-ready because it could be used by a printer to make the plates used in printing pages. Printers used cameras to make these plates. (Use of systems to create camera-ready copy involved even more complex programming codes.)

In addition, specialized software applications that supported other publishing tasks emerged during this period. One, called spell-checkers could check the spelling of a document and identify misspelled words, another, "grade-level checkers," could analyze features of text and indicate the likely reading level of a document. A third was for preparing indexes (Southworth, 1989). Although a publications specialist needed to identify index entries, the entries could be linked with a particular passage of text on an automated system, and the system could automatically generate an index without someone needing to verify the page numbers. This system also reduced the time needed to update indexes.

However, the text processing and publishing systems developed during this era worked only on mainframe computers. Because these systems were costly (usually in the hundreds of thousands, or millions of U.S. dollars), they were used only by the largest organizations who could afford to install and support them.

During this period, technology for preparing illustrations and graphics was not in commercial use; it was still being developed in research laboratories. Illustrators typically hand drew technical drawings, like those of the interiors of products with exploded views. As former STC president Ken Cook reports, drawings "were first done in pencil; then, upon proof approval, inked for creating camera ready copy" (2008).

In addition, while developing text processing and publishing systems, computer scientists realized that the computer display screen used to follow entry and editing could also be used to display the content, and they experimented with the first online help systems. Given the limitations of the character interfaces they used, these systems typically displayed just a few lines of explanatory text. These limitations included displaying only characters, using fixed spacing (that is, each character used the same amount of space), displaying only a fixed number of lines because scrolling was not available, and not easily displaying graphics or colors. Help was not widely used in systems during these years, but by 1985, several research projects with online help had been conducted (Wallace, 1985).

Although the development of text processing and related tools more tightly integrated the work of technical communicators into the production process, most technical communication groups considered production separate from the work of writers. Similarly, in production, the editors still focused on preparing text for production, rather than performing production tasks themselves. As a result, most organizations hired technical communicators for either their knowledge of technical content or their ability to communicate (Shirk, 1989). At most, some employers inquired about the typing speed of job applicants, but most employers considered typing skills and the ability to use publishing systems a desirable trait, not a required skill.

Phase Two: The Desktop Revolution (Mid-1980s to Early 1990s)

The second phase in the development of technology for technical communication was characterized by growth in personal computing and a corresponding growth of tools to assist technical communicators with automating publishing tasks.

The cumbersome, tag-based automated text processing systems used on mainframe computers, which had required extensive training to use, were replaced by software applications for personal computers. Word processing applications handled the entry, revision, simple formatting, and printing of documents. Because these personal computer-based word processors incorporated some elements of WYSIWYG text entry and editing, they did not require the extensive tags of mainframe-based word processing and were perceived as easier to use and therefore required less training (Scally, 1989). Word processing software was also considerably more affordable than mainframe-based software; it cost just a few hundred (rather than tens of thousands) U.S. dollars per license.

Although word processing systems simplified the entry of text, the first word processing systems had their limitations. The first was the quality of the output. The only affordable PC-based printers were dot matrix, which only printed in a small number of typefaces and produced low-quality print images that were not suitable for mass printing. In response, low-cost laser printers were developed, which provided a selection of fonts and could produce output of sufficient quality for printing.

A second set of challenges pertained to the availability of tools in the software that simplified specialized formatting tasks, like creating tables, using scientific notation, and adding footnotes. Handling these tasks often required work-arounds or complex actions that did not always produce the desired results. Other challenges pertained to automating complex, error-laden tasks, such as having systems automatically generate cross-references, tables of contents and indexes (tasks that were already being automated in mainframe-based text processing systems).

A third set of challenges pertained to graphics. Computer-aided design tools, which let users create, store, and reuse graphics online, were just then being developed for commercial use. These complex systems required specialized hardware and software, were more expensive than personal computers, and required extensive training and additional equipment to use. Most significantly, although the images could be produced, saved, and changed online—thus reducing rework costs and the creation of related images—not all graphics could be easily integrated with text, thus requiring manual tasks for operations that, in theory, should have all been feasible online. The problem was most acute with mainframe-based text processing systems (which were still widely used) on IBM PCs.

In response, a new class of software emerged called desktop publishing programs, which handled all of these tasks—entering and formatting text, adding cross-references, and integrating text with graphics—as well as more complex layout tasks. The ultimate goal of desktop publishing systems was preparing materials for submission to printers in camera-ready form. At their best, desktop publishing systems let users prepare entire documents exactly as they should be printed, and print them out in camera-ready form (from which materials could be prepared for printing presses). Desktop publishing systems worked like word processors in that users could automatically enter text into them, but these systems also let users take documents prepared with other word processors and prepare them for publication. These systems were complex because they used complex codes, had a non-intuitive screen layout, or both.

Because online preparation of text, graphics, and layout is inherently a visual activity, and because only graphical user interfaces could perform these activities in such a way that what appeared on screen matched (or closely matched) what would eventually be printed, computers that featured graphical user interfaces were preferred for publishing activities. During early days of this period, only the Apple Macintosh (the Mac) featured such an interface, so it became a preferred tool for desktop publishing activities among many technical communicators. But because the organizations for which technical communicators worked often used IBM-based PCs that ran under a character-based interface, a dilemma emerged because the systems that worked best for publishing were not compatible with those used by the rest of organizations used for the rest of their business activities. Some organizations continued to use IBM-based PCs and to deal with the technical problems; others chose Mac-based publishing systems and figured out how to handle the incompatibility of systems.

In addition to the emergence of desktop publishing systems, other software emerged that benefited technical communicators. Versions of spelling checkers, grade-level checkers, and index preparation software that had already been available for mainframe-based text processors were now available for personal computers. In addition, software for checking grammar also became widely available, first as separate products and, within a few years, as part of most word processing software.

Although the major developments in technology for technical communicators primarily occurred in the then fast-growing branch of personal computing, developments continued to occur with mainframe-based text processing systems, which had been the staple of the previous period (remember that these were the text processing systems that ran on software that used codes like .p to indicate different parts of text). Many organizations still preferred mainframe-based text processing because their primary business systems were also mainframe-based. These systems also provided for more effective centralized storage and online transmission of documents (though available, networks of PCs were still emerging during this time, and most PC-based information was available only on a single PC and transferring to other PCs could pose significant challenges). To facilitate the easy exchange of mainframe-based documents, standards for markup languages emerged. One of the best known is Standardized General Markup Language (SGML), a standard that was adopted by the U.S. government for use in its documents, especially those with defense purposes (Davidson, 1993).

Other standards emerged for user interfaces (that is, the parts of the hardware and the software with which users interact) as research indicated that consistency in interfaces among different types of software simplifies the learning of new applications, because users could transfer some skills from a familiar application to a new one. The consistency also minimized errors resulting from inconsistencies. One of the most widely followed set of standards was that of the Mac interface. IBM tried to mimic the concept with its 1987 Common User Architecture for all its products, but that met with neither the critical or commercial success of the Mac interface (Berry, 1988).

In addition, more content was presented online during this period. Although experimental work in online help continued, the real excitement in presenting information online emerged from Apple's Hypercard, a WYSIWIG software application that let users create groups of these online cards, called stacks (Babcock, 1989; Bernstein, 1989; Walker, 1989). Each card could contain short bits of text and visual information, and that information could be linked together as presentations or fact sheets, or for whatever purpose an author could dream up. The ability to link the content—called hyperlinking—created strong interest among technical communicators. Apple provided Hypercard software free with its Mac computer, which promoted its use. Toolbook (Carliner, 1999), a similar product for the PC, was eventually developed and made available at a low cost, though it never reached the popularity of Hypercard.

Further facilitating this use of online information was the increasing availability and decreasing cost of disk storage on PCs. The first PCs in the early 1980s used 5.25-inch diskettes, which only held 360,000 bytes of information. By the end of the 1980s, systems had internal hard drives with up to 50 MB of storage capacity.

Interest also grew in online multimedia. The videodisc and tools for using it to create computer-based training first appeared in the mid-1980s (Dell, 1985; Elser, 1985). But tools for producing multimedia use were still expensive and not widely available. For example, the cost of reproducing the first videodiscs was $US 1,500 per disk. Similarly, playing sound required use of an expensive, separately-installed sound card in a computer and, because of the concerns of the impact of *sound bleed* from one person's computer onto the work performance of others in an office, this feature often was not purchased for early PCs.

Toward the end of this period, networking of PCs became common and the Internet—then still in an experimental stage—grew. People who worked at large companies and those affiliated with universities had access to it. The first *browsers*—software for locating and displaying material that was stored on any computer linked to the Internet (Webopedia, 2008)—appeared too, though they were text based (that is, they could display only text, not graphics). These included MOSAIC and the University of Minnesota's GOPHER system (Computer History Museum, 2006).

In response to the increasingly ubiquitous use of computers in the workplace, employers started demanding that technical communicators have, at the least, word processing skills and, at the most, familiarity with certain classes of software, especially desktop publishing software. Because desktop publishing required extensive skills, companies initially hired desktop publishers to handle these tasks. Although few of these desktop publishers actually wrote content, many identified themselves as technical communicators, because many of their job opportunities were in this field. The rise of skilled desktop publishers resulted in a downturn in employment for editorial assistants who had been overseeing production tasks and typesetters who had been working with more dated publishing systems. But by the end of this period, many organizations realized that, with training in these publishing systems, the same person who writes the text could also be responsible for designing and producing it, and employment opportunities quickly flattened for those who did not provide a wide-ranging base of skills that covered the publication process end-to-end.

Phase Three: The GUI Revolution (Early to Late 1990s)

The third phase in the development of technology for technical communication is characterized by the move to Graphical User Interfaces (GUIs) on IBM-based PCs. Although Apple's Macintosh always boasted a GUI (based on a predecessor product, the Apple LISA), IBM PCs running under the character-based DOS system continued to dominate the business market. Although many technical communicators felt that Macs were more appropriate for publishing work, many were compelled to continue working on PCs, because those were the dominant systems in their employers' organizations.

Recognizing that the graphical interface offered countless advantages, IBM tried to upgrade its operating system with the 1987 introduction of its second generation of PCs. As a result of both a failure to properly define the capabilities of this new operating system and a series of delays in fully launching it, the new operating system, OS/2, never had the impact of its original. Meanwhile, Microsoft, which had worked with IBM to develop the original operating system for the PC, developed its Windows extension to DOS and, by version 3.1 of Windows, what was once a minor add-on (to make DOS appear like a GUI) became a widely used GUI product. PC-based applications were then redesigned for the new interface. This, in turn, sped up the development of PC-based versions of desktop publishing programs that once only worked on the Mac. Similarly, moving to a GUI simplified visual communication tasks such as page layout and the creation of illustrations. Although some character-based work continued, all desktop publishing effectively was GUI based by this time (for example, PageMaker, originally designed for the Mac only, was now available for the PC).

Three other significant developments in desktop publishing occurred during this period: the emergence of specialized desktop publishing tools, an even tighter integration of desktop publishing into the printing process, and changes to printing systems. The first development was the emergence of specialized desktop publishing tools. Some applications, including Adobe PageMaker and Quark Express, worked well with small documents, like those intended for marketing (Brewer, 1995). Others, such as Interleaf, were better suited for larger documents. Only one, FrameMaker, seemed equally adept for both small and large documents. As a result of this versatility, FrameMaker eventually became the dominant desktop publishing product in the field of technical communication. (Its versatility eventually extended beyond printing; it could produce print and online versions of the same document.)

The second significant development in desktop publishing was an even tighter integration of it into the printing process. Rather than merely produce camera-ready copy from which the plates used on printing presses could be made, desktop publishing programs could now produce the plates themselves, eliminating another step in the printing process, and further reducing print costs. Some organizations banked the savings, while others used the savings to print color documents (costs of using color in the past had been prohibitive).

The third significant development pertains to printing systems. Significant developments in copier technology allowed copying machines to provide printing quality that was similar to that produced by the more traditional printing presses. For smaller volumes of printing, these copiers could handle printing at a more reasonable cost than traditional printing (which required setting up a printing press). In some branches of communication, this new generation of printers meant that organizations could prepare several versions of the same document for different markets and provide users with materials tailored to their specific interests and needs (a process known as mass-customizing).

As desktop publishing and printing technology further evolved, online publishing moved into the mainstream. To encourage application developers to provide online help and as a means of increasing its own use of online help, Microsoft published interface and other guidelines for its Windows-based help, known as WinHelp. This step facilitated a rapid rise in the use of online help. In response, several software applications emerged that helped organizations easily prepare online help. In time, the product RoboHelp from BlueSky Software (later sold to Macromedia which was sold, in turn, to Adobe) came to dominate the market.

The other major development in online information was the movement of the Internet from a limited-use network by those working in the defense industry and at universities, to a ubiquitous communications network. This growth, started by MOSAIC, exploded with the emergence of Netscape, the first browser with the ability to display graphics. Its free distribution quickly facilitated its acceptance. Microsoft soon offered a competitive browser to get some of the market for itself. As part of making information easily available to anyone at any time, the rise of the browser also facilitated standards for sharing information. Through browsers, organizations could conceivably distribute sound and video in addition to text and graphics, but most users did not have software for playing these media on their systems. Users could download additional software to play this content—called plug-ins—but many were reluctant to do so (Carliner, 1999).

As both desktop publishing and help authoring tools further integrated the publishing process into the writing process, thus increasing the possibility that the person who initially wrote the text would also oversee its publication, employers started expecting technical communicators to have skills with desktop publishing and authoring tools as well as specific knowledge of specific versions of the tools used in their organizations. Reasons for this new expectation included the increasing sophistication of the systems, but also the increased use of contract services (contractors were expected to be able to be productive on their first day of an assignment, not requiring training on any outside skills or tools) and high unemployment in the field of technical communication. As companies were forced to restructure due to a shift from a manufacturing to a knowledge-based economy, many technical communicators lost their jobs in fading industries. Flooded with applications, hiring managers gave priority to applicants with technical skills (Carliner, 2001).

Phase Four: Web 1.0 (Mid-1990s to Mid-2000s)

The fourth phase in the development of technology for technical communication was characterized by the emergence of the Internet as a primary means of communication, and the World Wide Web as a source of information. Although the Internet had existed in some form for over two decades, the rise at the end of the previous period of browsers with the ability to display graphics and the growth of low-cost services for connecting to the Internet led to a rapid rise in the use of the Internet between 1996 and 2000.

The Internet and the World Wide Web together facilitated unprecedented levels of communication and access to information. Email became one of the primary means of interpersonal communication and people could exchange files through email and other easy-to-use file transfer mechanisms.

Electronic file transfer had many effects on technical communication. It affected the process of reviewing drafts, because technical communicators increasingly sent drafts of publications out for review by email, thus eliminating the costly and time-consuming process of duplicating and mailing drafts. (The ability to include comments in computer files also facilitated electronic reviews.) Even reviews of scientific articles began to occur online. *Technical Communication*, STC's journal, began using electronic reviews at the beginning of this period. The resulting savings in review costs and time translated into increased productivity of technical communicators. Electronic file transfers also facilitated remote work, as workers in one location could now easily collaborate on or manage projects across multiple locations (Dziak, 2001).

But perhaps the best-known impact of the Internet is the rise of Web sites. At first, most Web sites were primarily intended for promotional or experimental purposes, but then Web-based applications, such as e-commerce, emerged. E-commerce, in turn, created the need for other Web applications and the promise of a new model of business in which the primary commodity exchanged was knowledge. Hoping to capitalize on the unprecedented growth of the Web, venture capital firms funded many—some might say any—ideas for Web sites. This sudden influx of capital and rise of countless Web sites is known as the dot-com boom, because the sites all had universal resource locators (URLs) ending in .com. (Similarly, the sudden closure of many of these Web sites that failed to generate a profit in a reasonable period became known as the dot-com bust.)

In addition to launching Web sites, the growth of the Internet affected other aspects of technical communication activities. It created new opportunities for some to become actively involved in designing Web sites and assessing their usability. Others started preparing material for delivery over the Web. To do so, technical communicators needed to learn how to use several new classes of authoring tools. Web pages are formatted using a standard markup language called Hypertext Markup Language (HTML), whose standards were approved by the World Wide Web Commission (W3C). For those who had used the tag-based text processing programs on mainframe computers, HTML looked familiar because it was based on those. For those who had never learned how to use tag-based systems, however, HTML seemed complex. In response, a new class of authoring tools emerged that would help people create Web sites without having to learn much or any of the HTML codes. Some of these tools focused on the preparation of entire Web sites, and included the ability to merge changing data (called dynamic data) with more static text. Some tools were capable of creating entire Web sites, like the extremely complex ColdFusion and the moderately complex Dreamweaver (useful for designing individual Web pages), and simpler tools, like Front Page, were designed for personal and small business pages.[1] In addition, some Web sites had changing elements and required some level of programming knowledge in languages suitable for the Web, so some technical communicators learned how to write programming routines called scripts in languages like CGI, PHP, and C++.

During this time, too, applications like Photoshop and Illustrator made graphics software accessible to mainstream users, both in terms of price and usability (although still complex, people could learn these applications relatively easily). So technical communicators needed to learn how to use other tools intended to assist with the development of visuals and graphics. Although Photoshop and Illustrator were not developed specifically for use with the Web, the visual nature of Web sites facilitated growth in their use. In addition, the rise of a few nearly ubiquitous media players that most large organizations pre-installed on computers led to an increased use of sound and video in Web documents.

As communicators increased their use of the Web to deliver information, they took advantage of its ability to display ever-changing content and its increasing capabilities to display both audio and visual content. These functions, in turn, generated microgenres of content that became synonymous with the Web, such as Frequently Asked Questions and online forms. (Both of these microgenres had actually existed in print, but they gained new visibility and generated new interest online.) Note, however, that most of the content was relatively static—that is, produced, published, and controlled by an organization like a commercial enterprise or a government agency. Users could not directly contribute to this content, although tools like message boards and discussion lists (which had been available since the early uses of computers for communication) provided users with opportunities to comment on content.

Although the uses of the Web started to vary, the interface standards started to converge, as certain practices became common conventions, such as the use of underlined green or blue type to indicate hyperlinks and the placement of navigation bars at the top and to the left of most Web pages.

Although experts in the design of Web pages increasingly emphasized visual and interactive characteristics, most technical communicators continued to prepare material for online use as static, text-based online help. At this time, too, Microsoft quickly upgraded its help interface from the original WinHelp to HTML, and upgraded most of its tools for creating help. As a result, although many technical communicators wrote about applications affected by the Web, the materials they prepared actually looked more like Help than Web pages. This might have resulted from a desire to mimic the look and feel of Help provided with Microsoft software, which had a unique look and generally did not include any visuals, much less audio content.[2]

Although developments in desktop publishing were limited during this period, the primary ones provided technical communicators with tools for ensuring that they could produce a single source file to publish output in print and online. One such tool was Adobe Corporation's portable document format (PDF). Originally, PDF was intended to address a serious printing problem: when printed on different computers, the same file prints differently, possibly ruining carefully planned formatting such as pagination, margins, and layouts. By printing a document from a PDF, a technical communicator could ensure that the file would look the same when printed on any computer and printer. In addition, the PDF ensured that documents would display the same on any computer screen. Organizations realized that they could use this ability to distribute documents online. In some cases, this meant that organizations would prepare documents only as PDF files and distribute these files to customers. Customers would then print documents themselves, eliminating both the time and cost of printing (no small savings as production and printing adds between 5 and 13 weeks to a cycle). In other situations, organizations distributed PDF files expecting that people would use them only online.

Other developments in publishing technology sought to further extend this type of versatility with documents. Specifically, the World Wide Web Commission developed a more versatile markup language—Extensible Markup Language (XML)—that would allow organizations to prepare a single source file and use it as different types of output: print, online, and mobile (that is, used on small screen devices known as personal digital assistants). XML also let users create their own tags so that their documents could address situations not addressed by the standard. XML addressed some practical challenges faced by organizations preparing technical documentation, such as those in the aircraft industry, which needs to produce documents for maintenance formats for presentation online, in print, and on PDAs, but cannot risk producing different source files for these different formats for fear of introducing errors. This ability to publish a material in a variety of formats from a single source file is known as single sourcing.

With the increasing ease of publishing content, and the growing numbers of versions of a single document, organizations needed systems that would help them organize all of this material, control versions, and make sure that only material that was approved would be published. Systems that accomplished these management tasks are known as content management systems (CMS) and they first emerged during this period. At first, these systems were intended primarily for internal use within organizations to manage content that was under development. More recently, such systems have been used, as well, to publish content. When doing so, these systems ensure that the content is formally approved before publishing, provides tools for ensuring that content is appropriately formatted, and tracks all links to, and usage of, the content.

In another development, not only did the volume of content expand, but so did its reach; significantly, the use of technical content increased outside of the countries in which it was produced. Products, services, and related technical content were marketed in several countries in a process known as globalization (Hoft, 1995; Bosley, 2000). Globalization led to the need to translate documents, but also to localize content (that is, adjust terminology and examples so that they use local terms like the term "lift" instead of "elevator"). Growth in demand and volume of translation and localization led to new systems for automating part of this task and changes in the process of developing technical content, which were intended to minimize the number of words altered in a document to ultimately contain the cost of translation.

For technical communicators, a new tiering of work emerged. At one end were technical communicators who designed the user experience of a Web site, from determining the purpose of the site, to preparing its flow and interface, to designing the content and conducting assessments of its usability. Although many people performing these tasks had backgrounds in technical communication, they did not necessarily have job titles of technical communicators, and in many instances did not work in technical communication groups. At the other end were technical communicators working in groups primarily to prepare online help, user's guides, references, and similar technical content. This pattern was identified in a survey of the workload of technical communication departments (Carliner, 2004).

With the advent of online help and online distribution of documents in PDF, and the elimination of printing from many processes, and in response to increasing competition, most organizations shortened their product development cycles from 1–3 years (which had been common in the 1970s) to ongoing product releases (common in the first decade of the twenty-first century). Many technical communicators worked in a state of continuous production of information, rather than going through peaks of work followed by valleys, in product cycles that had characterized work processes 20 years earlier. At the same time, managers who hired technical communicators for these roles intensified their focus on applicants' (and workers') facility with tools.

Phase Five: Web 2.0 (Since Mid-2000s)

Writing about this phase poses a challenge because it's not yet history—it's current life (at least, when this chapter was written). As a result, developments in the field have arisen over the year since the chapter was first drafted that have significantly informed the conclusions presented here. Further developments in the time between the completion of the last draft of this chapter and the time it is published could further inform it, but practicalities of publishing prevent them from being reflected here.

With that caveat in mind, the most current phase in the development of technology for technical communication seems characterized by the growth of technologies that promote a continued increase in the publication and distribution of content online, as well as interactive capabilities of computers and communication networks.

Standardization and simplicity characterize the most recent technologies for promoting publication and distribution of content online. Some standardization efforts are invisible to end users, but facilitate the exchange of information. One of the most significant is the Darwin Information Typing Architecture (DITA). DITA is an XML-based architecture for technical information that divides content into small, self-contained pieces that can be used in several different communication products.

Some of these standardization efforts result from the emergence of dominant software applications, such as Microsoft Word for word processing, Robohelp and Madcap Flare for preparing help, Dreamweaver for preparing Web sites, and Captivate for preparing online demonstrations. Certainly technical communicators can and often do choose other applications that perform the same tasks. In fact, as a means of avoiding the costs of purchasing or leasing software, many technical communicators now choose to use open-source software, which is made available to everyone without charge and that anyone can modify and distribute, without violating a copyright license. Furthermore, open-source applications prepare content that can be used easily with dominant commercial applications.

In a related development, content management systems continue to simplify the process of managing different versions of content and have emerged as a primary tool for publishing content online (Rockley, 2002). Early content management systems handled review and approval processes automatically. Newer ones add the capability of publishing material online once it is approved. Content management systems also promote the use of dynamic content; that is, content that changes frequently (e.g., the home page of newspapers changing every 15 minutes) (Shank, 2008).

Most technologies that promote use of interactive capabilities of computers and communication networks are referred to as Web 2.0 technologies, a term coined by Tim O'Reilly, the publisher of popular books on high-technology topics (O'Reilly, 2006)[3] to characterize in a single term three then-emerging trends in the World Wide Web, which, according to Shank (2008), included the following:

- The read/write Web, in which the Web is a two-way medium with people serving as both readers and providers of content, a situation made possible by software tools that let people create content easily. The read/write Web is characterized by tools like blogs (Web logs that let one person post thoughts and others respond) and wikis (a concept named for the Hawaiian word for fast, which allow many users to collaborate on the preparation of a single document).

- The Web-as-platform, in which Web sites are seamlessly knitted into applications, such as embedding calendars and maps into Web sites for making hotel reservations, so people can verify dates of a trip and see, for example, exactly where they're supposed to go and how much costs will be.
- Microcontent, which Shank (2008) explains, treats Web content in units that are smaller than full pages and involves pulling together pieces of content from various sources to make a single page. An example might be a home page for a technical support Web site, which includes updated announcements from a product development database, tips and techniques from an experts' blog, a podcast from a well-known developer, and a short satisfaction survey. Really Simple Syndication (RSS) informs regular users of the site about updates.

Applications that showcase the technical capabilities of Web 2.0 allow for social networking applications, like Facebook, LinkedIn, and MySpace, which let people tell their contacts what they are currently doing, comment on what the contacts are doing, send messages, and post announcements, calls for help, and photos (among other things) within a single interface.

Although most coverage of Web 2.0 applications has been about technologies that promote use of the interactive capabilities of computers and communication networks, technical communicators often find themselves working with another type of application and its related technologies, e-learning, which refers to content that is designed for instructional purposes. Although computer scientists first proposed the use of computers for learning in the 1940s and the first e-learning applications appeared in the 1960s, designing e-learning did not emerge as a significant assignment for technical communicators until the middle of this epoch, as evidenced by the growth of STC's Instructional Design and Learning Special Interest Group (which, as of 2008, was STC's largest special interest group with nearly 20% of STC members belonging to it).

The development of technology for e-learning followed a path similar to that followed by the technology for technical communication. By the time technical communicators became actively engaged in this pursuit, the common technologies had become the following:

- Authoring tools, which help course developers prepare content, much like help-authoring tools assist technical communicators with preparing online help. The most common tools for creating e-learning content include Dreamweaver (the same tool used to create Web sites with special features for creating learning programs) and Flash, a tool primarily used to create animation online, but often used to create engaging instructional sequences. Tools like Captivate, Photoshop, Illustrator, and Avid assist instructional course developers with specialized tasks like recording screens, creating visuals, and creating videos.

- Learning Content Management Systems (LCMS), which are specially designed content management systems that perform functions that are similar to those of content management systems. LCMS also manage track performance on tests in e-learning programs, both for record-keeping and choosing the most appropriate modules for learners based on their performance on tests.
- Learning Management Systems, which are basically electronic registrars that handle course registration, enrollment, and record keeping. (Their functions overlap with Learning Content Management Systems but these are in a different class of software.)

The stratification of work in technical communication that began in the previous phase, with one group of technical communicators designing the user experience of Web sites and another developing and producing the actual content, strengthened in this phase, as I found in two studies of work performed by technical communication groups (Carliner, 2005; Carliner, in preparation). However, those who develop and produce content have been facing dwindling work opportunities. Several factors have contributed to this. One is offshoring, in which organizations move clearly defined work assignments from markets where labor costs are high, like the United States, to those where labor costs are lower, like India. The types of assignments initially sent offshore are those can be completed without daily contact with subject matter experts. Another factor contributing to this has been the rise of content management systems, and the associated templates for creating and organizing content. These templates have simplified the task of subject matter experts creating their own documentation, with limited or no involvement from technical communicators. Seeking new work opportunities, these displaced technical communicators have sought opportunities creating and producing e-learning programs, especially those about software applications, as organizations have significantly increased their use of online tutorials and demonstrations to supplement online help and to provide an alternative to more costly classroom-based training sessions. However, these displaced technical communicators might experience the same consequences that they experienced earlier arising from the stratification of work in technical communication (Merrill and Wilson, 2006).

This stratification of work, predicted by Brown and Duguid (2000), might at first seem at odds with much literature in the field of technical communication that proposes new roles for technical communicators (e.g., the first quarter 2006 issue of *Technical Communication* and November 2006 issue of *Intercom* both focus on technical communicators and usability) and promotes "best practices" (such as Wilde *et. al's* idealized approach to assessing editing, 2006, and the fourth quarter 2008 issue of *Technical Communication,* which explores the then-emerging uses of virtual worlds in technical communication). But although such changes are considered by some experts to be ideal, they are not necessarily reflective of or feasible with typical practice.

Technology and Technical Communication: A Holistic View

I will now pull together the different technologies affecting the work of technical communicators (each of which appeared at different phases), and provide readers with a coherent framework for considering technologies that authors of subsequent chapters are sure to mention. Table 1.2 attempts to pull together the technologies that emerged and evolved over the five phases described in this chapter into a single framework, with three categories of components:

- authoring technologies, used to create and edit content;
- publishing technologies, used to prepare content for printing for publication;
- management technologies, needed to facilitate the flow of content from inception to withdrawal from publication.

The framework in Table 1.2 summarizes key categories of technology used in technical communication at the time this chapter was written within the context of the work of technical communicators. Although some products named admittedly could be classified differently, the classifications are based on the primary intended purpose of the product. Note, too, that product names provided are for example purposes only, and are not intended as endorsements.

Implications of Changes of Technology

Technology has always played a central role in technical communication. At first, it served primarily as the subject about which technical communicators wrote. As various publishing technologies emerged, the technology also became the tool that facilitated the work.

At the least, these trends have had a significant impact on various aspects of technical communication work. Consider the impact of technology on work processes. As technology developed, it reduced both the labor and time needed to take content from rough idea to published material. Work processes that once took one to two years have been condensed and now take three to six months. Through the capabilities that technology provided, technical writers have become their own designers, illustrators, and production assistants and, with the assistance of spelling and grammar

Table 1.2 Framework for considering technologies for technical communication (adapted from Carliner, 2004)

	Authoring technologies	Publishing technologies	Management technologies
Description	Hardware, software, and related standards needed to create and edit content.	Hardware, software, and related standards needed to prepare content for printing or for publication online or some other media.	Hardware, software, and related standards needed to facilitate the flow of content from inception (when someone first requests it), through publication until the content is withdrawn from publication.
Examples	Hardware: Computers, multimedia recording equipment, specialized graphics processors.	Hardware: Specialized graphics processors, specialized printing equipment.	Hardware: Technology infrastructure (including servers, routers, and wiring)
	Software: Word processing (like MS Word), audio and video recording (like Adobe Premiere), presentation graphics (like MS PowerPoint), photo finishing (like Adobe Photoshop), Illustration (like Adobe Illustrator), and screen capture software (like TechSmith SnagIt).	Software: Desktop publishing software (like Adobe Framemaker), Help authoring software (like RoboHelp and Madcap Flare), Web publishing software (like Dreamweaver and ColdFusion), video production software (like Avid products), animation software (like Adobe Flash), and presentation recording software (like TechSmith Camtasia and Adobe Connect)	Software: Content management software (which manages workflow, versions, and publishing of content in several formats), security software, learning content management software (which manages the creation of learning content, like OutStart) and learning management software (which acts as an electronic registrar, like Saba).
	Standards: Object Linking and Embedding (OLE) for interchanging content among applications.	Standards: For marking up content for publication, including markup languages like eXtensible Markup Language (XML), HyperText Markup Language (HTML),Darwin Information Typing Architecture (DITA), and Standardized General Markup Language (SGML) and programming and scripting languages (like PHP), file formats: portable document format (PDF), audio and video file formats (like MP3 and MP4),	Standards: Data transmission standards (like VOIP), data storage standards (like ASCII), security standards (like SSL).

checkers, their own editors, too. Companies have curtailed or eliminated printing, publishing much information as online help and, when choosing not to, preparing materials as PDF files that customers can print themselves. With publication processes simplified and capabilities expanded, organizations have added new software and human systems to handle the increased workload, such as the version control and workflow management capabilities of content management systems.

Consider, too, the impact of technology on the reuse of information. As content moved online and could be interchanged more quickly, organizations made a stronger effort to reuse existing information whenever possible.[4] Some reuse of information is simple, such as publishing the same procedure as online help and in a user's guide. Some reuse of information is more complex, such as publishing the same general product description for two different models, where the information is nearly identical except when discussing unique features, such as the distinctive characteristics of individual models (Hughes, 2009). Some of this type of reuse ensures consistency: using the same passages reduces or eliminates the likelihood of unintended inconsistencies. Some of this reuse is for economics: while organizations encourage their technical communicators to reuse content as liberally and as much as possible, other groups, including publishers and universities, actively discourage their constituencies from copying information, as these groups want to prevent copyright violations (Reyman, 2008).

Consider the impact, too, on industry and academic training for technical communicators. For practicing professionals, the primary issue is which technologies they should choose for investing their limited training dollars. In the 1980s and 1990s, dominant technologies and software applications changed so rapidly that technical skills became obsolete almost as quickly as professionals developed them. With the maturation of publishing technology in the past ten years, the tools have been more stable, though changes in their use continue to occur rapidly.

For academic programs in technical communication, a primary issue is the extent of training they need to provide. Most academic programs have limited resources to purchase costly publishing software; especially prohibitive financially is complex enterprise software like content management systems. More significantly, the purpose of an academic degree is to serve the student for decades after graduation by providing durable skills and knowledge. Technology skills and knowledge are perishable, often outdated within five years. On the other hand, employers expect students to develop skills with publishing technology as part of the education process, so avoiding technology altogether in the academic curriculum is not an option. Each program has to find its own balance.

Despite this wide range of impacts, curiously, no empirical study has systematically tracked how technology has diffused into the work of technical communication and has affected that work. Of considerable value, though, are case studies and experience reports that technical communicators publish in journals, professional magazines, and conference proceedings. Reviewing these transcripts provides technical communicators today not only with a nostalgic snapshot of the past, but also with insights into how our profession has evolved into its current place. Histories like this one meld these snapshots into a cohesive narrative from which others can reflect on how technology led the field to this point in its development, and provide a springboard for predicting how technology might affect the field in the years to come.

Histories can also help technical communicators make informed decisions about the future. It will be fascinating to find out which advances in technology continue to shape our work in the years and decades to come.

Notes

1 The product names are provided in this chapter for example purposes; they are not intended as an endorsement of the product or an indication of all of the products that might have been used.
2 In contrast, the material on the support site for Microsoft Office increasingly used interactivity, visuals and audiovisual media like video, but this was not considered part of the Help provided with the product.
3 In academic circles, Web 2.0 applications are generally associated with the broader term of social computing, which refers to people using software applications to interact with one another and exchange knowledge.
4 They always encouraged it, but with so much information available and few people knowing where to find it, taking advantage of that information was often more effort than was worthwhile, given the benefit it paid.

References

Arnston, A. (1998). *Graphic design basics* (3rd ed.). New York: Harcourt.

Babcock, L. (1989). Developing a hypertext document: Promises and pitfalls. *Proceedings of the 36th International Technical Communication Conference.* Arlington, VA: Society for Technical Communication. pp. VC-180–VC-183.

Beattie, H. S., & Rahenkamp, R. A. (1981). IBM typewriter innovation. *IBM Journal of Research and Development, 25*(5), 729–739. Retrieved March 19, 2009 from http://www.research.ibm.com/journal/rd/255/ibmrd2505ZH.pdf.

Bernstein, M. (1989). The shape of hypertext documents. *Proceedings of the 36th International Technical Communication Conference.* Arlington, VA: Society for Technical Communication. pp. RT-173–RT-175.

Berry, R. E. (1988). A consistent and usable human-computer interface for the SAA environments. *IBM Systems Journal, 27*(3), 281–300.

Bosley, D. S. (2000). *Global contexts: Case studies in international technical communication.* Boston, MA: Allyn & Bacon.

Brewer, T. (1995). Personal conversation.

Brown, J. S., & Duguid, P. (2000). Balancing act: How to capture knowledge without killing it. *Harvard Business Review, 78*(3), 73–80.

Carliner, S. (1999). *An overview of online learning.* Amherst, MA: HRD Press.

——. (2001). *Panel on upcoming trends in online learning and communication.* Clearpoint Communications. Lexington, MA. October 31, 2001.

——. (2004). *An overview of online learning* (2nd ed.). Amherst, MA: HRD Press.

——. (2005). What do we manage—and how do we assess it? Results of an exploratory study with executives in training, technical communication, and corporate communication. Annual Conference of the Association of Teachers of Technical Writing: San Francisco, CA. March 16, 2005.

——. (2009). The value of technical and professional communication: What managers track, what managers report. Canadian Association for the Study of Discourse and Writing Conference. May 25, 2009. Ottawa, Ontario

——. (in preparation). What measures of productivity and effectiveness do technical communication managers track and report?

Computer History Museum. (2006). Timeline of computer history—1990s. Retrieved March 19, 2009, from http://www.computerhistory.org/internet_history/internet_history_90s.shtml.

Cook, K. (2008). Review comments on this chapter. November 25, 2008.

Davidson, W. J. (1993). SGML authoring tools for technical communication. *Technical Communication, 40*(3), 403–409.

Davis, S. (1989). Do many technical writers really write well? (A benevolent diatribe) *36th International Technical Communication Conference.* Chicago, IL: May 15, 1989.

Dell, S. A. (1985). Introduction to interactive videodisk. *Proceedings of the 32nd International Technical Communication Conference.* Arlington, VA: Society for Technical Communication. pp. ATA-24–ATA-26.

Dziak, M. (2001). *Telecommuting success: A practical guide for staying in the loop while working away from the office.* Peachtree City, GA: Park Avenue Productions.

Elser, A. G. (1985). Producing courseware for interactive videodisk. *Proceedings of the 32nd International Technical Communication Conference.* Arlington, VA: Society for Technical Communication. pp. ATA-24–ATA-26.

Gillette, J. (1983). Strategic planning for text processing: How to proceed. *Proceedings of the 30th International Technical Communication Conference.* Arlington, VA: Society for Technical Communication. pp. ATA-26–ATA-29.

Hoft, N. (1995). *International technical communication: How to export information about high technology.* New York: John Wiley & Sons.

Hughes, M. (2009). Presentation to the Atlanta chapter of the Society for Technical Communication. Atlanta, GA: March 17, 2009.

Merrill, M. D., & Wilson, B. G. (2006). The future of instructional design and technology. In R. A. Reiser & J. V. Dempsey (Eds.), *Trends and issues in instructional design and technology* (2nd ed.). Upper Saddle River, NJ: Prentice-Hall. Retrieved April 3, 2009 from: http://carbon.cudenver.edu/~bwilson/ChoosingOurFuture.html

O'Reilly, T. (2006). *Web 2.0 Compact definition: Trying again.* Retrieved March 19, 2009, from: http://radar.oreilly.com/archives/2006/12/web-20-compact.html.

Reid, B. (1981). Scribe: A document specification language and its compiler. Doctoral dissertation. Carnegie-Mellon University. Pittsburgh, PA.

Reyman, J. (2008). Rethinking plagiarism for technical communication. *Technical Communication, 55*(1), 61–67.

Rockley, A. (2002). *Managing enterprise content: A unified strategy.* Indianapolis, IN: New Riders Press.

Scally, W. A. (1989). WYSIWIG and Batch. *Proceedings of the 36th International Technical Communication Conference.* Arlington, VA: Society for Technical Communication. pp. VC-74–VC-75.

Shank, P. (2008). Web 2.0 and beyond: The changing needs of learners, new ways to learn. In S. Carliner & P. Shank (Eds.), *The e-learning handbook: Past promises, present challenges*. San Francisco, CA: Pfeiffer. pp. 241–278.

Shirk, H. N. (1989). Humanists versus technologists: New challenges for publications managers. *Proceedings of the 36th International Technical Communication Conference*. Arlington, VA: Society for Technical Communication. pp. MG-4–MG-6.

Southworth, S. (1989). Balancing indexes: Using the INDAP software tool. *Proceedings of the 36th International Technical Communication Conference*. Arlington, VA: Society for Technical Communication. pp. RT-90–RT-92.

Walker, J. (1989). Hypertext and technical writers. *Proceedings of the 36th International Technical Communication Conference*. Arlington, VA: Society for Technical Communication. pp. VC-176–VC-179.

Wallace, J. E. (1985). What is on-screen documentation anyway? *Proceedings of the 32nd International Technical Communication Conference*. Arlington, VA: Society for Technical Communication. pp. ATA-39–ATA-42.

Webopedia (2008). Definition of browser. WebMediaBrands. Retrieved March 19, 2009 from: http://www.webopedia.com/TERM/b/browser.html.

Wilde, E., Corbin, M., Jenkins, J., & Rouiller, S. (2006). Defining a quality system: Nine characteristics of quality and the editing for quality process. *Technical Communication, 53*(4), 439–446.

2 The Effects of Digital Literacy on the Nature of Technical Communication Work

R. Stanley Dicks

With the rapid and intense increase in digital literacy, technical communication is, by many accounts, in the midst of a seismic shift (Hayhoe, 2003; Boiko, 2007; Spinuzzi, 2007). As recently as 25 years ago, most technical communicators were men who, according to Hayhoe, called themselves "technical writers or editors." Most documents were written in long hand on 8½" x 11" pads or typed on manual typewriters. Those documents often described hardware (e.g., airplanes, electronics, machinery, computers) or, in a few rare cases, computer software. Most of the documents were written with the assumption that their audience consisted of technologically savvy users so that the product could be described but its use did not have to be explained. Manuals, for example, often included a chapter or section on the theory of the device's operation.

Today, a majority of technical communicators are women (Society for Technical Communication, 2005–2006); all documents are prepared on computers; and technical communication is understood to encompass printed texts, online texts, help, tutorials, and Web sites, audio, video, and multimedia, and three-dimensional user interfaces. Changes are equally as dramatic in the nature of products and services and the tools used to create them as they are in the methods communicators employ and the relationships they must manage to be successful. Further, economic and management trends outside the discipline have had significant impacts on many practitioners. The nature of work for many technical communicators is changing so rapidly that many now perform an entire task set that they did not even know about five years ago. And yet, some are doing exactly what they were doing five, ten, and even fifteen years ago. It is too easy to look at the latest trends and assume that all workers will be doing those new, different tasks in the near future. Instead, what seems most useful for the discipline is to focus on implications of the tremendous expansion of the nature and scope of technical communication. What we do now covers the gamut from methods and procedures used during World War II to the latest, agile development methods used by distributed teams preparing single-source documents and working with colleagues around the world.

It is important to remember, when discussing current and coming trends in the discipline, that they largely have to do with the tools and technologies associated with the discipline, and not with the core competency skills that the discipline continues to require; that is, using words and images (whether stationary or moving) to inform, instruct, or persuade an audience (Schriver, 1997). Although there is a big difference in how communicators write for a single source database versus how they write traditional documentation, they still fundamentally use words and images to help people accomplish their goals.

Along with increased digital literacy on the part of technical communicators and their audiences, have come changes in the nature of their work due to new management philosophies, including those that are explicit and carefully crafted and carried out and those that are unspoken and perhaps not even consciously formulated. Several major changes in management philosophies in the last two decades have caused significant changes to the work that many technical communicators do, and they promise to continue to change that work in major ways. These changes come from three types of forces:

- *Economics*: Larger macro-economic changes affecting all work, fuelled primarily by the transition from the industrial age to the information age, and a perhaps larger transition from industrial age management capitalism to a post-capitalist society (Drucker, 1993) in which value is determined solely by customers, a phenomenon that Zuboff and Maxmin (2002) refer to as "the support economy."
- *Management*: Principles and practices that affect all workers, including reengineering, value added, outsourcing, downsizing, rightsizing, globalization, and flattening.
- *Methodologies*: Changes in methodologies and technologies that affect technical communication directly, including single sourcing, information architecture, knowledge and information databases, agile development, and Web 2.0 developments.

These three types of forces are not discrete and separate, but rather are interconnected in numerous ways. For example, one impetus for moving to single sourcing (the storage and reuse of modules or topics of information), aside from the obvious cost savings, is the necessity of preparing customized information products to accommodate the move toward individualized product configurations brought on in part by the support economy. This chapter examines how these trends are affecting current work practices and how they are likely to influence the work lives and careers of technical communicators in the coming decades.

Economics

Two major economic trends are influencing the way that everyone works, and technical communication is certainly included. First is the move from the industrial age to the information, or knowledge, age. Second is the move from management capitalism to the support economy in our post-industrialist society.

Movement from Blue Collar Work to Knowledge Work

Technical communicators who were working 50 and even 25 years ago were most likely developing paper documents to support hardware products being developed in factories with assembly lines. The document was seen as another "part" on the assembly line that was eventually added to the product. This era of assembly-line work was labeled as the industrial age, but at least in the most-developed countries, such assembly-line work has largely been replaced by what Drucker (1993) calls knowledge work, meaning work that cannot be performed by semi-skilled or unskilled laborers but that requires education and expertise. Rather than breaking down work into small enough pieces so that unskilled people can do the same task repetitively, knowledge work requires that workers can do many tasks well and can analyze and synthesize information. Robert Reich, the former Secretary of Labor, refers to this new more complex, synthesizing work as "symbolic-analytic work" (1991). As Johnson-Eilola (1996, 2005) has explained, technical communicators in the information age must move away from their previous focus on providing support for physical, industrial products (although someone will still have to do so) and toward providing much greater value through symbolic-analytic work that contributes more clearly toward an enterprise's definitions of value, which might be defined in a number of ways, only one of which is financial.

Along similar lines, Ames and Jensen (2003) have developed a value continuum for technical communicators that shows how the discipline must move from doing commodity work (wordsmithing, such as editing of text that subject-matter experts, or SMEs write without adding any substantive change or value except to "pretty it up") to making strategic contributions, including adding to the organization's profit. Ames and Jensen's value continuum stresses that commodity work adds little value to customers and thus to the organization creating products and services for them. As workers move toward more complex, symbolic-analytic work, they increase the value of the products and services to customers and hence increase their organization's income, or profit. Employees who are perceived as communicating effectively with customers and adding value to their experiences inevitably are perceived as strategic contributors who are important to retain. Those performing work similar to assembly-line efforts are providing commodities that can easily be provided by relatively unskilled employees. The value continuum model further demonstrates that to perform symbolic-analytic work, employees must have more leadership attributes, which they acquire and develop from greater education, training, and motivation. Having an advanced set of knowledge and skills allows them to improve communication both internally and externally and thus to improve the organization's financial goals, which means that they will be valued as strategic contributors rather than as commodity workers.

Becoming strategic contributors requires performing the kind of symbolic-analytic work that Reich and Johnson-Eilola describe, but technical communicators also need to do a better job of tying that work into the overall missions of their organizations (Molisani, 2003; Dicks, 2004). As Molisani put it, "We are ignorant of how business works. We need to be able to justify our costs against the bottom line. We need to speak 'CEO'" (Giammona, 2004). Writing or editing will continue to be important activities for many technical communicators. However, they are increasingly being viewed as commodity activities that business considers questionable in adding value and that are candidates for being outsourced or offshored. Outsourcing means that a job function, such as technical communication, is eliminated internally and is performed "out" of the organization, and, in some cases, out of the country (offshoring) by contract workers who are less expensive or who have greater expertise in performing the job function. As Moore and Kreth (2005) put it:

> The days of being grammar cops, wordsmiths, and software applications experts are not over for technical communicators, but those skills are diminishing in value as the global information economy becomes more cost-conscious, profit-driven, and focused on designing and delivering better experiences to individuals, groups, organizations, and entire cultures. Today, technical communicators who add value to their organizations do not merely write and edit documents. (p. 303)

So what is this symbolic-analytic work? Reich believes that in the post-industrial world the workers who add the most value are not those who create physical objects, but rather those who create conceptual and information objects. These workers analyze, synthesize, combine, rearrange, develop, design, and deliver information to specific audiences for specific purposes. Often, they deliver the same information that they or others will then modify for multiple audiences and for presentation in multiple media and formats. As Johnson-Eilola explains, "we might think of symbolic-analytic workers as technical rhetoricians or rhetorical technicians" (2005, p. 29). Symbolic-analytic workers tend to work online and require computers to do the heavy analytical part of their jobs. They can work with little supervision, which has implications for the flattening (reducing layers of management) of organizations, and they manipulate symbols and text to create their information products. Their work often is done collaboratively in teams with widely diverse knowledge and skill sets. Technical communicators, for example, often must work with scientists, doctors, product developers, graphic artists, human factors specialists, customer support personnel, subject-matter experts, information architects, product and system testers, editors, and those in many other disciplines. Symbolic-analytic workers' primary products are ideas (e.g., assertions, recommendations, value judgments) delivered in reports, plans, proposals, and other genres. With their increasing digital literacy, technical communicators have moved away from doing commodity work toward work that is increasingly analytical, can be done with minimal supervision, requires manipulation of symbols and language to produce information products, and includes the ideas in reports, plans, and proposals as well as many other types of information products. Communicators have come to realize and accept, since the formulations of Reich and Johnson-Eilola, that they need to move away from commodity work (wordsmithing) and in the direction of symbolic-analytic work, and that such a transformation, in turn, will require reshaping the discipline (see, for example, Mirel and Spilka's *Reshaping Technical Communication*, 2002).

Obviously, many technical communicators are already doing symbolic-analytic work, at least in part. The challenge for the future is to embrace this type of work more completely. It means technical communicators will have to change from viewing themselves as liaison agents or brokers between developers and users of technology. In this somewhat widely held view of the field, communicators "translate" difficult technological concepts or practices into something that the audience will be able to understand and use (Chu, 2000). According to this perspective, communicators are serving as brokers or middlemen between, for example, engineers, programmers, or medical experts and audiences with whom they need to communicate. In that model, it is too easy for everyone involved to question the value of the brokers and to assume that their roles could somehow be performed more cheaply or perhaps eliminated. In contrast, as symbolic-analytic workers, technical communicators will need to find more efficient methods for creating and manipulating (e.g., accumulating, storing, retrieving, combining, disseminating) information. Reshaping their status necessarily will involve learning technologies and methodologies such as single sourcing and information, content, and knowledge management, and then optimizing information development for multiple formats and media. At present, these abilities go beyond the typical knowledge base of many communicators.

The Support Economy: Movement from Management Capitalism to a Post-Capitalist Society

We are moving from the era when items were mass-produced, were delivered via layers of wholesalers and distributors, and were retailed by large chain operations to one in which those items can be custom configured for each individual consumer and delivered to them directly.

For example, several shirt companies allow customers to order customized shirts using a paper catalog or a Web site. The customer can designate neck size, collar type, button or cuff link sleeves, body size, etc. Squid Labs, an engineering design and technology company, specializes in making unique prototypes and finished products for customers based on their individual needs. Or, customers can even order a customized guitar from Squid, based only on paper drawings and specifications that they submit through their Web site. Norton (2005) did this, and she received a custom-built guitar unlike any other. The Dell Web site allows a customer to specify the exact components and peripherals desired in a computer system, so that each customer's order results in a configuration unlike any other.

These are examples of the coming wave predicted by Zuboff and Maxmin in *The Support Economy* (2002). Whether their predictions of a massive, paradigm shift in economic structures occur or not, the phenomena they describe are already happening in many industries. This shift to a support economy will lead to a change in how economic value is apportioned, away from mass-produced products and toward individuals and their needs and wants, where the real economic value resides.

Why has this change come about? Zuboff and Maxmin explain it using several different metaphors, but perhaps the most convenient is the solar system. In the old, industrial, centrally managed, capital model, the corporation is at the center of the universe and a series of planetary relationships revolve around it, including employees, suppliers, distributors, retailers, governmental agencies, and so on. Way out at the edge of the system somewhere are the customers, to whom occasional thought is given. In this model, price is everything, so every possible efficiency is exercised to reduce price. Constantly lowering price requires, ultimately, lowering quality both in the product itself and in the relationship with the customer. Consider, for example, the deterioration of most organizations' customer support functions and the impossibility, with many of them, of even speaking to another human being. The level of service has deteriorated so far that customers take it for granted that they will have an awful experience if they try to use customer support. Thus, the corporation–customer relationship has become so poisoned that something has to change.

What will change, according to Zuboff and Maxmin, is that the customer will become the center of the support economy universe. The customer's happiness will be the true measure of value, not the dollars that can be earned from selling products. Around the customer will be a series of support individuals and alliances, changing and recombining as necessary to bring to customers the products and services they want. With improvements to the communication system, customers will no longer stand for the conditions of the previous model, but will insist on getting the goods and services they want. As Carter (2003) points out, the authors are vague on how the details of all of this will work, and they tend to wander into a series of increasingly optimistic and even utopian revelries about the resulting world. Nonetheless, something like what they are describing is clearly happening and will continue to evolve. When customers can communicate instantly about products and services, rate them on online sites, publish and read blog reviews, and, in general, use Web 2.0 technology to exchange information, they are not going to settle for mediocrity and maltreatment.

If Zuboff and Maxmin are even partially right, we will see a significant restructuring of the way work is done. While it is too early to tell if Zuboff and Maxmin's predictions will come completely true, they are at least partially being realized in a push by organizations to allow customization of their products and services and, with Web 2.0 and other technologies, increased customer participation in product development, review, and maintenance. Many large, centrally managed corporations will disappear. Such corporations were based on the industrial model that counted on stable workforces performing a relatively standard set of operations that did not change quickly and that could be done in a single place, characterized by Spinuzzi (2007) as modular work. Due to management forces such as reengineering, outsourcing, and globalization, and to the tremendous increase in communication technologies and bandwidth, organizations are increasingly doing work in a distributed manner, with employees, management, customers, and suppliers all over the world. Dramatic improvements in communications and transportation allow work patterns and relationships that would not have been possible until recently. Those communications and transportation improvements have eliminated the necessity for modular work to be done in one place and allow, even encourage, distributed work to be done across spatial and disciplinary lines. The old industrial modeled organizations will be replaced by support organizations that specialize in managing a customer's interactions with service and product providers.

For example, if I want to take a vacation I have to wade through Web sites or telephone reservation systems for airplane reservations, hotel reservations, transportation arrangements, and restaurant reservations. In the support economy, however, I will have a support person who already has on file my preferences for all of those services; I will simply tell that person that I want to go on vacation; everything is then taken care of for me. To some extent, I can already access such personal assistance on some of the current travel Web sites, where I can reserve airline tickets, hotel accommodations, limo or taxi service, dining arrangements, and everything else associated with a trip. Rather than working on a single, repeatable series of tasks supported by the scientific model of industrial capitalism (Morgan, 2006), employees will move across multiple disciplines, constantly learning and performing a variety of job tasks and doing the symbolic-analytic work described earlier.

While many (Drucker, 2001; Zuboff & Maxmin, 2002) see this as positive and beneficial for both employees and customers, others (Haraway, 1991) characterize it as de-humanizing and necessitating a constant, unsettling round of deskilling and reskilling. From this view, for example, the travel agent I would have once hired to arrange at least some of my travel plans has now been replaced by my more general support person, so that the travel agent's job has been eliminated and the agent must develop a new set of skills to survive. But, then a newer support agent will emerge whose services encompass the newer set of skills, causing another loss of a job and the necessity for learning yet another set of skills. In part, this cycle is inherent in the rapidly changing information age, and if the support economy develops as Zuboff and Maxmin conceive it, more frequent deskilling and reskilling are likely to be ongoing for communicators and others.

People's lives are undergoing change both as employees who create and deliver some product or service and as consumers who assign value to the products and services others produce. In addition to customer interactions, employees' relationships with development organizations are affected by such a shift. Large, mass market, management capitalist organizations are yielding to project-based teams of collaborators who might all be self-employed. These shifts will have profound implications for technical communicators in the way they develop information about products, the processes they use to do so, and the pedagogy they will need to teach people how to do this type of work.

Many technical communicators have already been working in support economy style for years. Those who work as contractors have been following the employment model seen by Zuboff and Maxmin as most likely to emerge in a support economy. Rather than work for a single organization, contracting technical communicators move from project to project, sometimes with several team members in common and sometimes with wholly new teams.

Many organizations already have begun to move toward single-sourcing methodologies for producing easily customizable documentation and online solutions for customers. They depend on configurations of various product mixes that the customers have chosen. Increasingly, organizations are structuring Web sites so that they can translate and customize multiple versions for customers in multiple nations, and can present various versions of the information, depending on a customer's profile, interests, or previous access and buying patterns.

The products of technical communication also are changing in two fundamental ways. First, the products being documented often differ from those that are mass produced. They have multiple possible configurations and can be tied in with other products in unique configurations unlike those of any other customers. Second, due to the nature of the customized product configurations, the required outputs from communicators must necessarily be multiple in nature rather than single. Communicators must develop modularized documentation solutions that can adequately support the multiple configurations of customers' products. Doing this requires a completely different mindset from that necessary for preparing a user's guide or online help for a single, well-defined product. Developing individual documents for each of the possible configurations is, obviously, utterly impossible, but technical communicators are increasingly learning to develop information databases from which multiple variations of information can be extracted to meet multiple customer needs. Static, mass-produced documents are being replaced by databases with various front ends allowing access to information for a variety of purposes (e.g., training, reference, getting started, online help) to a variety of audiences (e.g., beginners, practitioners, experts) through a variety of media (e.g., paper documents, online documents, help systems, DVDs, and small interfaces such as cell phones and personal digital assistant screens).

The processes technical communicators follow are likewise changing. If predictions come true, many more technical communicators will be officially unemployed but constantly working. They will be following the consulting/temp agency model that already characterizes the work of many communicators. For example, Mir Haynes runs Anabo Studios, a successful design company that has created and modified Web sites for organizations ranging from small local companies to Fortune 500 corporations. Anabo Studios has no office space and no employees. For each development project, Haynes uses the services of a number of consultants, moving them onto and off of the project as their skills are needed. This is the model for employment that many will follow in the support economy. Project teams will be assembled as needed and constantly reconfigured to develop products and services with the appropriate expertise at the lowest possible cost.

The support economy has already started to happen. It will come more as an evolution than a revolution, but even if it never reaches the complete change that Zuboff and Maxmin predict, it is already changing the ways that technical communicators conceive of their jobs and careers, the methods they use for creating products and services, and the nature of those products and services.

Management Principles and Practices

We have all seen how management fads arise, hold everyone's attention for awhile, and then fade. Employees often cynically refer to them as the "flavor of the month" or the "trend of the year." Someone writes an article in the *Harvard Business Review*, CEOs read it and get excited, then a champion or guru publishes a book on the subject that becomes a bestseller, and the trend is in full force. Over the last 20–30 years or so, there have been many such trends: management by objectives, total quality management (TQM), chaos theory, excellence, one-minute management, six sigma, quality circles, empowerment, matrix management, corporate culture, reengineering, outsourcing, globalization, downsizing, rightsizing, and so on. Most of those trends have lasted a year or two or three as a dominating influence and then have faded, even though some of their assumptions and practices may have stayed in place in some organizations. Obviously, these trends do not arise in the absence of any context; they are usually a response to conditions and to economic, political, or geographical change. The Theory Z movement of the 1970s and 1980s, for example, wherein U.S. companies began to adopt the business practices of Japanese companies, arose because the Japanese were building better automobiles, electronics, and other products than were U.S. companies. U.S. managers reasoned that if they followed the same practices, they could match the Japanese in quality. Ironically, the Japanese practices were largely based on what they had learned from studying U.S. practices in the decades after World War II.

Some of these trends have lasted longer than a few years and have had significant influence on how managers conceive of and practice their discipline. Those trends have already had major impacts on technical communication, and will continue to do so in the future. While some communicators in some regions and in some organizations may not have been affected by them yet, it is almost a certainty that they will. Communicators need to be aware of such trends and then work proactively to take advantage of them, rather than be controlled by them. I will discuss next the following trends that have and will have the greatest influence on technical communicators: value added, reengineering, outsourcing, downsizing, rightsizing, globalization, and flattening.

Value Added

Technical communicators often have different backgrounds, knowledge sets, and processes than do the engineers, programmers, scientists, and physicians with whom they work. In many organizations the main culture and mission are dominated by those other groups of professionals, who often do not understand exactly what communicators do, or how they do it, or how they add value to the bottom line. It is, therefore, imperative for technical communicators to align themselves with the overall goals of the organization and to show others in the organization how they are doing so (Bryan, 1994; Plung, 1994; Hackos, 1994, 2007; Dicks, 2004).

Communicators need to make very clear to others, especially management, how they contribute value to the organization's main mission, whether that mission defines value as financial, political, or psychological. Toward this goal, they must demonstrate to those other professionals that they too are professionals who follow a regular set of procedures and processes. More specifically, they need to align their work patterns with those of the people with whom they work, to the extent possible, use the same tools for planning, scheduling, and budgeting, and write plans and specifications showing that they understand the goals of each project they work on and how they will contribute to achieving those goals (Hackos, 1994, 2007).

Many methods for technical communicators to measure and communicate value have been developed (Redish, 1995; Carliner, 1997; Mead, 1998;

Hart, 2001; Natchez, 2001; Dicks, 2004). In most organizations, value is measured against cost. Management looks at the cost of a given function and asks if it contributes that much value. If it does not, according to the reengineering credo, it should be eliminated or outsourced and done more cheaply. How do communicators show management how they add value? They can do so in four basic ways:

- cost reduction
- cost avoidance
- revenue enhancement
- intangible contributions.

Cost Reduction

In the global, information-age, support economy, all functions will be expected to reduce their costs as much as possible. For technical communicators, that means looking for better and more efficient development methods and tools. One method is to consolidate development of documentation, online help, and training to minimize the duplication of efforts in doing research, planning, and designing communication artifacts. Another method is to employ single sourcing, which allows information chunks to be reused for multiple types of documents (e.g., user's manuals, online help, marketing material, training manuals, job aids) and for multiple types of media and presentation (e.g., paper, large screens, small screens such as on cell phones, and PDAs). These methods mean that communicators will need to learn new talents and tools, but such is the nature of symbolic-analytic work.

Communicators can also reduce costs by changing current practices, such as moving from printed, paper documents to online or CD files, which are considerably cheaper. However, such cost reductions tend to become increasingly more difficult to achieve, as, once the largest inefficiencies have been eliminated, there are fewer cost inefficiencies to excise.

Cost Avoidance

Cost avoidance is difficult to calculate, but can be used as a strong argument by technical communicators. With insufficient or ineffective documentation, organizations often suffer considerably more costs, for example, from returned products; increased volume of calls to customer support hotlines, maintenance and service calls, and warranty repairs; fewer renewal sales; and greater legal costs associated with customer complaints or injuries. It is difficult to prove savings from the work of technical communicators, but, if everything else remains the same and technical communicators have made major improvements to the documents, they can claim credit for lower costs for, say, hotline calls.

Revenue Enhancement

Many technical communication groups have trouble showing obvious contributions to the bottom line, because they do not sell anything. However, technical communicators need to communicate that what they create is part of the product or service being offered and not some external, non-essential cost associated with creating it. For example, communicators should argue that documentation that goes along with a computer or a cell phone or an insurance policy is a crucial part of the product or service, just as the on/off switch is—the product is not usable without it. In the case of the insurance policy or a Web site, the document *is* the product. Technical communicators should communicate this message constantly, for example, in planning meetings, status meetings, and monthly reports. Another consideration for adding to the bottom line is to create something to sell. More companies are selling basic, user-friendly documentation with products to compete with other companies that are seen as the third-party (e.g., those who create the books for dummies series or the "idiot's guide to" series). See, for example, the publications sites for companies such as Microsoft and SAS. There, the companies provide barebones documentation with the product and then sell user manuals, training DVDs, reference documents, and other product-related information to users who want additional information.

Intangible Contributions

Intangible contributions are the most difficult to demonstrate, especially in any quantitative way. They are often anecdotal: a sales rep says that the customers love the new documents, your online help system wins an STC award, a magazine rates your documents the best in the field, or you receive unsolicited emails from customers praising your revised tutorials. What is important here is to publicize internally every such occurrence and to ensure that information about it is widely disseminated in status meetings, newsletters, and the intranet.

Because technical communicators often differ in education, background, and skill sets from other employees with whom they work, they must constantly justify and defend their roles and educate their coworkers and management. While technical communicators may resent having to prove their value when others do not have to do so, it is a fact that they are often doing something considerably different from their coworkers. Therefore, the communicators have to educate those coworkers constantly about what they do and how it adds value.

Reengineering

In any true reengineering effort, an organization looks at every task being performed by every employee and decides whether it needs to be done. It also looks at whether that task could best be performed by someone outside. For example, many corporations have decided that they do not need to have their own internal payroll department, that there are outside firms that are specialists in payroll and that have superior knowledge, personnel, and software for providing the service more efficiently and at a lower cost. In addition to reengineering how they will handle payroll, many corporations have decided to take the same step with other internal functions such as computing, building maintenance, cafeterias, accounting, legal services, and, yes, technical communication. In reengineering, management looks at each function and asks if it adds value to the organization's core competencies, those activities at which the organization wants to excel and that, it believes, will give them a competitive advantage that will allow it to succeed. Why, the thinking goes, continue to perform any functions that do not add such value? If it is perceived that technical communicators do not add value and do not contribute to the bottom line in some way, the organization will decide to eliminate the group or outsource it.

Reengineering was one of the trends that became prominent in the early 1990s, especially with the publication in 1993 of Hammer and Champy's *Reengineering the Corporation*. However, the practice of reengineering and some of its associated practices had been employed for decades before that, even if they called themselves by different names ("restructuring" in the 1980s, for example). Reengineering was indeed a reaction to larger economic forces, primarily the movement from the industrial age to the information age, but also from the capital, enterprise management model to the support economy model espoused by Zuboff and Maxmin. In fact, reengineering was one of the early indicators that the economy was changing in ways that Zuboff and Maxmin and others would soon be discussing. As Hammer and Champy describe it,

> For two hundred years people have founded and built companies around Adam Smith's brilliant discovery that industrial work should be broken down into its simplest and most basic tasks. In the postindustrial business age we are now entering, corporations will be founded and built around the idea of reunifying those tasks into coherent business processes. (p. 2)

Reengineering was not a call to fix, improve, or make more efficient current structures and practices; instead, it was a radical challenge to existing management conceptions and practices. To keep their customers satisfied (again, pointing to the support economy), it called for organizations to throw off those practices and to adopt completely new ones based on their core competencies.

Reengineering has led to major upheavals in many organizations, including, in some cases, massive layoffs. While it is easy to blame the champions of reengineering for the human suffering that has resulted, there was inevitably going to be significant change as we moved from the industrial, capital-based model to the information-age economy and support model. Some research has shown that layoffs resulting from reengineering have failed to produce better finances or profits for most corporations that have done them (Cascio, Young, & Morris, 1997; Morris, Cascio, & Young, 1999). Nonetheless, reengineering is not going to go away. It has become a permanent part of management arsenal, and most upper management now asks repeatedly whether every service in their organization is necessary or whether it could be done more cheaply or effectively somewhere else.

Technical communicators need to worry about how they are perceived and evaluated and whether they might be likely sources for being reengineered and either eliminated or outsourced. This growing reality introduces additional management trends spawned from reengineering: outsourcing, downsizing, and rightsizing.

Outsourcing, Downsizing, Rightsizing

Some organizations choose to adjust their employee pools, regardless of whether doing so is part of a larger reengineering effort, but the thinking behind it and the consequences are similar to what happens with reengineering. In this part, I describe three types of staffing adjustment: outsourcing, downsizing, and rightsizing.

Outsourcing is usually an effort to improve the bottom line so that a company's profits will be higher and consequently its stock will be more attractive to investors. The philosophy is similar to that behind reengineering: to identify what functions we have that are not part of our core competencies, and then have someone else do them more cheaply. Note that outsourcing does not always literally mean physically sending work out. Rather, it means hiring someone other than one's permanent employees to perform the work. Many companies, for example, have outsourced their grounds maintenance and cafeteria operations, even though that work is done on their premises. So, work can be outsourced and done in-house or outsourced to a contracting firm down the street or around the world.

Outsourcing has been a part of technical communication for decades. According to STC, 24% of its members identify themselves as consultants or contractors, and that percentage has been consistent across several of its contractor surveys (Society for Technical Communication, 2005–2006). That means, at least for STC members, that a fourth of all technical communication work is outsourced, performed by someone working for another organization. Such outsourcing can provide some substantial benefits for employers and contractors. For employees, the benefits include:

- filling in short-term gaps in their employee pools without having to go through the traumatic cycles of hiring and layoffs;
- covering the work of employees who are ill or on leave without having to hire permanently;

- using the services of someone with particular expertise that they need only briefly without having to hire them permanently.

In addition, doing contract work appeals to some communicators who prefer to work on a variety of projects and who might need a more flexible work schedule than working for a single organization would allow. Outsourcing, therefore, is not inherently evil; it is a business practice that can benefit both the employer and the contractor. Obviously, the person it does not benefit is the employee whose job is eliminated because someone else is doing it. Domestic outsourcing does not seem nefarious; if an organization decides to outsource 20 jobs to a firm down the street, that firm now has 20 job openings. But, if the organization sends the jobs overseas, we now have 20 unemployed workers in the United States. Indeed, at some U.S. companies, one or two technical communicators are retained to act as project managers working with groups of writers in other countries. As a reflection of this trend, STC membership has fallen from 22,000 (Sydow-Campbell and Hayhoe, 2000) around the turn of the century to 14,000 (Society for Technical Communication, 2009). Some of this dramatic decrease is no doubt due to the high-tech meltdown early in the century, a curiously growing trend for people not to join professional organizations in general, and technical communicators moving to other disciplines such as usability testing, or information architecture, but some of it is no doubt due to jobs being outsourced overseas.

How can technical communicators prevent their jobs from being outsourced? One strategy is to make sure that they are doing symbolic-analytic work in addition to or instead of commodity work. In technical communication, an example of commodity work is making non-substantive revisions to works written by technical experts (e.g., copyediting instead of comprehensive editing). Or, commodity work might include routine writing describing the features and functions of a product or service with no consideration for users or the tasks they will perform in their use of the product or service. Also viewed as commodity work are routine desktop publishing tasks, including design and layout of documents performed without making substantive contributions to them. Those routine, commodity tasks can be performed, at least at a perfunctory level, by people who are not necessarily experts about the technology being addressed and who are not in the same building with the people developing that technology. It is much more difficult to outsource true symbolic-analytic work: creating, accumulating, storing, retrieving, combining, and disseminating information for multiple purposes to multiple audiences. Such work requires knowledge of databases and the various methods for storing information files, meta-tagging and various other information tagging systems for efficient retrieval of stored information, scripting languages for combining and retrieving stored information in different ways for different audiences and purposes, and numerous additional skills that many communicators do not currently use. Being primarily responsible for those processes and demonstrating how they add value to the organization's mission and goals help prevent technical communication functions from being outsourced.

Other terms often used to describe outsourcing include downsizing and rightsizing. Downsizing is usually a euphemism that sounds nicer than saying a company fired part of its work force. Downsizing might be the result of reengineering or similar careful analysis of a workforce, or it might simply be a workforce reduction based on other criteria such as last-in, first-out; first-in, first-out (illegal if it involves age discrimination, but not enforced recently), or performance, or managerial whim.

Rightsizing, which means an organization trying to get to their proper levels the numbers of employees doing each function, is usually the result of some carefully considered evaluation, whether it be part of reengineering or some other endeavor. Thus, it might mean layoffs, but it might mean restructuring and moving people around without any layoffs, and it might even mean hiring more employees.

Globalization

Whether we like it or not, globalization is inevitable. While there may be some organizations and companies that operate only internally and thus do not feel the immediate effects of globalization, the vast majority of organizations are already feeling those effects. Improved methods of communication and transportation make it economically possible and desirable to work with and enter into commerce with people all over the world, and not merely those within our own borders. While globalization will cause political and economic perturbations, its course cannot be stopped. Globalization's effect on technical communication already means that some communicators are collaborating with colleagues in other countries. Hayhoe (2006) calls for technical communicators to support these new colleagues, help them establish academic programs, support and publish research to help us better understand their cultures, and anticipate changes in the membership and the operations of STC. Hayhoe further attributes to globalization at least part of the one-third reduction in the number of technical communicators in the last five years.

At least initially, much of the work outsourced overseas has been of the commodity type, as cultural, language, and geographical differences make outsourcing symbolic-analytic work very difficult (Johnson-Eilola, 1996, 2005). Some communicators are learning how to coordinate that commodity work being done overseas. They are learning how to use the communications technologies, including not just telephone, email, and instant messaging, but also more advanced systems such as online project management applications and synchronous collaboration applications. Further, they are learning how to work successfully with people from other cultures and to respect and accommodate cultural differences.

Translation and localization are activities of globalization that directly affect technical communicators. Although many methods exist for making documents easier to translate and localize, and not all of them are intuitive or follow stylistic guidelines that appear in many conventional writing and technical communication texts (Sanderlin, 1988; Hoft, 1995; Fernandes, 1995; Weiss, 1998; Kohl, 1999, 2008). Communicators are learning new writing habits such as reducing vocabularies rather than using variety, including the "that" or "which" of relative clauses that are often omitted when writing for English-speaking readers but that make it easier for a translator to understand the sentence structure; reducing the number of prepositional phrases and especially series of such phrases; preparing glossaries; and so on. (The need to consider rhetorical and cultural aspects of globalization is discussed in Barry Thatcher's chapter also in this collection.)

Globalization will soon affect how technical communicators work profoundly and in several ways. First, as discussed earlier, it will require technical communicators to move away from commodity work and toward symbolic-analytic work; to align themselves with the goals of their employers; and to demonstrate how they are adding value toward achieving those goals. Second, it will require communicators to move toward more efficient development methodologies (such as single sourcing and agile development, which I define and describe in the upcoming Methodologies section). And third, it will require that communicators design and develop documents with translation and localization in mind from the outset.

Flattening

In the traditional hierarchical, top-down management model, work was broken down into the smallest possible units and then supervisors watched over groups of employees to make sure that they were completing their units properly and in great enough numbers (productivity). It was generally assumed that a manager could successfully oversee about eight to ten direct reports, perhaps a few more. More than that and the supervisor could no longer ensure that the workers were doing enough and well enough. In the post-industrial age of symbolic-analytic work, such close supervision is not needed, and is, in fact, a detriment to the type of work that knowledge workers perform. Knowledge workers must be educated to perform complex tasks and to work in teams with other knowledge workers (Drucker, 2001). Hence, the workers are at least as well educated as their supervisors and, because they have the strength of the team, they require little direct supervision. A further impetus for reduced supervision is simply everyone's greater access to information and communication tools. When everyone has access to the same information, we need fewer managers to communicate it to workers.

The need for less management results in a flattening of organizations, with, in some cases, several layers of middle management removed. If one manager can now supervise the work of 30–40 people, an organization can eliminate two or three levels of management. However, this means that employees are much more responsible for their work and for working successfully with one or more teams. At one place where I worked we did testing on groups of employees and found that, not surprisingly, most technical communicators were introverted and preferred to work alone. That has been changing in the last decade or two, but technical communicators must learn to work well on teams and with minimal supervision. Working with less supervision requires that they develop strong project management skills and the discipline to work steadily on schedules rather than the procrastinate-and-then-work-extensive-overtime cycles of which some communicators have been guilty. Working without supervision may seem like a dream to some, but it requires that communicators take control of their daily work, their extended project schedules, and their careers, in ways that are more consciously planned and assertively acted upon than some of communicators, up to now, have found comfortable.

Methodologies

Just as the economic conditions and the management philosophies and practices are changing significantly for technical communication work, so are the methodologies and technologies changing, and rapidly. This applies to the types of documentation artifacts that communicators produce, the project methods they employ, and the tools they use. This section addresses how technical communicators are taking advantage of new digital technologies that allow them to produce information products more quickly and efficiently and to meet the needs of their audiences more effectively. Such methodologies include single sourcing, agile development, distributed work, and collaboration using Web-based development technologies.

Single Sourcing

In some organizations, when a new product is under development, a technical communicator is responsible for researching the product and preparing a user's guide for it. Another person might be responsible for developing online help for it. Another might be responsible for preparing a tutorial and in-class training. Another might have to write marketing and advertising materials. Yet another might be responsible for preparing materials to use in training the sales force about how to sell it. With all of those people doing essentially the same work, gathering the same information, and preparing artifacts that have many similarities, clearly a great deal of extra work is being done. And, in some cases, if different developers use contrasting or inconsistent models and metaphors for explaining the new product, they can be doing more harm than good. To further complicate the situation, the product or service may require documents that can be printed as conventional paper documents, but also viewed on large flat-screen monitors, cell phones, or PDAs, or listened to on a Web site using assistive technology or mp3 files.

Single sourcing provides solutions to the problems of multiple authors and the inconsistencies that result. Single sourcing can refer to both the creation process and the output process. One of its biggest advantages is that it allegedly separates those two, so that writers can develop content without worrying about the mode or media in which it will be presented. They can focus instead on developing the optimum-sized modules that will be labeled and stored in the content management system (CMS) database. On the other end, the output side, someone (technical communicators or programmers) will design various front-end programs to extract chunks from the CMS in an order and layout appropriate for specific audiences and specific media, so that, for example, telephone company personnel who carry PDAs can look up instruction manuals on those devices when they are out in the field and need a reminder about how to perform a certain task.

The implications for technical communicators are simultaneously exciting and ominously threatening (Sapienza, 2002, 2004; Weiss, 2002; Clark, 2002; Carter, 2003; Rockley, 2003; Williams, 2003). Many communicators receive considerable positive reinforcement from seeing and clutching their finished documents. (I still have the first ones I wrote over 25 years ago using WordStar and the CP/M operating system.) Merely developing content chunks removes the sense of accomplishment and pride that, for many technical communicators, is practically their only job satisfaction. Further, many communicators view information design as one of their primary tasks; they have had extensive training and take great pride in being able to arrange text, graphics, and space to communicate to certain audiences for certain purposes and do not believe that programmers and technology can replace that. Further, in some cases, specific industry practices, state and federal laws, and approval agency (e.g., Underwriters Laboratories, Canadian Standards Association) requirements demand that text and graphics be presented in very specific ways. In other words, no matter how much the proselytizers of separation of creating text and viewing output declaim that those two processes must be separate, at least in some cases they cannot be. Most successful CMS, therefore, will have to provide ways to save combinations of text, graphics, and space into usable chunks that have been designed to meet regulations and industry-wide templates and expectations. That continuing requirement to design text, graphics, and space should remove at least some of the fear technical communicators have of single sourcing.

The long-term savings and advantages to be realized from single sourcing are simply too great to ignore it and hope it will go away. Technical communicators are probably better off embracing it, learning more about it, and incorporating it at least in their own bailiwicks and, preferably, as part of a larger enterprise-wide endeavor (Hackos, 2002; Rockley, 2003). Technical communicators should even seriously consider learning how to take over the roles of designing and controlling the output side of single sourcing. It may require learning about Extensible Markup Language (XML), databases, and some light programming for pulling out chunks and arranging them, but this is where designing information for specific audiences for specific purposes is happening with single sourcing systems. Mott and Ford (2007) recommend that technical communicators essentially become information architects, as those are the people who are assured of jobs once single sourcing is implemented. Mott and Ford also provide a very good model and introduction to the subject. The role of those developing the information chunks is not clear. Some (Weiss, 2002) believe that that such a role will become so routine that it will be considerably marginalized or outsourced. On the other hand, we may learn that writing those chunks so that they work in multiple applications is sufficiently difficult that it continues to require the services of experienced technical communicators. In any case, the more symbolic-analytic jobs in single sourcing involve designing the front-end systems that combine modules and topics into various information deliverables.

Another reason for the inevitability of single sourcing is that it fits with the customized, personalized nature of products and services in the information-age, support economy. As customers demand more individualized product and service configurations, the accompanying documents, help systems, training manuals, maintenance instructions, and so on all have to be customizable to meet each specific configuration. Achieving that without single sourcing systems would simply be financially prohibitive, so at least for organizations that sell products and services of any complexity at all, some kind of single sourcing solution will be mandatory. Single sourcing will require that technical communicators learn new modes of thinking and new sets of tools, which many will find exciting and challenging rather than threatening.

Agile Development Methods

In the Internet age, the old waterfall, station-to-station approach to product and documentation development simply is not fast enough to keep up with the ever-changing demands of the market. One place where I worked estimated that the shortest time they could possibly take to develop a new piece of software using their entire quality control development process was 18 months. That is why some of the newer management theories and practices have evolved; the old methods are inadequate for meeting current market demands, where entire product life cycles are often much shorter than 18 months. Restructuring from industrial-age, functional, silo-like models to integrated teams of knowledge workers allows for work to be done more efficiently and rapidly. But the project management methods used must change also. Several methods have evolved to speed up product and service development, including user-centered design, iterative design, agile development, extreme programming, scrums, and variations of these with many other names (O'Connor, 2007). I will now describe each of these.

User-Centered Design

User-centered design came out of and is highly associated with usability testing. At its most basic level, user-centered design can involve simply adding a user to the development team or consulting with one about alpha and beta versions of products and documents. At its other extreme, it involves having users participate in every stage of development. With Web 2.0 collaboration tools, organizations are starting to develop products in completely transparent modes so that users can see progress and provide feedback throughout the process. Open-source projects use mailing lists, blogs, wikis, and other online collaboration tools to make an ongoing series of enacting initial changes, testing, enacting further changes, and so on to develop open-source software systems. Increasingly more product development work will be done using user-centered design methods, as the advantages over traditional development are too great. And, in the support economy described earlier, producing products and services that meet customers' demands becomes essential.

Iterative Design

Another method, iterative design, is a variation of user-centered design and also comes from usability work. Rather than developing extensive requirements or specifications as traditional designers did, iterative designers develop a set of criteria, based on user cases and user tasks, against which to test a product. They then go through a series of developing a prototype, testing it against the criteria, revising it, testing it again, and so on until the product meets the criteria and can be released. To those who have worked only on projects using traditional project management methods, this process can seem perilously dangerous, but, with some practice, it can lead to faster development times and to products and services that are much more likely to meet customers' expectations.

Agile Development

In agile development (explained in the Agile Manifesto at www.agilealliance. org), customers and developers write "stories" that are scenarios of tasks to be performed and features needed to be able to perform those tasks. The stories include how the processes will help them achieve their goals or define desired outputs. The programmers then design systems that deliver the desired results, with constant feedback from customers to make sure that the design will meet their needs. Agile development assumes that it will use iterative design, that the first version of the design will likely be a crude approximation of what is really needed, and that multiple redesigns and testing with customers will be required before a finished product is completed. This process can be a challenge for technical communicators, who may have to explain how to use features that are evolving swiftly, and that, in some cases, may be abandoned later for more elaborate features. On the other hand, because of the way agile development teams work, the communicators are more likely to have been involved in the project early and to understand more about the thinking that has gone into product design, because they have participated in developing the customer stories. That means that they will understand the inner workings of the product better than in traditional project management systems and hence will be able to continue making adjustments to the documents as the design changes.

Extreme Programming

Another variation of these methodologies is extreme programming (explained and illustrated at www.extremeprogramming.org). In extreme engineering, an initial "architectural spike" or innovative idea leads to a vision for a system metaphor. At that point, user stories (rather than the more traditional system requirements) are developed that inform planning and that also provide test scenarios against which the designs will be measured. During the planning stages, as the stories are refined and the system view becomes clearer, increasingly confident estimates about time and resources can be made. Programmers who work in pairs develop chunks of code that are tested against the user test scenarios and then iteratively revised and tested until they meet user requirements, at which point that small part of the code is released.

Once the iteration cycle begins, modules are developed and sent to acceptance tests. If they do not meet the predefined, acceptance test scenarios, they are sent back to be revised and to have bugs fixed. Once they meet the test scenarios and hence have customer approval, they are released. As is typical of agile development methods, everyone in extreme programming works together as a team in a physically open environment, and no one "owns" their code or their documents—everything is transparent and can be viewed by anyone else at any time.

Nuckols and Canna (2003) explain this process using what they call extreme documentation methods versus more traditional ones, and they enumerate several advantages for technical communicators, including improved communication, customer involvement throughout the design process, better access to subject-matter experts (SMEs), enhanced respect from SMEs, more communicator input to the entire design process, and better overall applications.

Scrum

Yet another variation of iterative design is Scrum (www.scrumalliance.org), which involves short-term iterations with small, physically co-located teams of developers who design applications based, again, on user "stories," and characterized by daily stand-up status meetings and intensive, ongoing communication among team members. While agile development methods have been pioneered by software developers, their use is inevitably spreading to other areas, as their advantages in reducing development times and costs are simply too important to ignore.

It is likely that most technical communicators will be using some kind of agile development methods in the next few years. Sigman's (2007) advice related to the Scrum methodology applies to all of these methods: technical communicators should enthusiastically participate in all team activities, even if they do not immediately relate to what the communicator will be doing. One major advantage of all these methodologies is that the communicator, rather than getting information piecemeal through requirements documents, and interviews with SMEs, gets the information first-hand as developers conceptualize and design the products and services. Most of these alternative project management methods require communicators to be even more team oriented, social, and proactive about obtaining information.

Distributed Work

Improved communication technologies mean that workers can collaborate without being co-located (i.e., without being in the same physical space, such as an office). In the example of Mir Haynes's Anabo Studios, large Web sites are developed by teams of information architects, programmers, graphic artists, and content developers who work at remote locations and who rarely, if ever, see each other. Such distributed work can be accomplished with fairly simple technologies such as telephones and email, or they can include more complex technologies, such as instant messaging and the use of online collaboration sites, where project management and file management tools enhance team productivity. Technical communicators will have to learn those tools and learn how to best take advantage of them. The most sophisticated of these tools will allow almost all project management tasks to be carried out on a collaborative Web site. Remote workers at numerous locations log in to access the documents they are working on, to exchange instant messages with coworkers, to leave email messages for workers in other time zones who are not currently logged in, to have team meetings where everyone looks at the same document simultaneously and offers comments about it, to submit time sheets each week, to read status reports from team members, and, in short, to do almost any task associated with the project. Among the most commonly used are Basecamp (www.basecamphq.com), Daptiv (www.daptiv.com), Microsoft Project, and Zoho projects (www.projects.zoho.com).

Much technical communication work in the future will be done using distributed work arrangements. Some communicators already work on multiple, distributed teams requiring constant communication and transitioning from one project to the next and from one set of tools to the next.

Web 2.0 and Transparency

Another trend involves an increase in the communication and involvement of users with product review, assessment, and documentation. Such involvement has increased due to the improved collaborative methodologies discussed above and to additional collaborative technologies including blogs, wikis, and other Web-based systems. Users now exercise much more power than previously over product evaluation. In the past, products might have been reviewed in a few magazine articles published months after the product was released. In the world of blogs, mailing lists, and collective sites such as MySpace and YouTube, opinions and experiences (positive and negative) about products and services are available instantly. It is much more difficult for an organization to get away with products, documents, or services that are flawed. And many customers, when they encounter a problem using a product, are going to resort to using search engines and searching through blogs for an answer rather than consulting the product's own documentation. Indeed, some people assume that they can find more accurate and honest information more quickly by consulting third-party sources than through official documents.

This growth of alternative information sources has interesting implications for technical communicators. Why not eliminate the product documentation altogether and simply institute a product blog? Communicators could provide a page or two of initial instructions and a link to the blog site, where customers with questions can pose them. Indeed, many companies have reduced or eliminated their paper documentation while supplying "knowledge bases" and customer support sites online. But the more interesting possibilities are with having customers essentially participate in developing an online system of questions and answers or problems and solutions, rather than preparing traditional documentation. Technical communicators have long complained that they could not get enough access to customers. Increasingly, at least some of them are finding that their jobs require constant customer communication on blogs, mailing lists, and user Web sites. Technical communicators should be actively involved in producing online knowledge bases and support sites. In many cases, those modes of communication are replacing the traditional paper documents they once developed, so if communicators want to be or stay employed, they need to learn how to develop the newer information products.

Technical communicators who are working with traditional project management systems may wonder about these newer models for conducting projects. Organizations using those traditional methods are coming under increasing competition from enterprises using more efficient methods, so they have no choice but to begin employing the same types of methods. In fact, it would be a good idea for technical communicators to begin employing single sourcing and agile development methods even if their larger organizations have not begun to do so.

Summary of Methodologies

To summarize, then, technical communicators' work is undergoing significant changes at a rapid pace. Some communicators will be working on traditional products and documents using traditional project management methods for years to come. But many communicators are seeing the nature of their work altered considerably. Rather than the relatively limited contributions of writing and editing in narrowly defined and conceived technical communication jobs, future jobs are more likely to require that communicators engage in the more complex symbolic-analytic work involving not just developing information but also managing, reconfiguring, disseminating, and customizing it for a diversity of audiences and in a diversity of media. Such work requires communicators to undergo constant education to learn better ways to analyze audiences and to conceive of and manipulate information in ways appropriate for those audiences. Also, doing that kind of work will naturally lead to job titles and responsibilities sometimes only tangentially related to technical communication. One reason that the STC's membership has dropped by 40% within the brief span of 2000 and 2008 is that many communicators have already morphed into related positions in customer support, human factors and interface design, quality assurance, marketing, and other areas, such that they no longer identify themselves primarily as technical communicators. Technical communicators are increasingly found on smaller teams working intensely with new, user-centered, iterative-development methods. More communicators are collaborating with at least some people with whom they are not co-located, and, in some cases, no one on the team is co-located. Some co-workers are located overseas. This means that communicators will do more work online using collaborative Web sites, instant messaging, conference calls, video conferencing, and other collaborative technologies. More communicators are working on translation and localization and on developing improved methods for preparing documents that can be translated as quickly and inexpensively as possible. Technical communicators, along with everyone else, have to keep up with such changes in order to contribute actively and explicitly to the missions and goals of their overall organizations and demonstrate how they are doing so.

Education for Symbolic-Analytic Work

Significant education is going to be required to do symbolic-analytic work, and ongoing education will be required to continue doing it successfully, so how do educators analyze the world of work and then introduce findings into their individual courses and overall curricula? How do they ensure that they teach knowledge and skill sets beyond the basic writing and editing skills, at least some of which have been deemed to be commoditized and hence eliminated or outsourced? While it is no doubt true that some education associated with symbolic-analytic work will be done in industry rather than in academia, especially for those facets of such work that are associated with specific technologies, educators should still concern themselves with the transition to more complex forms of work.

For educators, the first problem may be deciding with whom they should be talking. If they find people who are doing traditional writing/editing work that is in danger of becoming a commodity and being outsourced, they will likely develop a far different picture of the work world than if they find people who are doing complex, symbolic-analytic work, but who might not identify themselves as technical communicators. Part of the difficulty of researching the world of work, and this is one that has plagued technical communication all along, is in defining exactly what the discipline is. Nonetheless, if educators are going to prepare people for doing symbolic-analytic work, they need to find ways to study those who are doing it.

Up to a point, educators can continue to use the methodologies they have been employing to keep up with the world of work. They have borrowed most of those methods from other disciplines, such as, for example, ethnographies and field studies from anthropology and sociology. They can continue to develop internship and cooperative education opportunities and to encourage their students to take advantage of them. Educators can invite guest speakers from industry to their classes to inform their students about current work practices. Educators can also continue to develop industry advisory councils and to meet with them to learn about what types of work they are doing and what new trends they see in the work world. When possible, educators can try to collaborate on projects of common interest, either sharing in developing documents of some kind or doing research of some kind.

All of these methods have helped technical communication educators keep track of the nature of work in the world where their students will be going, but with these methods alone, they will not be able to immerse themselves significantly in the global, distributed work, agile development, symbolic-analytic, support economy. Such major changes happening so quickly may mean that educators need to use different, more involved methods. Bosley (2002), for example, proposes that technical communication educators become practitioners, that they develop direct experience in the field through research or employment. The technical communication program at North Carolina State University has a visiting professor relationship with SAS Institute (a vendor for business analytics software and services) wherein professors can work at SAS for a semester or a summer to help them keep up with the nature of work that communicators are doing and the methods and tools they are using to do it. Such immersion, even for a brief time, gives a far better idea about the true nature of current work than would other methods. Bernhardt (2002) also calls for "active-practice" collaborations allowing educators to work on extended, real-world problems. Despite challenges of scheduling and managing such exchanges, they can be more valuable than other, less immersive methods that educators typically use for gaining information about the work world. Extended ethnographic and field studies, lasting beyond several days or weeks, could also help provide a sufficient level of experience.

Conclusion

The world of technical communication work has changed radically in some ways in the last few decades. The audience operates in worlds that are filled with technological devices far more sophisticated and complex than those that existed 20–30 years ago. So, the nature of a communicator's basic task—developing text and graphics to inform, instruct, or persuade—is now more complex and difficult. Not only is what technical communicators write about more complex, but so are the tools and methods they use for doing their work. For the most part, these changes have occurred in an evolutionary manner, gradually enough so that most communicators could keep up with them.

Arguably, there have been two more revolutionary periods. The first came in the early 1980s when personal computers were introduced to the masses and technical communicators had to learn, first, how to develop information that would help users learn how to use such complex devices, and second, how to use the devices themselves to develop those information products. The second came in the early to mid-1990s when graphical user interfaces became universal and allowed computer use itself to become universal. That period further challenged communicators to develop information that would help even the least technology-savvy users succeed. But development of graphical user interfaces provided a still bigger challenge in that it gave communicators the ability to handle jobs that had previously been done by several other people: document design, page layout, graphic design, typesetting, and production. Further, communicators had to learn how to develop information that would appear on screens and not on paper, and they quickly learned that the two media had very different requirements. Technical communicators watched some people leave the profession because they chose not to change the way they worked and because they insisted that true writing involved writing for paper. Those who remained had to learn entirely new sets of information related to the new capabilities that desktop publishing software provided.

Technical communicators are now in a similarly disruptive, revolutionary era when several aspects of their work are changing at the same time. Most significantly, the overall economic models communicators follow may well be undergoing major changes. Management practices are also affecting the way communicators conceive of employment and will, of necessity, force them to redefine how they see themselves and how they want others to see them. The methods we use for managing projects are changing, in some cases quite radically. The tools and methods for developing, storing, and retrieving information are also evolving rapidly. While the period ahead may be at times unsettling for practitioners and educators alike in the technical communication discipline, it also promises to provide the kinds of challenges and rewards that such periods always yield.

References

Agile Alliance. (2007). Retrieved August 15, 2007 from http://www.agilealliance.org.

Ames, A. L., & Jensen, S. M. (2003). Transforming your career: Contributing strategically to your company or client. *51st Annual STC Conference Proceedings*. Baltimore, MD: Society for Technical Communication.

Anabo Studios (2007). Retrieved August 15, 2007 from http://www.anabostudios.com.

Bernhardt, S. A. (2002). Active-Practice: Creating productive tension between academia and industry. In B. Mirel & R. Spilka (Eds.), *Reshaping technical communication: New directions and challenges for the twenty-first century* (pp. 81–90). Mahwah, NJ: Lawrence Erlbaum.

Boiko, B. (2007). What's to become of the tech pubs department? *Intercom, 54*(3), 6–8.

Bosley, D. S. (2002). Jumping off the ivory tower: Changing the academic perspective. In B. Mirel & R. Spilka (Eds.), *Reshaping technical communication: New directions and challenges for the twenty-first century* (pp. 27–39). Mahwah, NJ: Lawrence Erlbaum.

Bryan, J. G. (1994). Culture and anarchy: What publications managers should know about us and them. In O. J. Allen & L. H. Deming (Eds.), *Publications management: Essays for professional communicators* (pp. 55–67). Amityville, NY: Baywood Publishing.

Carliner, S. (1997). Demonstrating the effectiveness and value of technical communication products and services: A four-level process. *Technical Communication, 44*(3), 252–265.

Carter, L. (2003). Review: *The support economy: Why corporations are failing individuals and the next episode of capitalism. Technical Communication Quarterly, 16*(3), 365–368.

Cascio, W. F., Young, C. E., & Morris, J. R. (1997). Financial consequences of employment-change decisions in major U. S. corporations. *Academy of Management Journal, 40*(5), 1175–1189.

Chu, S. (2000). Information as commodity: The state of technical communication in the new millennium. *48th Annual STC Conference Proceedings*. Washington, DC: Society for Technical Communication.

Clark, D. (2002). Rhetoric of present single-sourcing methodologies. *Proceedings of the 20th Annual International Conference on Computer Documentation*. New York: ACM Press.

Daptiv. (2007). Retrieved August 15, 2007 from http://www.eproject.com.

Dicks, R. S. (2004). *Management principles and practices for technical communicators*. New York: Allyn & Bacon.

Drucker, P. F. (1993). *Post-capitalist society*. New York: HarperCollins Publishers.

———. (2001). *The essential Drucker*. New York: HarperCollins Publishers.

Extreme Programming. (2007). Retrieved August 15, 2007 from http://www.extremeprogramming.org.

Fernandes, T. (1995). *Technical communication in the global community*. Boston, MA: Academic Press.

Giammona, B. (2004). The future of technical communication: How innovation, technology, information management, and other forces are shaping the future of the profession. *Technical Communication, 51*(3), 349–366.

Hackos, J. T. (1994). *Managing your documentation projects*. New York: John Wiley & Sons.

———. (2002). *Content management for dynamic web delivery*. Hoboken, NJ: John Wiley & Sons.

———. (2007). *Information development: Managing your documentation projects, portfolio, and people*. Indianapolis, IN: Wiley Publishing.

Hammer, M., & Champy, J. (1993). *Reengineering the corporation*. New York: HarperCollins Publishers.

Haraway, D. J. (1991). *Simians, cyborgs, and women: The reinvention of nature*. New York: Routledge.

Hart, G. J. S. (2001). Prove your worth! *Intercom, 48*(7), 16–19.

Hayhoe, G. F. (2006). The globalization of our profession. *Technical Communication, 53*(1), 9–10.

———. (2003). A golden opportunity. *Technical Communication, 50*(4), 439–440.

Hoft, N. L. (1995). *International technical communication: How to export information about high technology*. New York: John Wiley & Sons.

Johnson-Eilola, J. (1996). Relocating the value of work: Technical communication in a post-industrial age. *Technical Communication Quarterly, 5*(3), 245–270.

———. (2005). *Datacloud: Toward a new theory of online work*. Cresskill, NJ: Hampton Press.

Kohl, J. R. (1999). Improving translatability and readability with syntactic cues. *Technical Communication, 46*(2), 149–166.

———. (2008). *The global English style guide: Writing translatable documentation for a global market*. Cary, NC: SAS Institute.

Mead, J. (1998). Measuring the value added by technical communication: A review of research and practice. *Technical Communication, 45*(3), 353–379.

Mirel, B., & Spilka, R. (2002). *Reshaping technical communication: New directions and challenges for the 21st century*. Mahwah, NJ: Lawrence Erlbaum.

Molisani, J. (2003). As quoted in Giammona, B. The future of technical communication: How innovation, technology, information management, and other forces are shaping the future of the profession. *Technical Communication,* 51(3), 349–366.

Moore, P., & Kreth, M. (2005). From wordsmith to communication strategist: Heuristic and political maneuvering in technical communication. *Technical Communication,* 52(3), 302–322.

Morgan, G. (2006). *Images of organization.* Thousand Oaks, CA: Sage Publications.

Morris, J. R., Cascio, W. F., & Young, C. E. (1999). Downsizing after all these years: Questions and answers about who did it, how many did it, and who benefited from it. *Organizational Dynamics,* 27(3), 78–87.

Mott, R. K., & Ford, J. D. (2007). The convergence of technical communication and information architecture: Managing single-source objects for contemporary media. *Technical Communication,* 54(1), 27–45.

Natchez, M. (2001). Managing up: The overlooked element in successful management. *STC Management,* 5(4), 2–6.

Norton, Q. (2005). Squid labs: Suckers for novelty. *Wired,* 13(9).

Nuckols, C. E., & Canna, J. (2003). Extreme documentation. *Intercom,* 50(2), 6–9.

O'Connor, V. (2007). Agile development: Challenges and opportunities. *Intercom,* 54(2), 16–18.

Plung, D. L. (1994). Comprehending and aligning professionals and publications organizations. In O. J. Allen & L. H. Deming (Eds.), *Publications management: Essays for professional communicators* (pp. 171–187). Amityville, NY: Baywood.

Redish, J. (1995). Adding value as a professional technical communicator. *Technical Communication,* 42(1), 26–39.

Reich, R. (1991). *The work of nations: Preparing ourselves for 21st-century capitalism.* New York: Alfred A. Knopf.

Rockley, A. (2003). Single sourcing: It's about people, not just technology. *Technical Communication,* 50(3), 350–354.

Sanderlin, S.(1988). Preparing instruction manuals for non-English readers. *Technical Communication,* 35(2), 96–100.

Sapienza, F. (2002). Does being technical matter? XML, single source, and technical communication. *Journal of Technical Writing and Communication,* 32(2), 155–170.

———. (2004). Usability, structured content, and single sourcing with XML. *Technical Communication,* 51(3), 399–408.

Schriver, K. A. (1997). *Dynamics in document design.* New York: John Wiley & Sons.

Scrum Alliance. (2007). Retrieved August 15, 2007 from http://www.scrumalliance. org.

Sigman, C. M. (2007). Adapting to scrum: Challenges and strategies. *Intercom,* 54(7), 16–19.

Society for Technical Communication. (2005–2006). STC salary surveys. Retrieved March 6, 2009 from http://www.stc.org/stcmembers/boardNews_docs.asp.

———. (2009). About STC, vision and strategic plan. Retrieved March 26, 2009 from http://www.stc.org/about.

Spinuzzi, C. (2007). Guest editor's introduction: Technical communication in the age of distributed work. *Technical Communication Quarterly,* 16(3), 265–277.

Sydow-Campbell, K., & Hayhoe, G. F. (2000). Teamwork requires cooperation, communication. *Technical Communication,* 47(1), 15–16.

Weiss, E. H. (1998). Twenty-five tactics to internationalize your English. *Intercom,* 45(5), 11–15.

——. (2002). The retreat from usability: User documentation in the post-usability era. *Journal of Computer Documentation, 19*(1), 3–18.

Williams, J. D. (2003). The implications of single sourcing for technical communication. *Technical Communication, 50*(3), 321–327.

Zoho Projects. (2007). Retrieved August 15, 2007 from http://www.projects.zoho.com.

Zuboff, S., & Maxmin, J. (2002). *The support economy: Why corporations are failing individuals and the next episode of capitalism.* New York: Penguin.

Part II
New Foundational Knowledge For Our Field

3　Shaped and Shaping Tools

The Rhetorical Nature of Technical Communication Technologies

Dave Clark

So what is a rhetoric of technology? It is the rhetoric that accompanies technology and makes it possible—the rhetoric that makes technology fit into the world and makes the world fit with technology.

(Bazerman, 1998, p. 385)

Bazerman's definition, relying as it does on repetitions of "rhetoric" and "technology," isn't terribly reassuring to those of us who might like to pin down a concrete definition of "the rhetoric of technology," a slippery phrase linking two terms that are themselves difficult to define. But what is clear in the quotation is that technology and rhetoric are, in his assessment, co-embedded in culture. Technologies are inseparable from the rhetorics that describe, promote, and of course document them, and are also themselves tools with rhetorical constructions and implications.

As I'm writing this in the spring of 2009, my current techno-rhetorical obsession is with Twitter, an increasingly ubiquitous "micro-blogging" tool that is capturing the popular imagination. The actual code that underlies Twitter is trivial compared to, say, Facebook; it's essentially a messaging service that allows users to post 140-character messages to the kinds of people who read Twitter (i.e., mostly other Twitter users). But the rhetoric surrounding Twitter and the rhetorical implications of Twitter are becoming fascinating and seem to be everywhere. Twitter is ideal for sharing quick messages with groups, but because so much of the traffic seems to be made up of mundane personal updates, it is accused of being stupid, pointless, narcissistic, and over-hyped. It therefore shows all the signs of a real cultural phenomenon. It has been widely mocked (featured on "The Daily Show" in a segment titled "Old Man Stewart Shakes his Fist at Twitter") even as its use broadens (it was recently featured during a NASCAR race), and it receives tons of mass media coverage, at this point mostly articles in *Time* and *Newsweek* with themes along the lines of "what's this Twitter thing?" And, of course, it is the constant subject of buyout rumors, most recently by Google.

From the perspective of technical communicators, most interesting are the still-emerging rhetorical implications of Twitter. Here are just a few:

- *Twitter is public.* Unlike text messaging or Facebook status updates, by default "tweets" are publicly readable and searchable, making new connections possible. For example, last month I was attempting to install a content management system on my server when I posted that "Dave Clark is finding the Moodle setup confusing. Stupid directory permissions." Within minutes, a Moodle specialist from Australia replied with a suggestion.
- *Twitter can be endlessly resorted and reorganized.* Because Twitter allows for and encourages outside software developers, we have countless interfaces and points of entry. Unlike with most messaging systems, which are designed for short-lifespan messages, users can track popular current trends in lists, search via location or key word, or create historical snapshots or follow key topics with creative searching (try a Twitter search for "#pman" to read the tweets used to organize the protests in Moldova).
- *Twitter is powerful in the aggregate.* Because all tweets are public, Twitter offers new and interesting possibilities for searching, allowing users to find and track events too new to appear on Google. I have software that continually searches Twitter for "Riverwest," which pays dividends. I get to see comments describing my neighborhood as "the ghetto," but I also get important news updates. I learned about the sinkhole that closed our major bridge hours before it made the news, because someone there witnessed the bridge closing and Tweeted about it, and was nice enough to use the word "riverwest."

These are pretty interesting implications for such a simple tool, and we have only begun to see the full range of possibilities. Technical communicators, who are by their nature intrigued by new rhetorical possibilities, have begun to explore Twitter's possibilities for discussions, information sharing, messaging, and other professional and workplace tasks.

But as the subject of this volume is "digital literacy," it's worth asking what it might mean for a technical communicator or any other user to be a "literate" user of Twitter. Does it mean being technically proficient with the tool? That's certainly not difficult. Being able to articulate its many uses to others? Developing a deep understanding of the political, social, ideological, and historical roots of the tool? Learning how the tool shapes linguistic activities such as reading, writing, and communicating within a variety of contexts? Yes, all of these. As Kastman-Breuch argues, comprehensive literacy requires multifaceted technological understanding in order to become "capable users of technology who understand broader implications and the potential influence of technology on linguistic activities" (2002, p. 280).

The key question guiding this chapter is this: How do technical communicators learn about and assess "broader implications" and "potential influence"? And subquestions I will explore include these: What methods and theoretical approaches do we rely on to study and articulate the ways that technologies structure, shape, and influence the ways we communicate? How do we answer the calls for communicators to "be critical" in their documenting, teaching, learning, and use of new tools? And what does it mean to be a rhetorically savvy user of technology, as opposed to uncritically allowing tools like word processors, social networking, and content management systems to structure our work?

I will not attempt to survey here the vast literature on the relationships of humans with their technologies. Instead, I'll provide a structured look at key literature in what many technical communication scholars call "the rhetoric of technology." As you will see, the boundaries of such work are not as tightly fixed as in, say, the rhetoric of science, and in many cases authors do not specifically use the term "rhetoric of technology." I will argue, nonetheless, that we can talk about the rhetoric of technology as a coherent category of literature that addresses specific concerns of technical communicators. In particular this literature problematizes conventional understandings of writing technologies, an incredibly important task in a field that is constantly expected to learn and use new tools like content management systems.

I begin with a working definition of "technology," and then define the rhetoric of technology, in part by characterizing its difference from the rhetoric of science, the related field from which it evolved. From there, I provide a structured examination of approaches used by technical communicators who theorize about the rhetoric of technology, including classical rhetorical approaches, technology transfer theories, genre theory, and activity theory.

What is Technology?

"Technology" is an extremely problematic term. Scholars who write books on technology tend to offer only sweeping definitions, acknowledging the difficulty of establishing a single, clear, universal definition that acknowledges the term's dense and complex history as well as its contemporary use. The term came into wide use only recently, around the time of the Second World War. As Hughes (2005) notes, there were earlier uses (the *Oxford English Dictionary* includes references as early as the seventeenth century), but before WWII, "technology" tended to reference texts and treatises "on the industrial or practical arts," (Nye, 2007, p. 12) a meaning that largely held until well past the Industrial Revolution, when those in the United States still talked primarily of "inventions" or "applied science" or "mechanic arts" (p. 12). It was only in the latter half of the twentieth century that the meaning of "technology" gained its present status as "an annoyingly vague abstraction" (p. 15) that can refer to "both cause and effect, or as both object and process" (p. 15) and more recently the term has become something of a synonym for computerized tools. At this point, we are often surprised to contemplate more humble tools as "technologies," as Petroski (2008) asks us to do (cf. *The Toothpick*), and the "technology" section of newspapers and Web sites like CNN's tend to focus on cutting-edge tools related to digital communication, space travel, and health care.

At the same time, the term "technology" has roots that are literally ancient, beginning at least as long ago as Aristotle's use in the *Nicomachean Ethics* of *Techne*, which he defined as pragmatic, context-dependent, practical reasoning, in contrast with *episteme* (theoretical, context-independent knowledge) and *phronesis* (practical and context-dependent deliberation about values) (Sage, 2005, p. 50). The objective of *techne* is "application of technical knowledge and skills according to a pragmatic instrumental rationality" (Flyvbjerg, quoted in Sage, 2005, p. 50). Aristotle's distinctions are instructive, as they anticipate the contemporary common-sense division of technology from *phronesis,* or discussion of values and civic good; culturally, we frequently see technologies discussed as value-neutral "tools." Aristotle is not always consistent with his use of *techne, episteme,* and *phronesis* and he does occasionally relate *techne* to the sciences, "notably through mathematics" (Nye, 2007, p. 7). Nye suggests that Aristotle's distinction was characteristic of the Greeks, who saw "work with the hands [as] decidedly inferior to philosophical speculation" (p. 7) and *techne* as subject to "strict moral–political supervision ... the good and wise city will determine which inventions are to be made use of and which are to be suppressed" (Strauss, quoted in Nye, 2007, p. 8).

Today, most definitions of technology are arhetorical and therefore, unsatisfactory. We see a philosophical division (similar to Aristotle's) of tools apart from their implications, a point of view that Feenberg characterizes as "instrumentalist" (1991, p. 5) and Downey characterizes as the "guns don't kill people, people kill people" viewpoint (1998, p. 12). This understanding of technology is extremely prevalent. I find many students, who are often resistant to works written to counter these beliefs, like Winner's (1988) *Whale and the Reactor*. From their point of view, surely it is the human application of those tools, not the tools themselves or their creation, that brings up questions of ideology, morality, and ethics, or that raise debates over the sociocultural implications of new technologies that tend to be managed not by "strict moral–political supervision" or "the good and wise city," but by the marketplace and by other technologies.

We do, of course, have some baseline, cultural agreements about what technologies should be allowed (we cannot, as of today, buy a grenade launcher at WalMart), but the adoption and use of more ordinary technologies are governed less by the state fiat, as was true with the Greeks, than by their perceived usefulness, marketing, pricing, and availability. The cell phone has its critics, but the problems it introduces are handled (however ineffectively) through the use of other tools (signs pleading with us to turn them off in the doctor's office, or jamming technologies used in some movie theaters). Opponents of new technologies tend to be branded Neo-Luddites, enemies of individual freedom, or both (Downey, 1998), and are generally doomed to the same irrelevance as people who hated "talking to a machine" when answering machines first arrived on the market. The technologies themselves often remain free of rhetorical and cultural analysis.

Consider, next, this useful and thoughtful but characteristic definition from Hughes:

> I see technology as craftsmen, mechanics, inventors, engineers, designers, and scientists using tools, machines, and knowledge to create and control a human-built world consisting of artifacts and systems associated mostly with the traditional fields of civil, mechanical, electrical, mining, materials, and chemical engineering. In the twentieth and twenty-first centuries, however, the artifacts and systems also become associated with newer fields of engineering, such as aeronautical, industrial, computer, and environmental engineering, as well as bioengineering.
>
> (2005, p. 4)

This definition, as Hughes acknowledges, emphasizes not the tools themselves, but their creative design, implementation, and use, paralleling Aristotle's definition of *techne* as practical arts. And Hughes, like Aristotle, sees cultural analysis and critique as external to the project of technology creation and certainly external to the technologies themselves. Hughes bemoans the lack of focus on the "aesthetic dimensions of technology, which unfortunately have been neglected in the training of engineers, scientists, and others engaged with technology" (p. 5), but he doesn't voice a concern about the lack of sociocultural or rhetorical training, and acknowledges a generally "tempered enthusiasm" for technologies and practitioners, a "sympathetic view [that] is qualified by what I have learned from critics of technology" (p. 5).

I have shown what is lacking in some current definitions of technology, which tend to see technologies as arhetorical objects. In what follows, my aim is to show how rhetorical scholars have sought to put rhetorical critique back into the mix of technology development and use.

What is the Rhetoric of Technology?

To develop a definition of "rhetoric of technology," let's begin by examining what it is not: the rhetoric of science. The terms "technology" and "science" have a complicated relationship, as do the "practical" work of technology and the more epistemic work of science. Technology is frequently viewed as "applied science," which seems reasonable. Consider the seed industry, where specialists with training in the hard sciences develop new genetic varieties of seeds, which Monsanto, for one, markets as "biotechnologies" or "seed and trait technologies" (Monsanto Corporate, 2009). We also have a rich history that celebrates the non-scientist inventor, working in his garage and producing technological miracles like the airplane and the personal computer. Technology scholars have argued that technology and science are fundamentally different in their epistemology, outlook, and objectives (Cahan, 2003, p. 244). As Layton argues:

> Engineering theory and experiment came to differ with those of physics because it was concerned with man-made devices rather than directly with nature. Thus, engineering theory often deals with idealizations of machines, beams, heat engines or other devices ... By its very nature, therefore, is less abstracted and idealized; it is much closer to the "real world" of engineering.
>
> (quoted in Cahan, 2003, p. 244)

The "rhetoric of science," for its part, has a fairly narrow and coherent body of scholarship that focuses primarily on a relatively small range of philosophical concerns. Gross, author of *The Rhetoric of Science*, summarizes the "existence of a substantial body of work in rhetoric of science" (2006, p. 9) in the introductory chapter of *Starring the Text: The Place of Rhetoric in Science Studies*. The rhetoric of science, he argues, began with a focus on the public policy of science, but became radicalized in that it began to view science itself as an object of study. The key debate, according to Bazerman, "has been precisely whether, and to what extent, science is rhetorical" (1998, p. 382):

> ... some rhetoricians and scientists still would like to consider science as knowledge that rises above the situated and purposeful use of language. Through the history of the rise of modern science, from the time of Francis Bacon to the time of Hans Reichenbach and Karl Popper, there have been explicit attempts to distance natural philosophy and then science from rhetoric. We can even trace to Plato and Aristotle the impulse to distinguish the uncertain persuasions of rhetoric from those domains of philosophic inquiry that provided access to certain knowledge.
>
> (p. 382)

The issue of whether science is rhetorical is assumed by most rhetoricians. The question of extent, however, has been the subject of internal discussion for decades, and Gross (2006) sees increased radicalization in claims by rhetoricians that rhetoric does not simply wrap a persuasive package around the truth of science. Citing McCloskey's rhetorical analyses of scientific texts, Gross suggests that her view, like that of other rhetoricians, is that rhetoric constitutes, and is therefore inseparable from, the knowledge production of science:

> What is McCloskey's view of rhetoric? ... She says: "a science is a class of objects and a way of conversing about them, not a way of knowing the truth" (1985, 105). This would seem to indicate that rhetoric is indeed epistemic in the deepest sense; that it is fully constitutive of science. McCloskey's view of science seems virtually identical to the view espoused in my *Rhetoric of Science.*
>
> (2006, p. 13)

The rhetoric of technology is a younger line of scholarship, and has had to carve out a separate identity. Consider Winsor's discussion of rhetoric of technology in the 1998 special issue she edited of the *Journal of Business and Technical Communication.* Winsor notes that too often, technology has been an add-on in discussions of the rhetoric of science (as in: "the rhetoric of science *and technology*"). This is true as recently as 2005, when Gross and Gurak (2005, p. 241–248) published a special issue of *Technical Communication Quarterly* on "The State of the Rhetoric of Science and Technology." But we should not simply "believe that similar rhetorical practices exist in both spheres" (Bazerman, 1998, p. 344), and a major aim of Winsor's special issue was to establish differences between the spheres. Among the differences between the rhetorics of science and technology, as suggested by Winsor, Miller, and Bazerman (in the same edited issue) are these:

- Science produces mostly symbols through rhetorical means such as the published article and the grant proposal. Technology aims at the creation of useful objects and material processes (p. 385).
- Science emphasizes the creation of knowledge (p. 308). Technology is more quotidian and practical, and having been designed to meet human ends, has always been part of "human needs, desires, values, and evaluation, articulated in language and at the very heart of rhetoric" (p. 383).
- Scientists working in academic or quasi-academic settings seek to validate their findings with outsider professionals; technologists must protect trade secrets and their success is evaluated internally and by market forces.
- Science has a more closely bounded rhetorical terrain, and a more limited direct impact. Technologies "must often enlist the support of numerous publics (financial, legal, corporate public, technical) long before it becomes anything like a material reality" (p. 384).

For these reasons, and in part due to the ubiquity of technological contexts and uses, the body of literature in the rhetoric of technology is still far less cohesive and self-referencing than that of the rhetoric of science; in fact, the phrase "rhetoric of technology" is far less likely to appear in an article or book than "rhetoric of science." It's a term that seems more likely to be used as a self-identifier ("I study the rhetoric of technology") or in the title of a graduate course.

I can easily imagine teaching a "rhetoric of science" course that would rely almost exclusively on authors who would consider some of their work to be "rhetoric of science" (e.g., Gross, Prelli, Fahnestock, Paul, Bazerman, Myers). However, doing the same with the rhetoric of technology would be more difficult, in part because there is such variety in the rhetorical approaches taken by its scholars. Most scholars in the rhetoric of science have relied on classical rhetorical approaches for their analyses. Work in the rhetoric of technology has tended to be broader in its approaches as well as its objects and contexts, relying fundamentally on rhetorical analysis but also on the technological expertise provided by scholars in other fields, most notably philosophy, history, and sociology, and including such notables as Heidegger, Habermas, Latour, Vygotsky, Feenberg, Foucault, Hughes, Lyotard, and Mumford. In what follows, I will not attempt to summarize the work of these foundational scholars, but will instead discuss some of their work as it is used in the rhetoric of technology as practiced by technical communication scholars.

Focuses and Approaches

As I suggested in the previous section, creating a coherent grouping of works in the "rhetoric of technology" is a difficult if not impossible task. My goal here is not to be comprehensive, but to create a means for categorizing some of this work in ways that usefully highlight key contemporary trends in the literature with special focus on theoretical approaches underlying these methods. I emphasize this point because I cannot claim that these categories are static or comprehensive or that there isn't significant overlap among them. Rather, my intention is to point to some key, interesting scholars and texts that readers might want to consult, and to acquaint readers with important terminology and concepts, and a basic familiarity with the many unique ways that rhetorical scholars provide theoretical and practical context to the technologies they study.

For these purposes, I have categorized readings in the rhetoric of technology in four groups: rhetorical analysis, technology transfer, genre theory, and activity theory (of course, there is much overlap in these groups). What differentiates these works, however loosely, is the foundational scholarship on which they rely, as I will show in the following sections.

Rhetorical Analysis

This category is, by necessity, only a loose grouping of related types of work that share a common goal: complicating common-sense understandings of technologies by analyzing them from a variety of rhetorical perspectives that demonstrate their immersion in social and rhetorical processes. What these works share in common, above all, is a foundation in classical or contemporary rhetorical analysis, and the application of rhetorical terms and theories to the analysis of technologies in context.

The last few years have seen the emergence of rhetorical studies of Twitter, including a recent panel at the South by Southwest Interactive Festival in which a group of rhetoricians spoke about Twitter in ways that demonstrate how thinking about technological problems from a rhetorical perspective can illuminate new tools and technologies. The "Is Aristotle on Twitter" panel (Brown, et. al, 2009) (pieces of which are viewable online at http://blogs.zdnet.com/weblife/?p=457) offered, for example, a discussion of how the classical concept of *topoi* can help us understand how social media problematize the "fixity" of text we've long been able to assume. While face-to-face speech has temporal fixity (listeners can only receive it in the order it is presented) and printed texts have spatial fixity (page 6 is always page 6), a network like Twitter opens up both temporal and spatial fixity.

Analyzed one way, it's easy to be skeptical of this line of work, which can be seen as a continual, nostalgic argument for the relevance of classical rhetoric to emerging problems, made by those most likely to benefit. But these works have made important contributions to the field by providing important sociocultural commentary from a rhetorical perspective enriched by predecessors in technology studies from a variety of other fields, including sociology, anthropology, history, and philosophy. Consider, for example, Johnson's *User-Centered Technology: A Rhetorical Theory for Computers and Other Mundane Artifacts* (1998). Johnson begins, as I do above, with classical rhetoric as a means to argue that the ancients saw technologies as arts in which the end was the civic good to be produced by the product, not the design and making of the product. Drawing further from philosophers and historians of science and technology, Johnson suggests that as a field we must argue for a rhetorical approach to technological design and implementation that places users, rather than systems, at the center of our focus, and that we have an ethical and cultural responsibility to learn and argue for collaborative approaches to technology design that incorporate users.

Gurak (1997), in *Persuasion and Privacy in Cyberspace*, similarly relies on publicly available texts, classical rhetoric, and philosophers and historians of technology to argue that a rhetorical perspective has much to offer to sociocultural interpretations of technology. In particular, Gurak is interested in leveraging the rhetorical concepts of interpretive communities and two key rhetorical elements—ethos and delivery—to evaluate the rhetoric used by online communities in their protests over two now barely remembered technological developments that once threatened user privacy. Gurak's book serves as an argument for the continued usefulness of rhetoric in technological settings, as she argues persuasively that classical rhetorical principles, when taken in light of the unique contexts of faceless electronic forums, can nonetheless enlighten and problematize our thinking.

More recently, Warnick (2001), in *Critical Literacy in a Digital Era: Technology, Rhetoric and the Public Interest,* analyzes the rhetoric of technology that has surrounded the development of new digital communication technologies. Relying, as Johnson and Gurak do, on rhetorical theory, Warnick evaluates and critiques the discourse of *Wired* magazine, an early-adopter publication that historically took an exceedingly libertarian, male, individualistic view of emerging technologies that propose technology as cure-alls for societal ills. She advocates the creation of a broader discourse, and in her subsequent book, *Rhetoric Online: Persuasion and Politics on the World Wide Web,* she adapts rhetorical theory to the study of Web-based discourse.

What these works and the many others in this grouping have in common is advocacy of a rhetorical perspective for analyzing the problems and issues raised by new digital technologies, through the examination of large-scale, publicly available discourse. For technical communicators, these works can provide critical background in rhetorical study as well as contemporary understandings of how that rhetoric can be adapted to new problems.

Technology Transfer and Diffusion

In basic terms this is the study of how new technologies are moved into organizations and then used, implemented, and in some cases, rejected. "Technology transfer" is an umbrella term for the study of complex processes by which new technologies are moved from the engineer's bench to the marketplace and then, eventually, are put into practice. "Technology diffusion" emphasizes the "market-driven process by which innovations are adopted and implemented" (Coppolla, 2006). Both are of obvious concern to technical communicators, who constantly are expected to design, evaluate, document, and implement new technologies.

The factors that determine the adoption and implementation of new technologies are of great concern to technical communicators. For example, Andersen (2009) conducted a longitudinal study of a "trial period" of a content management system by a technical communication workgroup. The rhetorical approaches and goals of the vendor and the trial participants were often at odds. The vendor saw their product as intuitive, their training as suitable for the needs of the workgroup, and the adoption unproblematic. The workgroup, for their part, found that the product did not align with their needs, the training did not help them develop the necessary information models, and the adoption was more trouble than it was worth. Andersen's study of the eventual rejection of the product points to useful implications for both vendors and practitioners who hope to integrate complex new rhetorical tools.

The scholarship in technology transfer is enormous and multidisciplinary, and features a wide variety of approaches. Technology transfer itself can only loosely be called a "field" of scholars who study the design and implementation of technological innovations (Doheny-Farina, 1992, p. ix). The scholarship is growing substantially. When Rogers released the first edition of his *Diffusion of Innovations* in 1962, he reported on a survey of only 405 publications in the diffusion field. When he released the fifth edition in 2003, he estimated the existence of more than 5,000 works. In addition, the field has recently seen the creation, in 2003, of a new journal, *Comparative Technology Transfer and Society*. As Rogers put it, "No other field of behavior science research" he reported, "represents more effort by more scholars in more disciplines in more nations" (2003, p. xviii).

Much of the work surveyed by Rogers assumes an unproblematic, arhetorical transfer of technical information, processes, and products from developer to user. But from the perspective of technical communicators, much existing work on technology transfer is problematic because it fails to provide an adequately complex vision of the rhetorical situations. Williams and Gibson (1990) are widely acknowledged as among the first to problematize what they saw as a simplistic model of communication underlying the project of technology transfer. They summarize what they identify as three "traditional" models of technology transfer (summarized here by Perkins, 1993, p. 188):

- *Appropriability model (1945–1950s)*. This model "emphasizes the importance of the quality of research and competitive market pressures to promote the use of research findings ... Good technologies, according to this model, sell themselves."
- *Dissemination model (1960–1970s)*. "The objective is to transfer expert knowledge to the user who is a willing receptor." (This model is similar to the information transfer or conduit model, which Doheny-Farina's rhetorical perspective counters.)
- *Knowledge utilization model (current)*. "Although this model begins to reflect the complexities of transfer ... it suffers from an inherent linear bias ... The stated or implicit notion is that basic research moves from researcher to client, in one direction, to become a developed idea and eventually a product."

Doheny-Farina (1992) describes Williams and Gibson's work as among the most promising, but still finds it lacking a fully rhetorical perspective. Writing not long after them, Doheny-Farina suggests that technology transfer is deeply rhetorical in previously unrecognized ways:

Every aspect of technology transfers must be negotiated, constructed, and reconstructed in the minds of the participants. There is no clearly objective fact or physical entity that proceeds uninterpreted from the lab to the market. The entire process is one of interpretation, negotiation, and adjustment. Moreover, it engenders a reciprocal shaping as it develops; the innovators, the innovation, and the users of the innovation are all changed through the process.

(p. 6)

In the near future, we are very likely to see technology transfer studies of such innovations as the implementation of Twitter by workgroups. Ideally, some of this work will come from technical communicators, who until recently have produced remarkably little literature between Doheny-Farina's 1992 book and a special issue of *Technical Communication Quarterly* (edited by Coppolla) in 2006: as Coppolla puts it, "After the mid 1990s, technical communication publications dwindled to a few isolated cases, a handful of conference papers, and passing references critical of the social constructivist approach used in technology transfer" (p. 288).

This lack is unfortunate at a time when technical communicators more than ever need to develop and use rhetorical tools for evaluating and implementing new technologies. There is promising new work, however, like Andersen's, and the work on which she structures her own, Dayton's (2006), which calls for work in technology transfer that moves beyond the social constructionist approach favored by Doheny-Farina in favor of a "hybrid approach" that incorporates Rogers's adoption and diffusion theory, cultural-historical activity theory, and the theory of the social construction of technology. Taking such an approach—along with turning away from the historical focus on retrospective studies of large-scale innovation diffusion and toward real-time investigations of organizations and work groups—can help scholars develop nuanced critiques that will help us better understand successes and failures.

Genre Theory

In comparison to work in technology transfer, scholarship that focuses on tight readings of individual technologies can at first seem myopic, but when employing rhetorical theory as well, such an approach can provide a focused, nuanced examination of both particular tools such as PowerPoint and broad and complex content management systems. Genre theory, in particular, because it focuses so closely on the rhetorical construction of the writing produced and encouraged by particular tools, can be invaluable to gaining new understandings.

Genre theory in technical communication is derived largely from Miller's work in the 1980s that defined genres as "typified rhetorical actions based in recurrent situations" (1984, p. 159). For rhetoricians, Miller's work implies that we should not think of genres, such as a memo, a report, or a manual, simply as different *formats*; instead, they are most usefully seen as regularizing structures, that is, as socially recognized types of communicative actions that become habitual, regularized, and institutionalized templates that shape the work of members of organizations (p. 69).

Genre theory has been applied often to regular printed genres in workplaces. For example, Winsor's work on work orders in an engineering setting (2000) made clear that genres aren't simply a particular, regularized format, but are instead an institutionalized means of social action that can take many forms and have real impacts on workplace "power and territory" (p. 155). In the case of the technicians and engineers she studied, work orders, whether formally presented or scrawled out long hand, had the effect of both triggering and concealing the work of technicians; the status and use of work orders in the organization allowed engineers to subsume technicians' work into their own without due acknowledgement.

Scholars in the rhetoric of technology use genre theory in numerous ways. Yates and Orlikowski (2007), for example, rely on it to dissect PowerPoint presentations, arguing that genres create expectations of purpose, content, participants, form, time, and place, and that PowerPoint presentations, despite their variations, share a set of such similar discursive characteristics that they are recognizable as a genre, with all the attendant enabling (facilitating the completion of particular organizational tasks) and constraining (limiting the range of possibilities for social action) effects. Yates and Orlikowski suggest that the ubiquity of PowerPoint structures the contemporary workplace in particular ways, and that the common use of PowerPoint slides as standalone artifacts raises new questions about genre.

Similarly, I rely on genre theory in my investigations of content management systems. Single-sourcing content management often has as a goal the perfect reuse of standardized text, in the process hard-coding the elements of individual genres, eliminating some of the communicative complexity and flexibility that is normal for genres. In my analysis of one content management implementation (Clark, 2007a), I found that each manual was identically formatted, as would be expected, but also, in order to promote cost savings, each one was composed of the same components structured in precisely the same ways, thus limiting options for the kind of flexibility expected of most organizational genres, which evolve and morph over time to serve new functions. Also made more difficult were the tasks of internationalization and localization, which have commonly and historically meant rethinking the structure and organization of documents.

Recently, genre theory has been expanded in ways that allow rhetoricians to use it for larger, contextual analyses. The concept of "genre ecologies," drawing from ecological metaphors developed by Nardi and O'Day (1999) and by Hutchins (1995), allows technical communicators to think of the relationships of workers and their technological tools in more complex and useful ways. As argued by Spinuzzi (2003), "technical communicators have seen the texts that they produce—manuals, references, instructions— as 'bridging' or mediating between a worker and her tool ... [but] upon many workers often draw simultaneously upon many different textual artifacts, including official genres but also [the] ad hoc" (p. 97). As we move forward, these understandings of genre can give us rich understandings of the collaborative and distributed work so common to the contemporary workplace.

Activity Theory

By far the largest category of current work in the rhetoric of technology consists of studies that use a variety of theoretical perspectives, including genre theory, work in technology transfer, and classical rhetoric, to investigate the specifics of particular organizational contexts. The publication in 1985 of Odell and Goswami's *Writing in Nonacademic Settings* anticipated a flurry of organizational studies that appeared in the late 1980s and early 1990s and relied on "the social perspective," which valued the examination of writing and its associated technologies within organizational contexts. The work can be difficult: getting access to nonacademic settings can be a significant obstacle, and learning to conduct studies properly meant learning new theoretical and practical research methods. Technical communicators relied heavily on the work of anthropologists and other social scientists in developing these approaches.

In the early to mid 1990s, the most common approaches continued to be based on social construction theory. More contemporary approaches see early theories of social construction as not yet accounting for power and agency (Thralls and Blyler, 1993, p. 14) and for the particulars of the larger circumstances in which knowledge work is accomplished. As Winsor notes, such analyses are "incomplete because [they] ignore the circumstances in which much knowledge work is done, that is, in for-profit hierarchical corporations ... we must remember that systems of distributed cognition are not always collaborative, egalitarian, and harmonious" (2003, p. 7). More problematic for rhetoricians of technology, social construction offered few ways to consider the nonlinguistic material realm, such as the technologies used to accomplish communication in these contexts (Clark, 2007b, p. 160).

Activity theory, on the other hand, designates useful, structured ways for incorporating discussions of material tools and technologies. Activity theory was developed from early twentieth century Russian psychology, particularly from the work of Vygotsky and Leont'ev, and was adapted for work in professional communication through the work of Cole and Engestrom (1993). Activity theorists argue that an "activity system," the basic unit of analysis, is "any ongoing, object-directed, historically conditioned, dialectically structured, tool-mediated human interaction," for example, "a family, a religious organization, an advocacy group, a political movement" (Russell, 1997, p. 510). In the case of technical communicators, the focus is most often on work groups or organizations. Groups and individuals are analyzed with a triangular approach that emphasizes the multidirectional interconnections among subjects (the individual, dyad, or group), the mediational means or tools they use to take action (machines, writing, speaking, gesture), and the object or problem space on which the subject acts. Activity theory analysis can provide us with a broad cultural understanding, as activity systems share a common language and structure, allowing scholars to compare and contemplate similar contexts. As Flower (2003) suggests, "In Engestrom's (1993) powerful model [activity analysis] includes not only the actors, the object of action, and the community which shares those objects, but also divisions of labor and power, the rules and conventions, and the material or symbolic tools that mediate the activity" (p. 242).

Activity theory calls for active attention to analysis of artifacts, whether written genres or digital technologies. Consider Cheryl Geisler's look (2003) at the Palm Pilot, which incorporates, as guided by activity theory, a sociocultural history of the artifact, a consideration of its diffusion (what motivated users to adopt a Palm?), and reflection on how Palms become incorporated into the activity patterns of everyday life. Geisler argues that the roots of the device in systematic management make it an unusual candidate for incorporation into our personal lives, but its persuasive character and roots in professionalization make it a compelling object of study. Will, she asks, the Palm Pilot become the antecedent of further professionalizing, multitasking technologies? As a result, theories such as genre theory, activity theory, and actor-network theory have become commonplace as analytical tools in workplace studies in the rhetoric of technology. Activity theory is most often used to examine tools within organizational contexts, allowing researchers to balance their interests in particular technologies with the necessary practice of seeing those tools being used in action toward specific objectives.

For a detailed application of activity theory, see Longo's chapter in this volume.

Conclusion

As I have suggested throughout, my brief survey of the rhetoric of technology cannot be comprehensive. I have of course only glossed the surface of these important theories and approaches, and have omitted others in favor of those I've selected. In particular, actor–network theory (ANT), developed by Latour and other science studies scholars in the 1990s, has recently seen something of a resurgence in technical communication literature; I recommend Spinuzzi (2007) for an overview of ANT and its relationship to other network theories.

My aim in this chapter was to highlight some theories and foci of key approaches within the scholarship, and to point readers to useful resources for learning more about them. Ultimately what these approaches share, in addition to their interest in technology, is their emphasis on the importance of examining the rhetorical contexts in which technologies are embedded.

Understanding those contexts is critical to developing a deeper understanding of technologies that can lead to their more effective use.

References

Andersen, R. (2009). The diffusion of content management technologies in technical communication work groups: A qualitative study on the activity of technology transfer. Unpublished doctoral dissertation.

Bazerman, C. (1998). The production of technology and the production of human meaning. *Journal of Business and Technical Communication, 12*(3), 381–387.

Brown, J., Burdette, W., Jones, J., Roberts-Miller, T., & Sayre, J. (2009). Is Aristotle on twitter? Panel presented at the South by Southwest Interactive Festival. Austin, TX: March 17, 2009.

Cahan, D. (Ed.) (2003). *From natural philosophy to the sciences: Writing the history of nineteenth-century science.* Chicago, IL: University Of Chicago Press.

Clark, D. (2007a). Content management and the production of genres. In *Proceedings of the 25th annual ACM international conference on design of communication,* El Paso, Texas (pp. 9–13). New York, ACM.

——. (2007b). Rhetoric of empowerment: Genre, activity, and the distribution of capital. In M. Zachry & C. Thralls (Eds.), *Communicative practices in workplaces and the professions: Cultural perspectives on the regulation of discourse and organizations* (pp. 155–180). Amityville, NY: Baywood Publishing.

Cole, M., & Engestrom, Y. (1993). A cultural-historical approach to distributed cognition. In G. Saloman (Ed.), *Distributed cognitions: Psychological and education considerations* (pp. 1–46). Cambridge: Cambridge University Press.

Coppola, N. (2006). Guest editor's introduction: Communication in technology transfer and diffusion: Defining the field. *Technical Communication Quarterly, 15*(3), 285–293.

Dayton, D. (2006). A hybrid analytical framework to guide studies of innovative IT adoption by work groups. *Technical Communication Quarterly, 15*(3), 355–382.

Doheny-Farina, S. (1992). *Rhetoric, innovation, technology: Case studies of technical communication in technology transfer.* London: MIT Press.

Downey, G. L. (1998). *The machine in me: An anthropologist sits among computer engineers.* New York: Routledge.

"Episteme and Techne." *Stanford Encyclopedia of Philosophy.* Retrieved April 9, 2009 from http://plato.stanford.edu/entries/episteme-techne/#3.

Feenberg, A. (1991). *Critical theory of technology.* New York: Oxford University Press.

Flower, L. (2003). Intercultural knowledge building: The literate action of a community think tank. In C. Bazerman & D. Russell (Eds.), *Writing selves/writing societies: Research from activity perspectives* (pp. 239–279). Fort Collins, CO: The WAC Clearinghouse and Mind, Culture, and Activity.

Geisler, C. (2003). When management becomes personal: An activity-theoretic analysis of palm technologies. In C. Bazerman & D. Russell (Eds.), *Writing selves/ writing societies: Research from activity perspectives* (pp. 125–158). Fort Collins, CO: The WAC Clearinghouse and Mind, Culture, and Activity.

Gross, A. G. (2006). *Starring the text: The place of rhetoric in science studies.* Carbondale, IL: Southern Illinois University Press.

Gross, A. G., & Gurak, L. J. (2005). Special issue on the state of rhetoric of science and technology. *Technical Communication Quarterly, 14*(3), 241–248.

Gurak, L. (1997). *Persuasion and privacy in cyberspace.* New Haven, CT: Yale University Press.

Hughes, T. P. (2005). *Human-built world: How to think about technology and culture (science * culture).* Chicago, IL: University Of Chicago Press.

Hutchins, E. (1995). *Cognition in the wild.* Cambridge, MA: MIT Press.

Johnson, R. R. (1998). *User-centered technology: A rhetorical theory for computers and other mundane artifacts.* Albany, NY: State University of New York Press.

Kastman-Breuch, L. (2002). Thinking critically about technology literacy: Developing a framework to guide computer pedagogy in technical communication. *Technical Communication Quarterly, 11*(3), 267–288.

Leont'ev, A. N. (1978). *Activity, consciousness, and personality.* Englewood Cliffs, NJ: Prentice-Hall.

Miller, C. (1984). Genre as social action. *Quarterly Journal of Speech, 70,* 151–167.

Monsanto Corporation. (2009). Who we are. Retrieved April 14, 2009 from http://www.monsanto.com/who_we_are/default.asp.

Nardi, B. A., & O'Day, V. L. (1999). *Information ecologies: Using technology with heart.* Cambridge, MA: MIT Press.

Nye, D. E. (2007). *Technology matters: Questions to live with.* London: MIT Press.

Odell, L., & Goswami, D. (1985). *Writing in nonacademic settings.* New York: The Guilford Press.

Perkins, J. M. (1993). Social perspectives on technology transfer. *IEEE Transactions on Professional Communication, 36*(4), 185–189.

Petroski, H. (2008). *The toothpick: Technology and culture.* New York: Vintage.

Rogers, E. M. (2003). *Diffusion of innovations* (5th ed.). New York: Free Press.

Russell, D. R. (1997). Rethinking genre in school and society: An activity theory analysis. *Written Communication, 14*(4), 504–554.

SAGE Handbook of Qualitative Research. (2005). Thousand Oaks, CA: Sage Publications.

Spinuzzi, C. (2003). Compound mediation in software development: Using genre ecologies to study textual artifacts. In C. Bazerman & D. Russell (Eds), *Writing selves/writing societies: Research from activity perspectives* (pp. 97–124). Fort Collins, CO: The WAC Clearinghouse and Mind, Culture, and Activity.

——. (2007). Who killed Rex? Tracing a message through three kinds of networks. In M. Zachry & C. Thralls (Eds.), *Communicative practices in workplaces and the professions: Cultural perspectives on the regulation of discourse and organizations* (pp. 45–66). Amityville, NY: Baywood Publishing.

Thralls, C., & Blyler, N. R. (1993). *Professional communication: The social perspective.* Thousand Oaks, CA: Sage Publications.

Warnick, B. (2001). *Critical literacy in a digital era: Technology, rhetoric, and the public interest.* Mahwah, NJ: Lawrence Erlbaum.

Williams, F., & Gibson, D. (1990). *Technology transfer: A communication perspective.* Thousand Oaks, CA: Sage Publications.

Winner, L. (1988). *The whale and the reactor: A search for limits in an age of high technology.* Chicago, IL: University of Chicago Press.

Winsor, D. (1998). Guest editor's introduction: A call for the study of the rhetoric of technology. *Journal of Business and Technical Communication, 12*(3), 285–287.

——. (2000). Ordering work: Blue-collar literacy and the political nature of genre. *Written Communication, 17*(2), 155–184.

——. (2003). *Writing power: Communication in an engineering center.* Albany, NY: State University of New York Press.

Yates, J., & Orlikowski, W. (2007). The PowerPoint presentation and its corollaries: How genres shape communicative action in organizations. In C. Thralls & M. Zachry (Eds.), *Communicative practices in workplaces and the professions: Cultural perspectives on the regulation of discourse and organizations* (pp. 67–92). Amityville, NY: Baywood Publishing.

4 Information Design

From Authoring Text to Architecting Virtual Space

Michael J. Salvo and Paula Rosinski

By using the term "literacy" to describe digital work, this collection asserts that there is both an intellectual and a professional responsibility for maintaining the knowledge base of the field; that is, knowing not just how to do things with technology, but also why and when action needs to take place. That understanding of how and when to deploy knowledge is part of self-reflective (critical) professional practice. Using the word "literacy" carries with it an obligation to develop practice that is the result of thoughtful education in how best to construct or configure technical communication that should supplement training in current tools and practices. "Functional literacy" is a term used by literacy scholars to describe basic levels of literate activity, such as understanding words and initiating actions supported by those words (see Kanpol, 1999, p. 54). But full participation in any community requires higher levels of reflection, engagement, and understanding. Full participation, which we call "critical literacy," requires that one comprehend not merely the words, but also the purposes or uses for the selection of those words in a given context. Achieving critical literacy, of course, takes special effort because it requires the development of self-awareness of those aspects of practice that generally go unexamined and unarticulated. Articulated here as reflective practice, critical digital literacy has antecedents in the work of scholars like Gurak (2001) and Warnick (2002). Both Gurak and Warnick argue that to engage in digital literacy, one must have not only an ability to use new media technologies, but also a critical self-awareness that questions why and explores purposes digital communication technologies serve in culture.

As this chapter will show, proficiency in information design has become a key component of literacy in work contexts. It is now essential to include information design in any discussion of digital literacy. Search and retrieval—or findability—as well as navigability become increasingly important as the information age produces more documents than ever before.[1] As the volume of information increases, designing for storage and retrieval becomes more important in the planning stages of writing. After all, information that cannot be easily retrieved when needed is useless.

After providing a brief overview of how technical communicators are especially well positioned to manage information design in industry contexts, this chapter offers a description of emerging language developed and used in communities of professional practice. Technical communicators will find this language useful for articulating aspects of information design that are too often left unspoken. Our lexicon covers concepts important for reflective practice of information design. Concepts such as granularity and heterogeneity, mapmaking, and signposting highlight the kinds of organizational work technical communicators already do in terms of digital information storage and retrieval—they also reinforce the design of information as a critical part of maintaining searchability and findability. We also refer to the concept of pattern language, akin to digital versions of building codes. Pattern language is important because it influences the underlying structure of the World Wide Web. By knowing about this concept, technical communicators can reframe their expertise of traditional organizational strategies into digital organizational strategies and can design more usable and sustainable information spaces. Our lexicon is not intended as exhaustive, but rather offers a snapshot of valuable concepts relevant to information design at the end of the first decade of the twenty-first century. These terms will have alternative constructions and different practitioners will define the boundaries and taxonomies of these terms differently, so we offer them here mainly as a means of mapping practice (following the very useful precedent established by Barton and Barton, 1993).

Explaining emerging terms such as pattern language and ambience also has potential to assist in the future development of our field, and discussing key elements of information design can support critical efforts in professional development. The chapter therefore concludes by proposing a future of information design involving ambient searching mechanisms that extract contextual factors from a situation and then integrate them into the searching process—a far cry from current searches that rely exclusively on search terms. By staying engaged in information design considerations, technical communicators will be well poised to help usher in and shape a potential future of ambient contextual information storage and retrieval in the age of digital literacy. Savage (2004) envisions critical digital literacy, which he defines as a complex understanding of becoming responsible and responsive to the demands of the information age. Savage links the ancient rhetorical concept of *metis*, related to effective sailing, to meaningful deployment of contemporary digital tools in the workplace and the lifeworlds of users. According to Savage (2004), sailing is an apt metaphor for working effectively in a milieu of cultural and workplace change accompanying widespread use of new digital media; that is, for "not mastering but negotiating continually shifting technologies, institutions, discourses, and cultures" (p. 189). Negotiation requires articulation of desire: what does the technical rhetor want from proficiency and expertise in digital literacy, and how does this knowledge better prepare the professional to realize that desire? This chapter cannot give the reader a single definitive answer, but instead raises questions in order to articulate the stakes of this discussion.

More broadly, this chapter focuses on information design for two important reasons. First, by further refining expertise in information design, technical communicators have the potential to participate as leaders in digital literacy in the age of information. Attention to design most recently has focused on the placement and articulation of information (data) within documents as well as on finding, contextualizing, and placing any document within larger conversations and collections (metadata). As an example, Hart-Davidson's (2001) discussion of data and information about that data, or metadata, as a core competency of technical communicators leads to further widening of the focus of expertise in digital literacy, from the level of sentence and paragraph, to the level of the document and its design, to the context of its production and reception, and finally, to its response to the rhetorical exigency of its production. These concerns collectively are the domain of information design. As rhetorically trained, human-centered communication specialists, technical communicators are well situated to contribute to the development of usable, human-scaled virtual information spaces and to advocate for user needs in emerging digital spaces. In fact, some technical communicators are already doing just that. Because such familiarity, in large part, amounts to reinterpreting and refocusing the work already being done by technical communicators, they are not required to shoulder additional responsibilities.

Second, technical communicators are well positioned to bridge past and future work involving information design. Technical communicators have long been committed to designing information in written documents so that those who put ideas to work can access content when needed. As digital delivery becomes increasingly prominent, technical communicators must also consider how technological boundaries may hinder user access to digital content. Technical communicators have used numerous generic conventions (memos, letters, reports, and the like) to articulate content, and have been using the power of digital electronic networks to send and receive email, create Web pages, and interact with distant collaborators. Each of these writing situations shares an underlying similarity: each space, each genre, and each document is designed. That is, each is created for use by human beings for use by other human beings. One difference between paper-based and electronic communication is that the forms and designs of older analog media have been internalized and naturalized; whereas paper-based genres have cultural and organizational histories and are familiar to most readers, networked communications are relatively new, with their first widespread use in the middle to late 1990s followed by a surge in popularity through the early twenty-first century. Use, familiarity, and comfort within these newer information spaces are therefore, to some extent, generational, and technical communicators must now consider how to bridge these generational boundaries that are likely to express themselves as technological preferences.

An Overview of Technical Communicators' Unique Contributions to Information Design in Industry

Technical communicators have a solid foundation for making and arguing in favor of decisions related to information design. In this section, we identify three ways in which they are especially well positioned to do and manage information design in work contexts.

Technical Communicators in Information Design Have a Successful History of Applying Effective Design Principles

In the early years of the World Wide Web, digital designers untrained in technical communication tried to distinguish their online work from print design. Many principles of effective page design were ignored in their search for new designs on the screen. "We went through this with Web sites—the early designs ignored all that had been learned before and set us back many years in progress toward usability and understanding" asserts Norman (2002, p. xv), referring to the late 1990s. At that time, designers of new Web site construction ignored effective design principles, even at times asserting that effective document design developed for the page did not and could not apply online. Designers, once comfortable with digital display, learned to work with the new freedoms enabled online.[2] But these new freedoms and changes in design came at a cost: some best practices and traditions from the past that had been developed for print were abandoned now in online design. Many new Web site designers, as their attention moved from communicating on the page to communicating through the screen, ignored traditional principles of page design in their eagerness to invent new design styles and practices. But despite these rough, early attempts, the opening of the World Wide Web frontier ultimately did usher in new design styles and practices. Thankfully, since then, many have rediscovered the value of font design and use of white space, and perhaps most importantly, the benefits of collaborating with users (for example, through usability testing) toward the creation of readable and usable documentation.

Technical Communicators Understand Genre Historically, and Innovate in Work Contexts

As rhetorically trained, human-centered communication specialists, technical communicators are well situated to contribute to the development of usable virtual information spaces and to represent, and even advocate for, user needs in emerging digital spaces. Past approaches to information design in the field have provided technical communicators with a valuable long-term historical perspective, one that allows a variety of paper-based and digital documents to be understood as artifacts that represent genre historically.

Historicizing genre is significant, because it reminds writers that the ways in which emerging digital documents and virtual spaces are designed transmit values and reinforce or disrupt ways of working and communicating with one another. Such a historical perspective is articulated by Spinuzzi (2003), who explains that historically, genres have been fluid and aided by emerging technologies in impacting the design, context of reception, and mode (or media) of information transmission. For Spinuzzi, genres and their use change over time, and these changes reflect the values and potential impact of communication within the organizations producing these documents. Spinuzzi's study traces the impact of digital technologies on a variety of generic communication forms, showing how digital technology impacts not just the speed of communication but also the context of work, requiring re-articulation of genres that would otherwise no longer make sense in the new context. The network of people, the technologies they are using, and their institutional and cultural context create a unique mix of actors, one that impacts the shape and meaning given to documents, and that shapes the types of documents produced. As Spinuzzi describes it in *Tracing Genres Through Organizations* (2003), over time, purpose, content, and expectation for documents change, and accustomed genres not only fall in and out of favor, but also shift, becoming something new and unforeseen. In Spinuzzi's construction, these generic shifts emerge during larger cultural transformations, like the shift from paper-based to digital communication, Spinuzzi recounts how individuals at the Iowa Department of Transportation altered their documents' generic properties to respond effectively to change. These changes were neither wholly good nor wholly bad, but rather innovations developed in response to situations in which old patterns of behavior no longer yielded the desired results. Over time, small changes accumulate and result in new emerging genres. In the clearest example, memos have become email, but so too email has been altered quickly into instant messages, Twitter posts, and position papers and diaries rearticulated online as blogs.

Similarly, Johnson (1998) traces the development of a variety of genres developed to account for digital technology, asserting: "Genres are taxonomic devices that provide order and meaning to many everyday artifacts" (p. 139). As he points out, this position of generic convention as organizational, or taxonomic, destabilizes the relationship between author and text by recognizing an expanded agency of the author. For each document, the author (consciously or unconsciously) chooses to reify the existing relationship between one new document and other previous existing documents, for example, by deciding how much of the predecessors' visual and content clues are carried along into the new document. That is, Johnson asserts, each writing situation requires authors to accept accustomed structures in a given situation, for instance, by choosing to write a memo rather than trying to create a unique, new form of writing. Authors can use these social conventions to convey part of the text's meaning. Consider memos, parking tickets, wedding invitations, white papers, and reports for decision making: each of these genres carries part of the message in its visual design and physical presentation. The design indicates a range of possible responses to the text, and defines limits to how readers may choose to receive the text. One can accept or decline an invitation. On the other hand, a parking ticket under a windshield accuses the driver of breaking the law and requires response on the part of the recipient. Unlike an invitation, a ticket cannot be declined. Johnson reminds technical communicators of the power inherent in design and presentation: while innovation is possible, it comes at a cost. Innovative documents may not carry with them clear boundaries for readers' responses.

Yates (1989), like Spinuzzi and Johnson, is interested not only in the content of these institutional genres of communication, but also in ways in which emerging communication practices, codified into generic formats, represent values and relationships within organizations. Yates describes the nineteenth-century invention of some genres, like memos, that emerged in business communication alongside technologies such as the telegraph and railroad. These genres had power relationships encoded in them, as well as limits and potentials for individual action within organizations. For instance, during the railroad era, the "operator" was the technician who decoded the Morse signal into letters and the operator's initials were then added to the telegraph. A holdover from the telegraph era, early twentieth-century memos produced in corporate offices also often included the initials of the "operator." Typists added their initials to the bottom of the memos they typed. This example reflects how institutional values accompany emerging practices during times of change. As Yates explains, the nineteenth-century emergence of modern corporate communication, in the form of telegraphs, memos, and reports that accompanied the emergence of railroad technology, was disruptive in a positive way, and brought needed change to patterns of life in the nineteenth century. The recent emergence of digital media in the late twentieth and early twenty-first centuries has also brought change, shifting distribution from paper to digital media, decreasing the cost of distribution, and lifting constraints imposed by paper-based printing. And of course, these changes impact use and context of business communication.

Technical Communicators Have Also Contributed, Historically, by Ensuring a Contextual Orientation to Design

From the perspective of information design, both the 1980s and 1990s challenged technical communicators to expand the scope of their work beyond a narrow consideration of text to consideration of the design of an entire document, and then to concern for the context and reception of documents. As Kalmbach argues (1997), interest in the visual aspects of page design emerged along with the widespread adoption of computers for desktop publishing applications in the 1980s, whereas Lipson and Day (2005) trace the development of the Web in the 1990s and beyond. Technical communication research expanded focus from producing sentences and paragraphs to a new concern for "effective labeling, headings and indentations, imagery, information mapping, definitions, objectives, summaries, and repetition" (Killingsworth and Rosenberg, 1995, p. 34). Attention widened from textual production to layout of pages to the design of entire documents, until document design became articulated as contextual awareness and rhetorical effectiveness or exigency. In the 1990s, Schriver's *Dynamics in Document Design* (1997) and Kostelnick and Roberts's *Designing Visual Language: Strategies for Professional Communicators* (1998) became popular; definitions of successful writing expanded to include the design of the document as an extension of content, and document or visual design was integrated into academic programs. More recently, cultural context (Longo, 1998; Scott, Longo, and Wills, 2006; Zachry and Thralls, 2007; Longo, this volume); institutional context (Porter, *et al.*, 2000; Simmons and Grabill, 2007); global trends (Thatcher and Evia, 2008; Thatcher, this volume); and digital technologies (Selber, 2004; Lipson and Day, 2005) have also greatly altered how texts are produced, disseminated, and received.

Information design as it is now understood is profoundly attentive to context by transcending sentence- and paragraph-level content and the design of written communication intended to be placed on paper; it now points, instead, toward the organization and storage of that information for future use. Today, being digitally literate and engaging in information design requires understanding how search engines and databases work within specific contexts to organize access to information, and how authors can also consider context as they assign keywords, create summaries, and otherwise prepare documents for a searchable future. Emerging new digital media, in particular, requires careful and thoughtful design to ensure the creation of usable systems for people who deserve them.

Lexicon: Spatial Metaphors Orient Users

Information architecture was first coined in the 1970s by architect Wurman, and its first public use was in his president's address to the American Institute of Architects in 1976. Ultimately, information architecture is a systems perspective (Yates, 1989), but software designers continue to use the term "information architecture" to describe the design of databases and complex programming structures. In the 1990s, with the widespread adoption and commercialization of the World Wide Web, information architecture became a way of describing the user's experience of the digital environment created by designers. And ultimately, it is this extension of the written and designed environment that is information architecture: the designed virtual space created by programmers, project managers, and Web site authors, the interdisciplinary group of creative authors of the Web, who are concerned with creating an effective experience for using the variety of multi-modal digital documents.

This concern for storing and retrieving information is not new, as professionals in previous historical ages have also felt overwhelmed by their information resources. Dewey developed his cataloging system to tame the tangle caused by proliferating texts. Indeed, Morrogh (2003) asserts that information architecture is an ancient and not a recent concern as he explains the emergence of communication systems with the spoken word and moves on to the written word, the printed word and what Ong (2002) refers to as technologies of secondary orality, that is, those forms of communications permitted by the electrical telegraph, telephone, radio, and television. When Morrogh describes the emergence of computing systems in the mid-twentieth century, the connections become apparent between the information architectures of earlier communication technologies, such as the printed word and radio, and later technologies, such as mainframes, desktops, email, and the Web.

Morrogh (2003) historicizes the development of information space and articulates the importance of applying the information architecture metaphor to creating virtual spaces. As Rosenfeld and Morville (2002) explain, "Information architecture involves the design of organization, labeling, navigation, and searching systems to help people find and manage information more successfully" (p. 3). And the act of organization is rather complicated given that language is imperfect: "Classification systems are built upon the foundation of language, and language is ambiguous: words are capable of being understood more than one way" (p. 52). Classification is imperfect because language is imperfect. But by grounding discussions of information design in the spatial metaphors developed for articulating information architecture, de-contextualized writing rules or guidelines, such as rules for how to write topic sentences or transitions or guidelines for organizing a Web site or report, are translated instead into "help[ing] people find and manage information more successfully" (p. 52) through features that guide the reader through a text, as well as to a text and its content.

The language of information architecture provides technical communicators with useful terminology for designing usable information spaces on the page and on the screen, even though the terms have diverse, sometimes competing definitions in each of the different communities of practice in which they are applied. As long as information is described through spatial metaphors, architectural language of navigation, signage, and mapping provides useful additions to discussion of information design, providing technical communicators with language to describe the relationship between themselves as information producers and their audience as information users. In what follows, terms such as granularity and heterogeneity are offered to discuss scale in information design, while the practices of mapping and signposting help articulate concepts in information navigation. Metadata, taxonomy, and pattern language organize information for readers. Finally, ambience and findability offer language for discussing the locatability and organization of the huge amount of information available through digital information repositories, whether open-access Web-based data or more specialized resources such as library-based databases of research journal holdings. Informed with these concepts for effective, open data mapping and organization, technical communicators are well poised to take advantage of opportunities in the digital age that include not just the micro-focused design of individual documents, but also the macroscopic design and implementation of information structures and systems: once armed with such knowledge, technical communicators can shape emerging digital culture rather than only adapt to the change it brings.

Granularity

Because effective digital spaces integrate several different modes of information delivery, designers must make decisions about integrating information chunks with different levels of granularity or "coarseness" (Rosenfeld and Morville, 2002, p. 5). Digital delivery of both text-based and multimedia documents allows for a greater variety and size of information chunks that can be included in any given artifact. For example, should an educational or stockholder report be delivered, in its entirety, via a PDF document on a Web site or email to interested parties? Or should the contents of the report be divided into individual chunks and posted on separate pages of a Web site? By using the concept and terminology of granularity, technical communicators can become more conscious of the relative size of information in different modes of writing, and therefore may be more likely to consider how best to deliver and organize these chunks of information for optimal reader comprehension.

Again, Spinuzzi (2003) offers language for discussing information granularity and articulates three levels of magnification worth considering: microscopic, mezoscopic, and macroscopic, representing close, middle, and far perspectives. Roughly equivalent to filmmaking's close-up, middle-shot, and long-shot, articulating granularity can support communication regarding the level of detail contained in information structures (for more connections between writing and film, see Blakesley, 2003). For instance, microscopic attention to information design may remain at the level of the individual document produced at a particular moment, articulating its use of white space, font choice, paragraph formatting, and so on. In many ways, this is the traditional and accustomed perspective of technical writing. In contrast, a mezoscopic perspective may look at numerous documents over a longer span of time, like Yates' articulation (1989) of the development of corporate communications in the nineteenth century. In contrast, Kostelnick and Hassett (2003) offer a long historical view of the development of visual communication through epical shifts, tracing practices not in days, or even in years, but through cycles of "emergence, evolution, decline, and revival" (p. 119).

Digital information foregrounds issues of granularity as users have specific needs when they search. Consider a user entering the term "broccoli" into a search engine. A home user looking for a recipe would be said to have a low "granularity" for searching. Recipes or uses of broccoli require a low granularity application. On the opposite end, a researcher at the U.S. Department of Agriculture would have a much finer level of granularity, perhaps searching for specific citations of research having to do with recent shifts in annual rainfall and how localized drought impacts the production of produce. Similarly, an organic farmer would also have a fine granularity for her search, but that search would be unlike that of the U.S. Department of Agriculture researcher. Fine granularity often, but not always, correlates with increased technicality. Both the organic farmer and agriculture researcher have highly technical and very different, or heterogeneous, needs.

Discussions of granularity and their impact on classification remind writing professionals how these containers for information may be effectively searched by specific communities of users. Information architecture gives us a critical meta-language to use, helping professionals see limitations of genre and opening up discussions of alternatives and of the historical dimensions of the creation and adoption of generic conventions. Information architecture provides practitioners with an array of terminology to describe Web-based rhetorical structure that can be applied and used for both paper-based and Web-based writing. While computer scientists wrestle with highly technical aspects of heterogeneity and granularity, technical communicators have taken on cultural, organizational, and practice-oriented challenges of information design.

Homogeneity and Heterogeneity

Homogeneity and heterogeneity articulate similarity and difference among given elements in a data set. For instance, locally at the campus libraries, if users can search only for books or for journals, these results are highly homogeneous—or not heterogeneous—as they have great similarity in the kind of information they contain and the way in which they are located. A similar query in a search engine on the World Wide Web would yield widely varied hits, and be considered highly heterogeneous. It might contain links to books, Web sites, blogs, and news sites, and probably links to images (e.g., commercial, scholarly) and to sites written for personal and idiosyncratic purposes. Each link is different, with different purposes and with different expectations of audience.

Awareness of the homogeneity or heterogeneity of information, and of an audience's information needs, would allow designers to plan appropriately for presentation of findings. If the results are homogeneous—alike in purpose, scope, and content—designers can customize the interface to best present the material without much concern for the flexibility of the display to handle different kinds of data. Meanwhile, a highly heterogeneous data source will require more flexibility in design. The interface for heterogeneous information challenges designers to account for display of different characteristics, accounting for displaying spreadsheets, email, images, and word processing, and producing sound. Compare YouTube's interface to Google. YouTube restricts content to a homogeneous collection of low-resolution video, whereas Google tries to account for all the different forms of Web-delivered content. Google indexes a vast, heterogeneous collection of materials, and does not even attempt to create an interface that accounts for all the different kinds of digitized resources it catalogs.

Recall the earlier example of the home chef, and consider the difference between a database of recipes with highly homogenous content. The content may be sophisticated and technologically advanced, but each database entry has the same fields: a list of ingredients, numbered procedures, time to completion, and even a video showing how the recipe is assembled and what the finished dish looks like. The information designer for this recipe collection can maximize the design for effective presentation of video and its accompanying sound and ensure the ingredients list is clearly presented and searchable. The interface can even allow for highly contextualized searches: 30 minute meals, recipes containing certain ingredients, and only videos of one particular chef. Homogeneity allows for a tight fit between the content and its presentation with the knowledge that the information will fit the design in each case because the contents are homogeneous, very similar in form or content (or both), and the information designer can use this knowledge to her advantage.

A more heterogeneous collection of data presents a different set of challenges to the information designer. Take, for example, a highly heterogeneous database of cooking information, from recipes and ingredients to celebrity chefs and nutritional guidelines, from videos and sound to image collections of special and unusual dishes. How does the interface display text information, if only some of the entries have text? How will the interface handle different levels of visual information, from low to high resolution images to different video formats, and to text-only files? Each design decision impacts the usability and technical specifications of the interface, and the designer has to be able to communicate effectively about the level of heterogeneity of the data and how this impacts potential design decisions.

Although different genres of writing, such as research papers, memos, lab reports, informal emails, or proposals, usually follow particular conventions or patterns, effective texts usually require innovation. When business or professional writing is taught as imitation of form, genre is depicted as rigid and decontextualized, unresponsive to rhetorical situation and inflexible to context. And although genres may be appropriate starting points, rarely do they serve as absolute models in actual writing situations where audience preferences, context, and purpose muddy the waters considerably. This complication corresponds with the information architecture concept of heterogeneity, which refers to the fact that, "[i]t is difficult and often misguided to attempt a one-size-fits-all approach to the organization of heterogeneous web site content" (Rosenfeld and Morville, 2002, p. 53). It is likewise inappropriate to apply a one-size-fits-all approach to using genres because "[t]o design usable organization systems, we need to escape from our own mental models of content labeling and organization" (p. 54) and create reader-centered designed information spaces instead.

Mapping

Sitemaps, which are the visual display of design offered to guide readers through architected space, are another information design practice emphasizing organization and arrangement of information. When designers create sitemaps, their attention becomes focused on document features or virtual space as a type of information design: organization becomes an invention strategy, a method of arrangement, and a way to increase the likelihood that the information will serve audience needs and correspond to user assumptions and expectations. In this sense, mapmaking becomes a practice of combining "organization, labeling, and navigation schemes within a [document]" (Rosenfeld and Morville, 2002, p. 3). Documents— Web sites, memos, reports, or resumes—if viewed as written information conveyance systems, little communication machines, need to be treated as devices for transferring information from the source, whether the source is one author or a team of writers, to the audience, with care taken to account for the conditions in which readers will be using the document. Johnson-Eilola (2004) explains that "the map has started to replace the story as our fundamental way of knowing." He argues that technical communicators should view themselves as mapmakers, not only as authors of texts. Becoming a mapmaker means selecting and arranging preexisting information in order to assist a user in learning something or accomplishing some task, often with visual extra-textual display of the data. Furthermore, the information design practice of developing sitemaps or indexes is a "postmodernist model of communication [that] prioritizes (or at least makes visible) the value of arrangement." This shift in lexicon emphasizes the importance of arrangement as a way to achieve effective information design for particular users with specific needs in specific contexts. The map also literalizes relationships between and among elements of information databases, allowing designers to see the information contained as landscapes of information that can be traversed by users.

Mapping requires technical communicators (as aspiring information architects) to see their own and others' texts as virtual spaces, as structures made of arguments as their primary building material. Designing sitemaps contributes to users' understanding of Web site design and their intended use. Information mapping requires technical communicators to articulate once-invisible organization as perceptible. Seen in this way, information design refers to the creation of spaces that support document design and the creation of spaces for user-creation. Mapping emphasizes identifying, selecting, and categorizing pieces of information; these acts of identification, selection, and categorization are not neutral activities, but rather moments replete with ethical decision making. As Johnson-Eilola (2004) explains, "Mapmaking isn't a neutral and objective reflection of an external reality. Maps, in fact, provide some of the most powerful ways of understanding communication as the selective arrangement of heterogeneous fragments and aspects, an activity that is social and political in very broad senses."

The process of creating a sitemap—for a traditional text, a digital document, or a virtual space—reminds information designers that their decisions to include and exclude certain information, and the very manner in which they choose to categorize this information (as sub-points of a larger point; as primary nodes of information; as secondary nodes of information) itself conveys meaning and value (see Barton and Barton, 1993). For example, information about potential dangers of a new drug carries different weight and will generate different levels of alarm if, in a traditional or online report, an entire chapter is dedicated to them, they are relegated to a footnote, or they are buried in a section about future research on the drug.

The acts of selection and arrangement require that information designers carefully gauge the context as well as audience need. Applying a mapping metaphor to the act of designing, or creating sitemaps of documents and virtual spaces, encourages practitioners to ask complex questions about their audiences' needs and their communication purposes. It is here that the most striking distinction emerges between textual composing of more traditional outlines and information designer's composing of sitemaps. While outlines are usually created as an organizational device for the writer to follow, sitemapping can be as a way to experiment with different ways of organizing information for different readers with different reasons for wanting to access the information. Hence, the metaphor of mapmaking allows technical communicators to rethink document design as "the processes of selecting, removing, and connecting pieces of information for various contexts and people" (Johnson-Eilola, 2004) As Johnson-Eilola notes: "The very reason we make and use maps is because they allow us to selectively omit things, to understand our stories within particular contexts."

While readers may not often use sitemaps, the benefits for practitioners of creating such information maps are still significant. Through information mapping, technical communicators increase their awareness of the importance of structure in effective information management. Working through various information design possibilities can increase focus on the kinds of information fragments included or omitted in the digital artifact based on their user's needs and their writing purposes.

Signposting

Mapping creates a macro-level, or bird's eye view, of an information design (see Chalmers, 1993). However, users often perceive themselves inside, or within, these structures, rather than looking in from the outside. For this point of view, users need help. Technical communicators can use signposting as a way to help users navigate virtual spaces, much the same way that people navigate physical spaces. Passini, an architect, developed the idea of signposting as a way to design physical spaces for human use. Signposting indicates a way to travel or move through real or virtual space, and as such it can help users make sense of information structures in which users perceive themselves to be immersed or inside the information landscape (Passini, 1992; 1999).

One way to use the concept of signposting as a way to discuss information design is by encouraging technical communicators to compare highway signs (which aid drivers in navigating complex roadways) with various structural signposting mechanisms in information spaces (which aid users in navigating complex information designs). Just as cities require signage to route automobile, train, and pedestrian traffic, information spaces require signposts so that users can orient themselves and locate the information they need.

Take, for instance, the redesign of an amusement park Web site from a text-based layout to a spatial virtual map. While redesigning the navigational scheme of the Web site to better serve the needs of the park's clientele, the designers could conceptualize the amusement park as a physical space through which people would move. First, designers could identify the essential signposts that people exploring the park would need to identify in order to accomplish important tasks (such as identifying the location of roller coasters, food courts, or restrooms). Second, designers could organize these important signposts into the Web site's navigational scheme, placing essential signposts into the primary navigation and relegating less-essential signposts (such as information on group rates or other attractions in the area) to the secondary navigation. Technical communicators can create more navigable and user-centered structures once they are provided with the alternative lexicon of signposting for structuring information spaces. They should be encouraged to apply what they already know about navigating physical spaces to navigating virtual spaces.

Signposting requires that technical communicators think about the reader's experience of text and communicators can learn much by watching users navigate information spaces. Observation allows them to see where instructions and descriptions fail and leave users confused. Designers can see where further guidance is needed, and what details are particularly helpful in orienting readers in the text. Finally, through observation and working with users, designers can develop a better sense of the range and variety of learning styles that audiences bring to communication tasks.

Signposting encourages greater awareness of the user's place within the larger information structure, as well as greater awareness of how readers move through, or, perhaps more importantly, become lost, in virtual information space. The process of signposting reminds designers that users inhabit texts, navigating through them to find pertinent information; designers have to consider how readers will interpret descriptions and relationships among elements of the text, and then provide ways for readers to move from idea to idea, or section to section, within the text.

Information About Information: Metadata and Taxonomy

Metadata and taxonomy are important to the practice of effective information architecture. Metadata is information about a document, including routing information. It can include the context of each document's creation, summaries, keywords, data, and information source. Commonly, metadata is shown on the small displays of mp3 players, indicating artist, song title, album title, date of release, and running time. Metadata can include descriptions of information structures and the ways that designers intend users to navigate these structures—that is, the ways in which users can "drill down" to the information that will ultimately prove helpful. This, in a nutshell, is the definition of metadata: it refers not to the data itself, but to the naming, organization, and descriptors attached to each record that will allow for later recollection, retrieval, and use. Effective labeling with metadata makes search and retrieval easier, and its use helps distinguish the text from information about the text. Metadata, therefore, supports information organizing, storing, and naming information.

Taxonomy is one form of metadata. Taxonomies are important in Web design, and the highest-level taxonomy terms often become the primary links in Web navigation. One common form of taxonomy on the Web is the use of "limited vocabulary" in which a small number of terms is used to describe all the content of a Web site, and every item must be placed under one and only one of the terms. This works well as long as the Web site is either highly specialized, such as a site dedicated to scholarship focused on a very specific subject (having a very fine granularity and low heterogeneity), or is a very limited collection of information, like a personal collection of links to Web resources with personal or professional significance (high heterogeneity and low granularity). Taxonomy has played an important role in information organization for some time. In libraries, the Dewey decimal classification scheme (Dewey) is one common taxonomic system. The Library of Congress Subject Heading Index (LOC Index) is another. These subject headings begin to break down when they attempt to classify all knowledge and all different kinds of resources (heterogeneity), as the strategies that users employ to search the headings, and the content they label, do not necessarily match the structuring logic of the designers of the classification scheme. The question of taxonomy for the Web has resulted in a number of recent books that discuss organization and classification in depth, with technical communicators with a background in library and information science producing readable texts such as *Glut* by Wright (2007) and *Everything is Miscellaneous* by Weinberger (2007). Both the Dewey decimal system and LOC Index are top-down taxonomies: they are controlled and edited by librarians for the use of patrons.

Currently, an alternative, user-participatory, taxonomy system, the folksonomy, is being developed online. The concept of a folksonomy was invented precisely as a way to make online information easier to retrieve and use. As Voss (2007) explains,

> Folksonomy (also known as collaborative tagging, social classification, social indexing, social tagging, and other names) is the practice and method of collaboratively creating and managing tags to annotate and categorize content. In contrast to traditional subject indexing, metadata is generated not only by experts but also by creators and consumers of the content. Usually, freely chosen keywords are used instead of a controlled vocabulary.
>
> (Voss, 2007)

Credited with coining the term folksonomy, Vander Wal (2007) has stepped away from its current use in community-tagged organization structures, insisting that he meant the term to be used for individuals organizing structures for private use. Nevertheless, so-called folksonomies are user-selected taxonomy terms that can be used to categorize Web texts. For example, when posting new content on a blog or similar user-generated content, users are asked to choose one or more keywords with which to label their posts. These user-generated tags are then used to populate the "tag clouds" that constitute a folksonomy.

The resulting tag cloud—or collection of user submitted keywords— is a user-generated, socially indexed, sharable category of content that users can refer to or search for when looking for particular information. As folksonomies currently are used, there is no authority to judge the usefulness or accuracy of the taxonomic labels, nor is there a way to limit the proliferation of taxonomic terms, all of which break the rules of effective taxonomy from the perspective of bounding and control. Johnson-Eilola (2005), among other scholars, refers to these displays as a DataCloud. However, there is much strength in the participation and willingness of users to address their own needs in structuring information and to participate in creating information structures. And there are ways for user-generated folksonomic structures to be revised: as terms fall out of favor, they shrink in size and eventually disappear from the tag cloud. While this process offers a picture of searches recently placed—presenting a clear sense of what is valuable now (and in the short-term past)—very little is useful for a longer-term past, for example, the librarian's interest in a long, historical memory. Perhaps more importantly, tag clouds currently have no apparatus for preserving previous key terms that have disappeared because of decreasing popularity.

Like tag clouds, Web 2.0 technologies also have short term memory and are unable to preserve and retrieve past content. It will be interesting to watch if these types of virtual spaces will be able to develop middle- and long-term memory and retrievability. Nevertheless, it remains important to teach future practitioners and teachers of these professionals about the usefulness and limitations of these emerging tools.

Pattern Language

Pattern language is a precursor to information design that highlights how human use of information is affected by how that information is presented or structured at a deep organizational level. Building codes are an example of pattern language because they can encourage certain behaviors; for example, walking will be more common if a grammar school, neighborhood grocery, and park are placed within a quarter mile of higher-density housing. Buildings will spring up, rhizome-like, within walking distance of a traditional neighborhood restaurant, dry cleaner, and convenience store. As these building codes proliferate and the town expands, the city will be more livable and neighborhood-based, and encourage healthier lifestyles than a randomly growing city might, or one that grows according to the rules of suburban sprawl. In a similar way, the Web uses this idea of building codes, or pattern language, and encodes each element of the underlying structure into standards that are articulated, negotiated, and then published for further discussion and development. The standards body for the Web is the World Wide Web Consortium, or W3C (http://www.w3.org/).

The Web is self-organizing in that it encodes its values and opens these standards to stakeholders for participation and negotiation. As the World Wide Web grows, it embodies the processes of structured growth asserted by proponents of pattern languages. These concepts were first proposed in architectural and urban planning in the mid-twentieth century, and are realized in the Web's scalability, openness, and emerging complexity, while also acting as a test case for the democratic potential of open standards. Even if one's individual experience of using the Web is accurately described as chaotic, it is a rule-governed complexity that emerges from the open, participatory nature of its underlying participatory structure and explosive growth, a chaos that results from the basic acceptance of the users' freedom to act and build the Web as they see fit. Stolley (2008) maintains an excellent Web resource that discusses open standards as part of the World Wide Web's pattern language (http://www.sustainablewebdesign.com). By naming his application of pattern language "sustainable," Stolley and others develop an ecological metaphor to characterize Web-based information development.

Keeping the concept of pattern language in mind when designing digital information spaces can help technical communicators make informed decisions about using open standards to better serve user needs and account for future expansion and change.

Ambience

Related to the concept of the democratic potential of open standards is the concept of ambience, which refers to human agency dispersed through technological artifacts (see Rickert, 2007). Patterns and open standards as described above can be understood as ambient intelligence: knowledge and processes are programmed into technological artifacts. Effective ambient design helps users understand the purpose and content of a Web site or other virtual object with a quick glance. Indeed, visual rhetorical cues can often help readers quickly discern the purpose of common documents: a wedding invitation's use of calligraphy on fine card stock distinguishes it from the bright envelope accompanying a parking ticket under a car's windshield wiper, both of which are distinguished from an online newspaper's mimicry of a printed newspaper. In each case, readers recognize designed elements of the document even before interpreting content. These are ambient elements, part of the designed content of a variety of texts, which prepare the user to understand the context for the document's use (e.g., inclusion in a wedding celebration, receipt of a parking fine, the world's daily events). In short, for information design purposes, ambience can be understood as the scaffolding for signposting and mapmaking. Integrated signage is a form of ambient intelligence in digital document creation, as well: complex programs have help systems presented within the interface, which the user can reference during use. Effective ambient integration of guidance and help may not be readily apparent to users. Instead, effective design is revealed during use (or may become visible during usability testing and user-centered research) when a user finds a system uncannily easy to use or when users indicate that whenever they needed help, the system provided the necessary guidance. Ambient information surrounds users, reminding them of options for action, and acting as an always-present guide.

Ambience follows one of Norman's key precepts about the limitation of human memory, and as such constitutes another facet of information design. Norman (2002) suggests putting important information into the world, and one way this idea has come to pass is by designing embedded documentation. Rather than asking people to remember how to use devices, hints and helps can be incorporated into the devices themselves. For instance, door handles can be placed on the side of the door where it needs to be pushed to be opened. Similarly, signage can be incorporated into the designs of buildings rather than added as an afterthought. One example of ambient instructions can be found on an office chair, which can have many levers and possible adjustments to the lumbar support, height, and angle of the seat and back, and tension controls. Rather than expecting users to remember the function and use of each lever, the designer provides a quick guide to the chair's levers and buttons (which constitute its user interface) integrated into the right arm. When a user needs to remember which of the many levers controls each seldom-used function, she can flip the information out into view and read the guide.

These examples of ambience gesture toward a new trend toward integration of help and user guidance. The goal is to deliberately incorporate guidance and reference information into the technological artifact's design, so that help works as part of the interface's usability. The text and the artifact are integrated, allowing the user to receive help without necessarily halting workflow with technology. On the surface, ambience may challenge traditional roles of the technical communicator, and it certainly does limit the after-market for documentation. However, integrating ambient help into software and Web site design requires that technical communicators be integrated into the technology design process. Technical communicators with an understanding and appreciation for ambience can help programmers effectively integrate instructions for common functions into designs, and can test for their most effective placement and appearance, resulting in a user-centered system where help and assistance can be integrated into the software interface.

Findability and the Future

Information architecture self-consciously creates information structures intended to aid use by human beings. Findability or relocatability is an important after-effect of successful information architecture. Such concern with findability is a key component of information design, and has been of particular interest to librarians. Indeed, librarians such as Rosenfeld and Morville (2002) ask about the value of documents that cannot be found when needed. They provide a name for the next generation of information designed for use: "Ambient Findability." Morville (2005) uses the terms "precision" and "recall" to discuss the findability of information:

> At the heart of these challenges and principles lies the concept of relevance. Simply put, relevant results are those which are interesting and useful to users. Precision and recall, our most basic measurements of effectiveness, are built upon this common-sense definition ... Precision measures how well a system retrieves only the relevant documents. Recall measures how well a system retrieves all the relevant documents.
>
> (p. 49)

This definition of search precision and recall is incredibly important as search tools like Google and Yahoo try to index the entire web. The challenge becomes sorting relevance among thousands and sometimes even millions of search hits. How can we find the individual texts, references, and materials that we want, when we want them? The challenges become contextual as well as semantic, because the value of the search results is different for different users, and may even change as a user searches.

Above, we imagined a user entering the search term "broccoli" into a search engine. Let us imagine this user again. Without contextual knowledge, the search algorithm does not know if the request comes from the home computer of a hungry individual with a family to feed, or from an agricultural economist searching for the same term "broccoli" to determine the value of a field damaged by hail, or from an organic farmer trying to determine the value of the crop raised and harvested with the intention to sell at the local market.

The meaningfulness and usefulness of these searches change, based not on the ability of the search engine to return results, but on the search engine, which understands the context from which the request for information is made. This is an opportunity for ambient findability, for the ability of the elements that make up the context for the search to precisely select relevant contextual cues. Search engines are just beginning to realize the potential value of using contextual cues for determining search applicability and relevance.

Currently, search engines barely register any distinction between users accessing from a desktop or laptop computer with large screens at resolutions of pixels dozens of times higher and wider than the small screen of a mobile device, most smaller than 3" by 4" with typical pixel depths of 120 by 160. Even these technological constraints change the usefulness and readability of the information accessed. Even a simple mechanism that recognizes the method of access, mobile or stationary, visually robust or constrained, would provide important information about the context for the use of the information delivered. Imagine the increased usefulness and readability if Web browsers delivered information not based on prioritizing, or on pushing advertisements on us (which skew the data on information accessed and delivered since the returns supported by ads are artificially ranked higher by virtue of producing revenue), but rather on maximizing applicability and relevance.

Imagine that a father with children sent the request for "broccoli" into a search engine, and imagine how his results might be improved if the search engine recognized that he was, first of all, at a home computer; such recognition might adjust the parameters of the search. Add that he is searching from a computer located in the kitchen at 5 p.m. and that dinner is usually a communal meal served at 6:30 p.m., which the terminal knows because all telephony connections are blocked between 6:30 p.m. and 8:00 p.m. by the user's request. So the database search interface now restricts the search term "broccoli" to recipes containing broccoli that take an hour or less to prepare. The same search from the same place made on another day at 6:00 p.m. would eliminate all recipes that take longer than 30 minutes to prepare.

Technical communicators are a long way off from this imagined, fanciful scenario, but it is meant to illustrate the potential for searches that extend the concept of information design to the concept of ambient information— of extracting information from the context of the search and taking cues from the user's situation that the user may take for granted and may not even think to incorporate into the parameters of the search. Defining a search result's relevance comes down to, as Morville (2005) articulates, the balance struck between precision and recall. The complex emerging world of information design is just beginning to be articulated. We have only reached the point of gesturing toward a rich future for the incorporation of ambient information into the concerns of technical communicators who use information architecture as a lens to see their work. After all, part of what is being accessed is the level of magnification of information the user is seeking, or its granularity.

Closing Thoughts: Designing Space for Habitation and Use

Effective technical communication has never been simply about writing clearly, but rather, about effectively organizing written communication for future reference and application. Instructions are written and stored to be referenced at some as yet unimagined future moment. Such storage is meant to save a user's time when working through new processes and assembling tools, keeping documentation near at hand, and becoming part of an organization's knowledge base. Reports collect and present information, becoming a data resource for future reference. Instructions help users navigate technologies that are new to them. Memos organize action and become part of the historical record of an organization's communication. Online, it sometimes feels like magic to find just the right resource when doing research. By being attentive to the ambient effects of technological artifacts and the ways designed elements interact with networks of communicating people, technical communicators, with an awareness of information design, see a less deterministic, more complex, yet nevertheless powerful impact of what Latour (1993) has called technological agents on our cultural interactions. Whatever the technologies are called, whatever the names for the skills employed, the technical rhetor is a literate agent working in the network of people, technologies, and other elements through which power and ideas flow. The digital revolution is the latest transformation in a long history of change in the means and modes of communication: *metis*, the ancient Greek term for effectively navigating change, offers an important touchstone. Digital literacy cannot be just the ability to use certain technologies. Rather, the term must apply to the thoughtful deployment of technologies that make intervention meaningful and informed by analysis, reflection, and historical representations of the field. As Kynell-Hunt and Savage (2004) put it,

> Technical writing as we find it today has emerged in relation to particular economic, political, and technological circumstances which combine in complex and contradictory ways that make the work our practitioners do both useful and disruptive, both materially rewarding and risky.
>
> (p. 189)

Accepting both risk and responsibility requires continual change and improvement in response to our decisions. Disruptions are changes in action, and each information product joins the network, changing the context for participation and altering the opportunities and problems present in the network. In turn, this requires further adaptation and results in further change that reveals other opportunities while closing others. Nonstop and fluid, these changes really do point to the sailor's expertise, *metis*, as an apt metaphor for critical engagement.

Churchill said it differently on the occasion of reopening the English parliament building in London after World War II, but the meaning is similar: "We shape our buildings, and afterwards our buildings shape us" (http://www.winstonchurchill.org/learn/speeches/quotations/famous-quotations-and-stories).

Churchill's is no simple statement. We build spaces and then we cannot control how users interact with them, and that horrifies and excites the "designer" and the "architect" inside each technical communicator. Information design is at its best when recognizing how the language used to describe content and practices reflects the history of the use of that language and the context in which it is used. Information spaces, digital, textual and otherwise, are built for people to inhabit. As soon as a design is out of the author's hand and launched in the world, we see how effective that design can be in use. At the same time, the virtual building impacts the very real symbolic interaction of living people, whether they are responding to printed documents, complex virtual worlds, or repositories of research. We make our information spaces, and then these spaces make us and impact our communication—always returning to the human genesis of the space, yet not always under the immediate control of the users (or designers) of that information space. Predictably, users become subject to (virtual) objects.

This chapter has introduced and analyzed concepts and language from information design and architecture as a way to familiarize the technical communicator with emerging trends in the digital workplace and to articulate the responsibilities facing communication professionals in the information age. While some of these trends in designing traditional and digital information spaces are already familiar to technical communicators, others reorient some institutional roles played by these professionals and offer new opportunities and potential for greater reward. Knowledge of and involvement in information design processes are important, natural extensions of technical communication work that do not require professionals to take on new or unaccustomed responsibilities, but instead, reframes technical communication work in a wider lens. Understanding the history and development of these concepts prepares technical rhetors to be critical, reflective practitioners. While each technical communicator may not work directly with design, understanding the language and concerns of information designers will prepare technical communicators to become productive members of the digital workforce and to take their place among techno-rhetorically literate professionals. This is important because we design virtual space, and afterwards, our virtual spaces design us.

Notes

1 For useful perspectives about the rapid proliferation of documentation, see, for example, Wurman's (1989) *Information Anxiety*, or more recently, Wright's *Glut* (2007).
2 The variety of digitally and Web-based display possibilities is mind-boggling; indeed, the solution is for designers not to account for all potential displays, but to code with affordances built in for user-selected elements like font size, image display, and color display depth. Decisions become those of relative and approximate placement on a screen rather than absolute placement on the page.

References

Barton, B. F., & Barton, M. S. (1993). Ideology and the map: Toward a postmodern visual design practice. In N. R. Blyer & C. Thralls (Eds.), *Professional communication: The social perspective* (pp. 49–78). Newbury Park, CA: Sage.

Blakesley, D. (2003). *The terministic screen: Rhetorical perspectives on film.* Carbondale, IL: Southern Illinois University Press.

Chalmers, M. (1993). Using a landscape metaphor to represent a corpus of documents. In A. U. Frank & I. Campari (Eds.), *Proceedings of the European conference on spatial information theory* (pp. 377–390). Lecture Notes in Computer Science (Vol. 716).

Gurak, L. J. (2001). *Cyberliteracy: Navigating the internet with awareness.* New Haven, CT: Yale University Press.

Hart-Davidson, W. (2001). On writing, technical communication, and information technology: The core competencies of technical communication. *Technical Communication, 48*(2), 145–155.

Johnson, R. R. (1998). *User-centered technology: A rhetorical theory for computers and other mundane artifacts.* Albany, NY: State University of New York Press.

Johnson-Eilola, J. (2004). Stories and maps: Postmodernism and professional communication. *Kairos* 1(1). Retrieved from http://english.ttu.edu/kairos/1.1/features/johndan/stories_and_maps_029.html.

———. (2005). *Datacloud: Toward a new theory of online work.* Cresskill, NJ: Hampton Press.

Kalmbach, J. R. (1997). *The computer and the page: Publishing, technology, and the classroom.* Norwood, NJ: Ablex Publishing.

Kanpol, B. (1999). *Critical pedagogy: An introduction* (2nd ed). Santa Barbara, CA: Greenwood Publishing Group.

Killingsworth, M. J., & Rosenberg, M. E. (1995). The evolution of document design since 1985: A response to Richard E. Mayer's "structural analysis of scientific prose." *ACM SIGDOC Asterisk Journal of Computer Documentation, 19*(3), 31–35.

Kostelnick, C., & Hassett, M. (2003). *Shaping information: The rhetoric of visual conventions.* Carbondale, IL: Southern Illinois University Press.

Kostelnick, C., & D. Roberts. (1998). *Designing visual language: Strategies for professional communicators.* Boston, MA: Allyn & Bacon.

Kynell-Hunt, T., & Savage, G. J. (2003). *Power and legitimacy in technical communication: The historical and contemporary struggle for professional status,* Vol I. Amityville, NY: Baywood Publishing.

———. (2004). *Power and legitimacy in technical communication: Strategies for professional status,* Vol II. Amityville, NY: Baywood Publishing.

Latour, B. (1993). *We have never been modern.* Cambridge, MA: Harvard University Press.

Lipson, C., & Day M. J. (Eds.) (2005). *Technical communication and the World Wide Web.* Mahwah, NJ: Lawrence Erlbaum.

Longo, B. (1998). Technical communication constituted as an object of cultural study. *Technical Communication Quarterly, 7*(1), 53–74.

Morrogh, E. (2003). *Information architecture: An emerging 21st century profession.* Upper Saddle River, NJ: Prentice Hall.

Morville, P. (2005). *Ambient findability.* Sebastopol, CA: O'Reilly Media.

Norman, D. (2002). *The design of everyday things* (2nd ed.). New York: Basic Books.

Ong, W. J. (1975). The writer's audience is always a fiction. *Publications of the Modern Language Association, 90,* 9–21.

———. (2002). *Orality and literacy: The technologizing of the word* (2nd ed.). New York: Routledge.

Passini, R. (1992). *Wayfinding in architecture.* New York: Van Nostrand Reinhold.

———. (1999). Sign-posting information design. In R. Jacobson (Ed.), *Information design* (pp. 83–98). Cambridge, MA: MIT Press.

Porter, J. E., Sullivan, P., Blythe, S., Grabill, J. T., & Miles, L. (2000). Institutional critique: A rhetorical methodology for change. *College Composition and Communication, 51,* 610–642.

Rickert, T. (2007). Toward the chora: Kristeva, Derrida, and Ulmer on emplaced invention. *Philosophy and Rhetoric, 40*(3), 251–273.

Rosenfeld, L., & Morville, P. (2002). *Information architecture for the World Wide Web* (2nd ed.). Sebastopol, CA: O'Reilly.

Savage, G. (2004). Tricksters, fools, and sophists: Technical communication as postmodern rhetoric. In T. Kynell-Hunt & G. J. Savage (Eds.), *Power and legitimacy in technical communication: Strategies for professional status* (pp. 167–193), Vol. II. Amityville, NY: Baywood Publishing.

Schriver, K. (1997). *Dynamics in document design.* New York: Wiley.

Scott, B., Longo, B., & Wills, K. V. (2006). *Critical power tools.* Albany, NY: SUNY Press.

Selber, S. (2004). *Multiliteracies for a digital age.* Carbondale, IL: Southern Illinois University Press.

Simmons, W. M., & Grabill, J. T. (2007). Toward a civic rhetoric for technologically and scientifically complex places: Invention, performance, and participation. *College Composition and Communication, 58*(3), 419–448.

Spinuzzi C. (2003). *Tracing genres through organizations: A sociocultural approach to information design.* Cambridge, MA: MIT Press.

Stolley, K. (2008). *Sustainable web design.* Retrieved May 22, 2008 from http://www. sustainablewebdesign.com.

Thatcher, B. L., & Evia C. (Eds.) (2008). *Outsourcing technical communication: Issues, policies and practices.* Garden City, NY: Baywood Press.

Vander Wal, T. (2007). Folksonomy coinage and definition. Retrieved July 9, 2009 from http://vanderwal.net/folksonomy.html.

Voss, J. (2007). Tagging, folksonomy and co-renaissance of manual indexing? Retrieved April 4, 2009 from http://arxiv.org/pdf/cs/0701072v2.

Warnick, B. (2002). *Critical literacy in a digital era: Technology, rhetoric, and the public interest.* Mahwah, NJ: Lawrence Erlbaum.

Weinberger, D. (2007). *Everything is miscellaneous: The power of the new digital disorder.* New York: Times Books.

Wright, A. (2007). *Glut: Mastering information through the ages.* Washington, DC: Joseph Henry Press.

Wurman, R. S. (1989). *Information anxiety.* New York: Doubleday.

Yates, J. (1989). *Control through communication: The rise of system in American management.* Baltimore, MD: Johns Hopkins University Press.

Zachry, M., & Thralls C. (Eds.) (2007). *Communicative practices in workplaces and the professions: Cultural perspectives on the regulation of discourse and organizations.* Amityville, NY: Baywood Press.

5 Content Management

Beyond Single-Sourcing

William Hart-Davidson

As scholars such as Manuel Castells (1996) remind us, a consequence of the transformation to an "information society" is that information itself is a valuable commodity. Organizations view the content types they produce as assets, and they look to get the most value from those assets that they possibly can. Regardless of where technical writers find themselves working, odds are that they will be charged not merely with the activity of writing, but also with the task of supporting or managing a network of people who develop content for a variety of internal and external types of communication channels. Often, it falls to them to look after the information assets of the organization. Today's technical writer, with expertise in writing, editing, and communication, typically is expected to create templates, establish editorial guidelines, create metadata formats, and perform a host of other tasks that relate directly related to the management of content and not necessarily to its creation. In short, today's technical writer could very well be a content manager.

Content managers face the twin pressures of simultaneously reducing the total investment a company must make to produce content and increasing the quality, quantity, and sustainable value of that content. While any committee can write a mission statement, technical writers often are charged with maximizing the utility of such high-stakes bits of content. One way they do this is by making content reusable. For example, a technical writer might be the one to ensure that the mission statement is as close to "evergreen" as possible, designed to be easily reused in places as diverse as the company's marketing and branding materials, its internal training materials for employees, and its technical manuals for customers.

Recently, I needed to describe a course in our curriculum meant to prepare technical and professional writing majors for this sort of work. The course, called "Content Management for Professional Writers" is designed to help these majors acquire the knowledge, skills, attitudes, and leadership qualities associated with managing content assets in an organizational setting. Just as other courses in our major ensure that our students are skilled "pilots" of complex documents of various shapes and sizes, this course prepares them to become air traffic controllers, helping to make sure a host of projects take off and land safely, efficiently, and effectively.

Where does the need for such a course, and the corresponding skill set, come from? Two key trends have converged to make content management (CM) commonplace for technical communicators in the United States and Europe: advances in networked information technology, especially in the World Wide Web, and a shift toward a global information economy (Castells, 1996; Zuboff and Maxmin, 2004). These two trends combined have created new markets for information products and services, by opening new channels for distributing and selling customized information. Despite these trends, we can argue that the field of technical communication has viewed CM practices and the arrival of content management systems (CMS) rather narrowly. With a few notable exceptions (Applen, 2002; Clark, 2002; Hackos, 2002; Rockley and Kostur, 2003), literature in the field has largely viewed CM through the lens of a single concept—single sourcing—which is the process of producing and distributing content in multiple formats from one, centrally maintained repository. The field has also occasionally viewed CM as a threat to what some perceive as the already marginal status of technical communicators (Albers, 2000). The source of the perceived threat is, in some ways, real. In an information economy, more workers will write. Computer technologies will be increasingly employed to take care of editorial concerns, such as maintaining a consistent design and establishing a uniform tone and voice. Content creation will be more broadly distributed across organizations rather than concentrated in the work of a few people who are hired to be "writers." So what can technical communicators do?

In this chapter, I aim to present a broader, more nuanced view of CM and CMS than is typically found in the technical communication literature. My aim is to explore the range of expertise required to ensure that large groups, not merely individuals or small teams, write well together. This is the role that many technical communicators will likely fill in their organization. If we accept that high-quality information cannot be produced, maintained, and managed solely by a few select members of the organization, any more than other key processes like accounting can, we do not have to concede that this trend necessarily dilutes the technical communicators' roles. On the contrary, as I will argue in this chapter, this trend implies that the core expertise of technical communicators is perhaps more important than ever to CM goals and operations (Hackos, 2002).

By analogy, consider how pharmaceutical companies must do "good science" and scientists who work there are charged not with doing *all* the science, but making sure the organization as a whole does good science. Similarly, organizations in an information economy must create and distribute information and they should do so with an explicit and managed approach. CM, seen as a set of practices, is the name for such an approach. By virtue of their expertise, technical communicators should play the key role in making sure an organization can succeed in this critical endeavor (Hart-Davidson, *et.*

al, 2008). Technical communicators can and should orchestrate, coordinate, and negotiate CM. But for this to happen, they will need to take on increasingly varied organizational roles and responsibilities. In this chapter, I present a framework that articulates these roles and responsibilities. I hope the framework is useful as way to generate conversations about technical communication work and curriculum and professional development.

What is Content Management?

The term "content management" generally refers to a set of practices for handling information, including how it is created, stored, retrieved, formatted, and styled for delivery. Calling this sequence of events "content management" allows us to focus on what is sometimes called the content life cycle apart from more specific and limited activities involving information review and approval, such as the way many conceive of the editorial process. We can recognize systems that support CM as complex tools that support this life cycle. And we can see in the term "management" the goals of making practice explicit and repeatable, identifying and correcting inefficiencies, and providing for some mechanism of process control.

When we look carefully at what it means to *do* CM, we can see a collection of practices that commonly have the following aims:

Goal 1: Distributing authoring tasks and responsibilities among members of a group.

Goal 2: Authoring and storing content in ways that enable multiple-audience adaptation, including the translation and localization of content for specific groups.

Goal 3: Authoring and storing content in ways that permit multiple output formats to be derived from a single repository of information (single-sourcing).

Goal 4: Authoring and storing content in ways that facilitate systematic reuse within and across organizations.

While none of these practices, on their own, are entirely new (and certainly the motivations behind them are not), it is still a relatively novel idea to group them together and present them as explicit goals to which one or more people in an organization might be answerable. Indeed, for skeptics, it may be something of a relief that we can trace back to these goals what we now understand to be best practices of CM today, including the need to separate content from presentation (cf. Clark, 2008) or to tear down content silos (cf. Rockley and Kostur, 2003); both of these can be traced back to the goals listed earlier.

We hardly need to convince experienced technical communicators that it is best to separate content from presentation, but for others the implications of such a move are not so obvious. We need to explain, then, that separating content from presentation makes it far easier to use the same bits of information in multiple output formats (Goal 3), throughout an enterprise (Goal 4), all while customizing format and style for the needs of particular audiences (Goal 2). Experienced writers also understand that content "silos," a metaphor for storing information in ways that prevent anyone other than the author(s) from seeing or making use of that information, are barriers to systematic reuse (Goal 4) and lead to authoring bottlenecks, meaning that only a few people in the organization can effectively contribute to content development (the opposite of Goal 1).

But these goals, which are core to technical communicators' understanding of their own work, are not obvious or intuitive. Rather, typically they are hard-won lessons, underpinned by sophisticated theories about what a genre is, or what it means for an organization, rather than an individual, to be an author, to cite just two enduring questions. Perhaps what is most new about CM is our need to make it an explicit and well-understood area of expertise, and then to teach it to other technical communicators, most of whom will step into the kind of distributed authorship environments that recently have become more prevalent in companies, now that technologies have enabled them to become more commonplace.

Content Management and Technical Communication: Historical Notes

For many technical communicators, CMS—software meant to help organizations systematically index content assets in ways that do not lock them into specific presentation formats—represent relatively new features of the workplace. But what I would like to suggest is that despite the recent emergence of the term "content management" and the even more recent development of the technological means by which we do CM, in fact, the goals or ends of CM practices, listed earlier, have much longer historical roots. Most accounts of the origins of the term "content management" come in the context of a related area, knowledge management, that is usually construed as being broader. Wallace (2007) traces the appearance of "content management" in the literature of several disciplines and specialty areas including business, operations research, and graphical information systems, concluding that it emerged in the mid-1970s, began to appear more regularly in the 1980s, and was in wider use by the mid-1990s as corporate intranets began to be built (p. 142).

CM's Early History in the Technical Communication Literature

There have been a few attempts to trace the history of CM practices, such as distributed authorship or single-sourcing, published recently in the technical communication literature (Clegg-Gilbert, 2004; Sapienza, 2007).

Some have looked outside the field to find the motivations that come to mind when we think about managing content to ensure maximum potential for reuse. For example, as Clegg-Gilbert (2004) and Sapienza (2007) point to artistic movements in the twentieth century to explain the mechanics of single-sourcing, both focus on how an intense concentration on form can also permit a focus on function and meaning. Sapienza turns to the poetic movements of Russian Acmeism and Anglo-American Imagism to show how the field might begin to understand the principles that underlie single sourcing, and the expertise of those who do this work, in terms of a craft tradition. For example, Sapienza uses the Acmeist technique of constructing poetic superstructures that draw upon previously constructed poems, to highlight ways that a poetic tradition can foster multiple voices while honoring conventional structure by following strict structural rules. The superstructures also provided a means for highly specialized forms of expression. Clegg-Gilbert reminds us of the democratic political underpinnings associated with the Bauhaus design movement, arguing that the emphasis in that tradition on modular, reusable components that we see echoed in CM practices can be understood as user-centered. Whittemore (2008) finds similarities between CM and the well-known Ciceronian construct of the five canons of rhetoric—invention, arrangement, style, memory, and delivery—seen as a representation of the full scope of rhetorical performance. Focusing on the canon of memory, Whittemore explains why technical communicators might struggle to perform rhetorically in CM systems that are meant to promote reuse, but, perhaps unwittingly, introduce (or reintroduce) obstacles to information recall and retrieval. This can happen when these systems fail to make obvious (and, at times, deliberately obfuscate) what a skilled writer wants to see: rhetorical information regarding how and where a particular bit of content has been incorporated into a document with a genuine audience, context, and purpose. If a writer is unable to find or identify rhetorical evidence, she is left to her own devices to recall and gather the details of past use in order to best strategize content reuse or adaptation. This might involve, for example, tracking down the last person who used a particular document or content fragment, though this is not always possible to trace within a given system.

Embracing CM While Remaining Critical of CMS

The literature in technical communication has critiqued ways in which CM practices have become manifest in CMS (see especially, Clark, 2002) in addition to the core technologies and standards that make CMS work. But Whittemore (2008), Clegg-Gilbert (2004), and Sapienza (2007) share an overall optimism for CM practices and what nobody can deny is the importance of markup languages such as Standard Generalized Markup Language (SGML), Hypertext Markup Language (HTML), and Extensible

Markup Language (XML)—tools that permit us to define and share structural and semantic metadata standards—to the development of CMS.

Our field acknowledges the importance of these technologies. One visit to the exhibition floor at the annual Society for Technical Communication (STC) convention is enough to convince you of their ubiquity. In 1999, the STC recognized Charles Goldfarb and Tim Berners-Lee, inventors of SGML and HTML respectively, as Society Fellows, the group's highest honor given to nonmembers who have had a significant impact on the field. Goldfarb's work on SGML began in the late 1960s, and Berners-Lee's work on HTML culminated in the invention of the World Wide Web in 1986. By 1999, it was clear that the work of these two men had forever changed technical communication in ways they themselves had not originally foreseen. But the impact of Goldfarb's work is not lost on him today, as he notes in his online press kit:

> SGML literally makes the infrastructure of modern society possible. It supports the documentation of nuclear plants, oil rigs, government laws and regulations, military systems—anything that is too complex for a single person to understand and that has life-and-death significance.
>
> (2008)

Of course SGML and its now more familiar markup progeny, HTML and XML, are just tools. Goldfarb, of course, is referring instead to the set of practices that SGML, HTML, and the World Wide Web have enabled and that forms what he calls the "infrastructure of modern society." I find it useful to call these practices, taken together, "content management."

To our credit, the field of technical communication has had an eye on these practices for some time, well before they became the coherent software-based CM systems that we know today. In the late 1980s and early 1990s, groundbreaking contributions by scholars (such as Sullivan, 1989; Schriver, 1993; Bernhardt, 1993; and Redish, 1993, among others) expanded the scope of technical communication work as the field contemplated the future of electronic documents. We recognize this group of writers, in particular, as pioneers who helped us imagine how our field's care in thinking about issues of audience translated, in the digital era, to thinking about usability. This work created the space for a more specific set of conversations to emerge focusing on the core ideas of CM. Weiss (1993) questioned the way document databases and markup languages were shifting the balance of power to the reader/user and away from the writer. Bist (1994; 1996) and Price (1997) offered early conceptual frameworks for CM practice, pointing to the potentialities that languages like SGML offered, but focusing more on the conceptual and strategic differences associated with authorship and with texts as artifacts. Both Bist and Price anchored their discussions of CM in the practices of object-oriented modeling associated, at the time, exclusively with computer programming. Heba (1997) clearly framed the conceptual shifts implied by an object-oriented approach to writing. He argued that technical communicators need to understand that they are creating user environments rather than static texts, that these environments' core structure is modular rather than hierarchical, and that a "document" can be a combination of complete elements but, due to its ability to adapt and change as users' needs change, may never be complete (p. 281).

Heba's perspective was shaped by another conversation about hypertext that had been going on in technical communication and the allied field of computers and writing. Before the advent of the World Wide Web, a group of scholars explored the implications of texts that included dynamic links and embedded multimedia elements for technical communication (Mehlenbacher, 1993; Selber, *et al.*, 1996). The conversations about hypertext by Johnson-Eilola (1996), Selber, and others were interdisciplinary, ranging across literary theory (Landow, 1992), information science, and computer engineering (Nelson, 1964; 1974; Nielsen, 1990), and stretching back, famously, to Bush's 1945 *Atlantic Monthly* article "As We May Think." Bush's article, known for its description of a mechanical hypertext prototype machine called a memex was more accurately a call to develop CM processes. We have, for the most part, fulfilled Bush's 1945 vision today, though our capacity to create information has grown in ways that make the impressive gains in managing it seem just as inadequate as Bush predicted they would be: "He [sic] has built a civilization so complex that he needs to mechanize his records more fully if he is to push his experiment to its logical conclusion and not merely become bogged down part way there by overtaxing his limited memory" (p. 4).

Indeed, Bush's most impressive bit of forecasting may well be the acknowledgement that our society would not only produce more information, but at the same time, this information would grow increasingly more valuable. And the need to manage it, and to acknowledge the expertise required to do so effectively, is precisely what motivates me to turn next to a kind of proto-job description for the technical communicator as content manager.

Mapping Technical Communicators' Expanding Roles and Responsibilities: Developing a Content Strategy

Perhaps the best way to understand both the scope and the specific aspects of technical communicators' role in CM is by creating a conceptual map of what is involved in developing a content strategy for an organization. This kind of macroscopic view of CM work allows us to consider how technical communicators typically come to play many different roles and deploy diverse sets of skills over the course of a career, even advancing to the point where they, themselves, may be marginal to the field (Anschuetz and Rosenbaum, 2002). We are not merely writers any more. Now we are editors, information architects, usability analysts, interaction designers, project managers, client liaisons, and more. All these roles can be viewed as critical in a service-oriented, knowledge-intensive economy like the United States at this time, where companies live and die based on how well they communicate. This is true, moreover, not simply because communication is how companies operate, but fundamentally because communication has become *why* they operate. Information, knowledge, content—these are now products in our economy. Naturally, technical communicators cannot be the only ones creating and managing content. They can and do and should, however, play key roles in the way an organization as a whole creates and manages content.

The following are three perspectives, or categories for creating and managing content.

• Making texts—here texts are understood as more or less coherent wholes, sometimes called "information products" or "information types;" these are the genres that a particular organization makes for its clients, users, and customers, and its own members or workforce.
• Creating and managing information assets, defining relationships among these, and specifying display conditions for specific views of these—an object-oriented worldview prevails in this perspective, ideally balancing the interests of users/readers with those of content producers; unlike the text-making perspective, the focus here is on ensuring that all the elements are in place to make text-making possible, scalable, and effective for all those involved.
• Designing and managing workflows and production models—the third perspective focuses on the roles and responsibilities of those involved in content creation and management, including users in some production models; within organizations, this third way of seeing offers a managerial perspective; across organizations it incorporates the interests of partners and clients (think, here, of a supply chain).

Interpret each of these three categories as something the entire organization must do and do well. What technical communicators do within those categories flows from this idea: they must perform simple tasks that fall under these, but they must also help the organization and its employees perform them well, too.

There is no high theory driving the construction of these categories; rather, they arise from what technical communicators do every day: make texts; manage everything that goes into making texts; and manage the processes of making texts. The three categories, then, no longer belong to the individual writer, but to the larger organization. But this new perspective of ownership doesn't diminish or threaten the value of the technical communicator. As we will see soon, Table 5.1 will make this argument by demonstration. It will serve as an answer, of a sort, to the question, what does a technical communicator do, now that the whole organization writes?

Table 5.1 Mapping technical communicators' expanding roles and responsibilities in the context of an organization's content strategy

CM perspective	Foregrounds the interests of	Sees the enterprise as	Typical workday includes	Technical communicator roles include	Tangible outcomes include
Text-making	Users (inside and outside the organization), customers, and readers	A genre system or ecology that sustains the organization	Genre tracing (Spinuzzi, 2003) Rhetorical analysis Audience analysis Usability evaluation User-centered design	Writer Document designer Information designer	Document templates Style sheets Design guidelines Use cases User profiles
Creation and management of information assets, relationships, and views	Writers, designers, and others involved in the content lifecycle	A networked archive of resources that must be able to grow while remaining available and accessible	Content auditing (Rockley 2003) Information modeling Creating semantic markup Prototyping new user environments	Information architect Editor Interaction designer Archivist curator	Taxonomies Object metadata Document type definitions and schema Customized markup
Design and management of workflows and production models	Managers, partners, clients	A social network of humans and technologies that must work smoothly together	Contextual inquiry Work process analysis Task modeling Workflow visualization	Manager Team leader Training consultant Field researcher Client liaison	Work process descriptions & training materials Job descriptions Work evaluation metrics New software tools

What Does a Writer Do When the Whole Company Writes?

Table 5.1 associates the three categories, described in the previous section, with the total effort to develop a content strategy for an organization. A grid like this is useful, because when these three responsibilities are shown as goals for an entire organization-wide enterprise, the technical communicator recognizes the critical need to be able to shift smoothly among all three. Also, such a mapping of focus areas can help technical communicators see how these three focus areas, together, become an organizing force for work as a whole.

To interpret Table 5.1, imagine an organization as an entity that produces content. Starting from the CM Perspective column on the left, read across each of the three rows to see how that organization might function on a strategic level. The first row maps an organization's content strategy from the "text-making" perspective, a point-of-view that tends to foreground what that organization produces that is of value to its users and customers. Reading across row one, how technical communicators figure into the overall content strategy begins to come into sharper focus. From a text-making perspective, the enterprise appears to be what Spinuzzi and Zachry (2000) call a genre ecology, a kind of textual-ecosystem sustained by the interdependencies among species of texts. Technical communicators, as I have argued elsewhere (Hart-Davidson, 2000), look after the ecosystem by acting as gardeners of a sort, nurturing growth, tending to the soil, and yes, occasionally getting our hands dirty and actually writing. The work practices listed in the "Typical Work Day Includes ..." column make this work possible. They are, for the most part, inquiry practices, knowledge work rather than routine production work. They result not only in the texts being made, but also in the kinds of tangible outcomes that improve text-making across the organization: model documents, templates, guidelines, style sheets, and use cases.

Reading across the other two rows invites you to shift perspectives, looking at the same basic phenomenon—content creation and management—but with a different set of priorities in focus. Row two is something of a behind-the-scenes look at content management inside an organization, emphasizing the interests of those directly involved in enacting a content strategy. Note that this group was also represented in row one, but as only one of several groups of users (and likely not the most important one, since customers or end users are emphasized there). This perspective is the one that may seem the most alien (or perhaps robotic!) to outsiders; the organization, itself, appears to be a collection of ever-growing, digitally stored bits of information, and technical communicators take on roles and titles that are increasingly difficult to explain to friends and family outside of the field: Information architect? Interaction designer? Librarian? Yes, but not *that* kind of librarian ... Tangible outcomes associated with row two, like those in row one, create critical infrastructure for knowledge work: semantic schema, customized markup languages, categories for organizing information.

Row three puts in motion the humans, texts, and machines referenced in the other two rows. Focused on how *ad hoc* practices can be routinized, and how routine practices can be optimized, the perspective in row three foregrounds the interests of managers and partners. The organization appears as a social network, but one that includes nonhumans as important social actors. Machines and texts stand in for people when possible for a host of reasons, most having to do with improving efficiency and lowering costs, but also minimizing risk and inconvenience to people, and enhancing people's capacities. Here, technical communicators take on supervisory roles at the level of a team, a project, a critical business process, or the organization as a whole. They study how people work to create and manage information and they then look to make improvements. They document practices, specify standards, and invent new tools. Their work produces metrics for evaluating critical processes to their organizations, materials used to train new workers, and even new work environments.

Seen from such a high level, the array of roles and responsibilities for technical communicators depicted in Table 5.1 can be dizzying. Odds are, there are sections that do not, or do not yet, make sense to everybody who consider themselves to be technical communicators. To help bring this discussion closer to ground level, I talked to a technical communicator who has one of those ambiguous-sounding job titles: content analyst. I asked her to characterize her work. As you'll see, Sonia's description shifts among all three perspectives discussed above. What follows below are her words, as she wrote them. I include them here without editing because I believe it is important to hear the way she uses specialized terminology, and the way she talks about her work and the concepts that are involved. I acknowledge, at the same time, that it may be a bit unfamiliar. If you have ever been on a long commercial airline flight and flipped by all the music channels to discover that one of them carries the radio transmission between pilots and air traffic controllers, you might recognize the feeling of being able to follow the flow of the action without knowing all the terms, at first. But if you listen long enough and carefully enough, you start to understand. More importantly, your appreciation for the knowledge these specialized terms represent, particularly as they are in use, grows. This is my intent in presenting Sonia's words here. They come from an email she sent to me (and which I've obtained her permission to share here) about her work.

> What I do now is broad, but at the core of the many aspects of the Content Analyst's job is to translate the various "raw" code formats we get from the various publications whose feeds we license to one of our two internal formats, depending on the electronic pipeline we want to push the content through.

One of these pipelines is older and does not support image or a lot of other useful text fields (like a References, Illustration (descriptions), Author Affiliation, and others), but the advantage of this pipeline is that it can deliver the content to resellers (and InfoCorp) quicker than the newer, more advanced pipeline. In addition to supporting said fields and images (PDFs), the more advanced pipeline also has more built-in catches that prevent bad data from loading/displaying to customers and is more likely instead to error out the docs containing data that does not match the provided DTD/Schema or contains encoded characters which are not supported/converted by the entity files provided for it.

Based on the reseller list (some will not tolerate the content delivery delay associated w/the newer pipeline, even at cost of poorer content) and the complexity of the content, we decide which pipeline a feed is best handled in, and then my job of filter spec writing begins. What I do is convert the raw data into one of the internal formats (again, dictated by destination pipeline) to create filter specifications which the developers will then use to write coding for the filter. The specifications incorporate both generic scripts and callbacks as well as data-specific explicit treatments of raw fields and parts of fields. Before a spec is submitted for development, it must go through an interdepartmental "spec review" which is a formal and required meeting at which defect logs are completed by colleagues from all involved departments and then these defects are marked as "Accept," "Discuss" or "Reject" and discussed one by one in the review meeting. During the filter design process we work closely w/developers to treat the data as desired per our internal standards and the Provider's specifications, if any.

The entire process from the time a contract memo is issued (Publisher Relations dept. doc verifying that the feed was licensed) until after the data is in production (ie: we are receiving ongoing feeds and loading them to InfoCorp web client via the filter we have in place for that particular Provider) is called "electronic startup", and the Content Analyst is responsible for getting the data up and running and looking good, at which point, after the in-prod test (preceded by multiple testing environment tests and multiple filter iterations), the Providers are "turned over" to the Acquisitions/Manufacturing manage for ongoing maintenance and QA. Besides the filter spec, we are also responsible for "turnover and processing notes" which highlight any manual processing instances and instructions for the Acq./Man. Folks that manage ongoing content.

We are also responsible for format changes, which, like new content, require a brand new filter, as well as ongoing maintenance items which we receive in the form of Remedy (an itemized problem/ solution tracking software) tickets, edit for developer's understanding— doing true technical writing, where we bridge gap layman's terms and technical terms/requirements—and see these filter changes through to satisfactory resolution, always providing 'raw files' for developers testing, and reviewing the tested output before release of filter changes to production.

Besides communicating w/developers during the startup process, we are also work closely with our technical contacts on the Provider side, which communications vary in their degree of helpfulness ☺ Proficiency in both internal and external email (and sometimes phone) communications is useful/necessary, as well as aptitude in ftp operations.

I like the job because it's largely logic work—at the end of the day I don't feel dumber (most of the time)—lots to learn, which was at first overwhelming but once learned, continues to be stimulating. And, of course, the tech field in general is continuously morphing and advancing, so boredom isn't a concern.

This company's implementation practices are very much ad hoc, as I remember was your experience while working at ABC. Did I mention our developers are ABC contractors? As you probably know, ABC is now outsourcing many of their employees, so we do have a 24 hr disconnect w/India, where most of our developers reside, though there are a few onsite, who attend the spec reviews and facilitate coordination and communicate w/offsite.

Sonia's job is like a high-tech version of plumbing, or as I prefer, a textual version of air traffic control. Her company does not make the content; it simply makes sure that those who need it get it in just the ways they need. She attends to the practices and products of those who create and use the content her company provides the conduit for, and smoothes things along by intervening to modify both the content and, when needed, the transmission system itself. We see Sonia playing a critical role in achieving the aims of content management discussed earlier: enabling distributed authorship and facilitating content reuse across formats and across organizations, all the while making sure that the information is customized to suit her clients' needs.

Considering the Risks and Rewards of CM for Technical Communicators

Acknowledging the conceptual expansion of the work of technical communication is an attempt to address, in a serious way, the reality of the risks and rewards for technical communicators associated with CM and the adoption and use of CM systems. There is tremendous opportunity for those who understand how critical writing is for the success of organizations in an "information economy." But there is also risk. Both are real. Rethinking the value technical communicators can bring to CM will be critical to the long-term development of our field.

Two important trends that speak both to important critiques and invoke impassioned defenses of CM inside and outside the field illustrate these risks and rewards. One is the combined threat that many technical communicators have confronted firsthand: outsourcing and work fragmentation. Another is the rise of user-generated content, and the broader phenomenon of Web 2.0, something that is perhaps best understood as a significant shift in user behavior from passive consumer to active contributor of content. Features such as content syndication and tag-based organization of information (folksonomies) are pieces of an alternative production model that operates alongside, though not in direct opposition to, our current best-practice standard: the "user-centered design" lifecycle (see Hart-Davidson, 2007 for more description and a visual diagram of this model). The bottom line, I argue, where Web 2.0 is concerned is this: we must devise ways to listen carefully and move quickly to support the emerging needs of users by documenting new uses, supporting them with new features or services, and scaling-up capacity. The focal areas represented in Table 5.1 factors in the kinds of changes associated with Web 2.0 in order to emphasize that trends that might otherwise appear threatening to the role of technical communicators—users providing their own help content on a group-edited wiki, for example—actually present dramatic new roles for technical communicators to play. But these shifts are obvious if we consider that our work should influence not merely the means, but also the ends toward which our organizations work. Better relationships with customers could be one result, for example, when a technical communicator assists a user community in developing standard formats for help information, encouraging their contributions but also ensuring that these mesh well together as a wiki grows.

A Closing Thought: CM Is Not Magic

Outsourcing and work fragmentation are potential negative consequences of a short-sighted view of CM, one that the model represented in Table 5.1 attempts to correct. The importance of CM to organizations in an information economy, I have argued here, is that, if their expertise is used properly, technical communicators can help organizations avoid the pitfalls and prosper. CM systems provide resources for enacting the kind of work reflected in Table 5.1, but they do not do that work by themselves. Nor do they help those who lack expertise in writing studies learn best practices.

It is not shameful, by the way, to lack formal training in writing. It simply means that professionals who must write as part of their work responsibilities are not, themselves, experts in what technical communicators should be. From today's academic programs, most technical communicators do receive training, not in "how to write," but rather in how to perceive writing as a social and cultural practice and in how to take an inquiry-based, problem-solving approach to understand this practice in particular contexts. But managers do need to recognize the following: that writing needs to assume a high status in corporate work, and be viewed as a critical means to just about every organizational end. The lingering idea that writing is somehow a "basic skill" rather than an area of strategic activity for a whole enterprise sometimes causes managers to make poor choices when implementing CM practices and systems. Many see these as a chance to automate or, worse, eliminate the work that writing specialists can do.

I hope this chapter helps to dispel that myth and prevent such decisions. I also hope that technical communicators will recognize that one route to conveying this message will be to use the framework provided here to make a compelling case for their potential value and contributions to an organization.

References

Albers, M. (2000). The technical editor and document databases: What the future may hold. *Technical Communication Quarterly, 9,* 191–206.

Anschuetz, L., & Rosenbaum, S. (2002). Expanding roles for technical communicators. In B. Mirel & R. Spilka (Eds.), *Reshaping technical communication: New directions and challenges for the 21st century* (pp. 149–164). Mahwah, NJ: Lawrence Erlbaum.

Applen, J. D. (2002). Technical communication, knowledge management, and XML. *Technical Communication, 49,* 301–313.

Bernhardt, S. A. (1993). The shape of texts to come: The texture of print on screens. *College Composition and Communication, 44*(2), 151–175.

Bist, G. (1994). Single source manuals. *IEEE Transactions on Professional Communication, 37*(2), 81–87.

——. (1996). Applying the object-oriented model to technical communication. *IEEE Transactions on Professional Communication, 39*(1), 49–57.

Bush, V. (1945). As we may think. *Atlantic Monthly.* Retrieved April, 2009 from http://www.theatlantic.com/doc/194507/bush.

Castells, M. (1996). *The rise of the network society. Volume 1: The information age: Economy, society, and culture.* Cambridge, MA: Blackwell Publishers.

Clark, D. (2002). Rhetoric of present single-sourcing methodologies. In M. Priestley (Ed.), *Proceedings of the 20th annual international conference on computer documentation,* Toronto, Ontario, Canada (pp. 22–25). New York: ACM Press.

——. (2008). Separating content from presentation. *Technical Communication Quarterly, 17*(1), 10–34.

Clegg-Gilbert, C. (2004). Engineering creativity: *Proceedings of the SIGDOC 2004, 22nd annual conference on design of communication* (pp. 48–63). New York: ACM Press.

Goldfarb, C. (2008). Charles F. Goldfarb's online press kit. Retrieved April, 2009 from http://www.sgmlsource.com/press/index.htm.

Hackos, J. (2002). *Content management for dynamic web delivery.* New York: John Wiley & Sons.

Hart-Davidson, W. (2000). Confessions of a gardener: A review of information ecologies. *ACM Journal of Computer Documentation, 24*(2), 79–84.

——. (2007). Web 2.0: What technical communicators should know. *Intercom,* Sept/Oct, 8–12.

Hart-Davidson, W., Bernhardt, G., McLeod, D. M., Rife, M., & Grabill, J. (2008). Coming to content management: Inventing infrastructure for organizational knowledge work. *Technical Communication Quarterly, 17*(1),10–34.

Heba, G. (1997). Digital architectures: A rhetoric of electronic document structures. *IEEE Transactions on Professional Communication, 40*(4), 275–283.

Johnson-Eilola, J. (1996). Relocating the value of work: Technical communication in a post-industrial age. *Technical Communication Quarterly, 5*(3), 245–270.

Landow, G. (1992). *Hyper/text/theory.* Baltimore, MD: Johns Hopkins University Press.

Mehlenbacher, B. (1993). Software usability: Choosing appropriate methods for evaluating online systems and documentation. *Proceedings of the 11th annual international conference on systems documentation* (pp. 209–222). New York: ACM Press.

Nelson, T. (1964). A file structure for the complex, the changing, and the intermediate. *Proceedings of the 20th ACM National Conference,* Cleveland, OH (pp. 84–100). New York: ACM Press.

———. (1974). *Dream machines/computer lib.* Redmond, WA: Microsoft.

Nielsen, J. (1990). *Hypertext and hypermedia.* New York: Academic Press.

Price, J. (1997). Introduction: Special issue on structuring complex information for electronic delivery. *IEEE Transactions on Professional Communication, 40*(2), 69–77.

Redish, J. C. (1993). Understanding readers. In C. Barnum & S. Carliner (Eds.), *Techniques for technical communicators* (pp. 14–41). New York: Allyn & Bacon.

Rockley, A., & Kostur, P. (2003). *Managing enterprise content: A unified content strategy.* New York: New Riders.

Sapienza, F. (2007). A rhetorical approach to single-sourcing via intertextuality. *Technical Communication Quarterly, 16*, 83–101.

Schriver, K. (1993). Quality in document design: Issues and controversies. *Technical Communication, 40*(2), 239–257.

Selber, S., Mcgavin, D., Klein, W., & Johnson-Eilola, J. (1996). Issues in hypertext-supported collaborative writing. In A. H. Duin & C. J. Hansen (Eds.), *Nonacademic writing: Social theory and technology* (pp. 257–280). Mahwah, NJ: Lawrence Erlbaum.

Spinuzzi, C. (2003). *Tracing genres through organizations: A sociocultural approach to information design.* Cambridge, MA: MIT Press.

Spinuzzi, C., & Zachry, M. (2000). Genre ecologies: An open systems approach to constructing documentation. *ACM Journal of Computer Documentation, 24*(3), 169–181.

Sullivan, P. (1989). Beyond a narrow conception of usability. *IEEE Transactions on Professional Communication, 32*(4), 256–264.

Wallace, D. P. (2007). *Knowledge management: historical and cross-disciplinary themes.* Santa Barbara, CA: Libraries Unlimited.

Weiss, E. H. (1993). Of document databases, SGML, and rhetorical neutrality. *IEEE Transactions on Professional Communication, 36*(2), 58–61.

Whittemore, S. (2008). Metadata and memory: Lessons from the canon of memoria for the design of content management systems. *Technical Communication Quarterly, 17*(1), 88–109.

Zuboff, S., & Maxmin, J. (2004). *The support economy: Why corporations are failing individuals and the next episode of capitalism.* New York: Penguin.

Part III

New Directions in Cultural, Cross-Cultural, Audience, and Ethical Perspectives

6   Human + Machine Culture

Where We Work

Bernadette Longo

When I work at my computer, I may feel that my primary relationship is between myself and my machine. But whether I am writing an article, visiting an immersive world, or writing on a friend's wall in Facebook, I have a sense that other people lurk behind my screen—and I want a relationship with those other people, even if it is mediated by the machine that is a physical manifestation of the virtual relationship. Because I sense that there are human relationships beyond my machine and because I can communicate with other people in a virtual environment, together we will form some kind of community and culture based on those relationships and communication. Together, we will create a common computer-mediated context for forming, valuing, sustaining, and ending relationships, and that will become a culture.

Community formation relies on acts of inclusion and exclusion. As technical communicators and information designers, we rely on our understanding of audience, community, and culture to guide our decisions about what to include in, and what to exclude from the documents and other media we develop. Our implicit assumptions about communities and cultures within which we work shape our notions of what is (in)appropriate and what is (in)effective in our communications.

Just as we rely on our assumptions about culture to guide our decisions, at the same time, culture is shaped by decisions we make about inclusion and exclusion. This culture then becomes an implied, tacit context within which people make decisions, form opinions, adopt values, generate desires, initiate, maintain, or end relationships, and so on, whether in the physical world or in a computer-mediated environment.

In the computer-mediated environment, however, the presence of the mediating machine adds a technological sensibility to the culture that is created. Because this digital culture is comprised of human + machine, it is important for us to investigate and characterize this new culture rather than assuming that it is simply equal to the human + human culture that has become a nearly invisible medium for our activities, something like the air we breathe. Technical communicators especially need to understand the human + machine culture, since we operate within it and it profoundly influences the communications we craft and their effects on groups of people. These effects could be buying habits, social networking patterns, expectations for social inclusion/exclusion, or other explicit or implicit outcomes from human+machine interactions.

In this chapter, I will begin by exploring the term "culture," which is a complicated term even though we often assume we know what it means. This is an important definition to start this chapter, since I am arguing for a new understanding of our culture when we become profoundly coupled to machines that facilitate our communication and networking with other people. I then explore another term that we often take for granted: "community." Like the term "culture," we often assume we know what we mean when we call a group of people a community. We often argue that we can form an all-inclusive community through the use of computer technologies, yet I argue in this chapter that this goal is not achievable or even desirable. The idea of community has also been incorporated into the model of activity theory that seeks to confine the idea of community to a component that can be isolated in an organizational research setting. Yet I argue here that the idea of community must be studied within its cultural context in order to come to an understanding of why people make the decisions they do in a given circumstance. The idea of community has been especially attractive to people who advocate building communities through virtual, online groups or social networks. Yet these virtual communities encourage simulated social interactions that lead to simulated human connections. The question that I am left with at the end of this chapter is this: Can virtual social connections established within a human+machine culture satisfy our human need to connect with other people? As technical communicators, each of us has the power to craft an answer to this question.

Whose Culture?

Culture is a slippery concept, so I will explain how I am using it in this chapter. Williams (1976) claimed that the word "culture" is "one of the two or three most complicated words in the English language" (p. 87). Sometimes people think of culture as tied to citizenship in a nation, thus they speak of the "Japanese culture" or the "French culture." Usually, people using these phrases refer to culture as something that is inherent in groups of people who are somehow unlike themselves. Even within the United States, we might conceive of a "Southern culture" or a "New England culture" as having distinct characteristics that manifest themselves in such aspects as how readily people speak to strangers or what types of foods are traditional to these areas of the country. But this concept of culture as related to a physical place is not one that pertains to this discussion of human+machine culture.

The concept of culture that informs critical cultural studies and this chapter reflects centuries of evolving meanings for this term. Williams traced this term's evolution back to its earliest meaning as "tending of natural growth"

(1983, p. xiv). Over time, by analogy, this term extended to include tending a person's growth and development. This sense of the word then took on a noun form and "culture" became the effect of personal growth on a social scale—"a thing in itself" (1983, p. xiv) related to "civilization" (1976, p. 89). Williams found that in the nineteenth century, this latter understanding went through the following development:

> It came to mean first, "a general state or habit of the mind" ... Second, it came to mean "the general state of intellectual development, in a society as a whole." Third, it came to mean "the general body of the arts." Fourth, ... it came to mean "a whole way of life, material, intellectual, and spiritual."
>
> (1983, p. xvi)

Williams further argued that the complex relationships between the different senses of this term:

> ... indicates a complex argument about the relations between general human development and a particular way of life ... and between both and the words and practices of art and intelligence ... in archaeology and in cultural anthropology the reference to culture ... is primarily to material production, while in history and cultural studies the reference is primarily to signifying or symbolic systems.
>
> (1976, p. 91)

In this understanding of the term, "culture" refers to the ways in which people relate to each other within a particular social context—how their values, beliefs, assumptions, worldview, and so on are manifested through everyday actions and decisions. These relations take place within the largely invisible context of culture, yet the traces of this culture can be seen in the language and other symbolic systems that we employ. Thus, technical communicators can learn about cultural contexts by studying language and the social relationships embedded in how people use it.

The concept of culture that I am using views it as the social milieu or context in which individuals and groups of people carry on their daily lives. Culture is like the air: it is all around us and we rely on it; we breathe it in and out, but we don't usually notice it. We take for granted that our cultural values and beliefs are "normal" and we notice what is different about other cultures. We attribute this understanding of normalcy to the "nature" of things, or to what is "natural." And our common sense tells us that some things are "natural" or "normal." If something belies our common sense, it is "foreign," "unnatural," "abnormal," or even "dangerous." We struggle to make meaning of whatever does not agree with our common sense beliefs about how the world is and how people act in the world.

In a virtual world, sometimes it may seem that everyone is "normal"–from rabbit avatars to dorm roomies streaming their lives via webcam. One of the stories we tell about digital culture is that it is all-inclusive—almost acultural—a realm in which everyone seems equal in what Rheingold (1993) describes as an "electronic democracy" (Chapter 10). Computer technology, some believe, homogenizes cultures into one universal digital culture "embodied" in one all-encompassing virtual community. Yet any information designer contemplating the intended audience for a Web site knows that the digital culture is not universal, nor is it culturally homogenous. Instead, digital culture is so diverse as to defy definition. Human+machine communities tend to be fragmented and localized and not universal.

Whose Community?

Logically, the idea of an all-inclusive, universal community does not make sense. So it is curious how some information designers and theorists continue to perpetuate an enduring desire to form such an acultural community.[1] Bruffee (1984) once explored how a universal community might function. He articulated a desire to form a community in which everyone understands expectations and conventions for collaborative knowledge-making. Citing a social model of science based on work by the philosophers Kuhn (1962) and Rorty (1979), Bruffee envisioned a community in which "normal discourse" is universally understood: " ... everyone agrees on the 'set of conventions about what counts as a relevant contribution, what counts as a question, what counts as having a good argument for that answer or a good criticism of it'" (p. 643). According to Bruffee, in this system, knowledge is stabilized through "normal discourse" and new knowledge is generated when "abnormal discourse" gains acceptance through social consensus.

In many ways, Bruffee was describing an idealized community that appeals to our sense of harmony and well-being, an idealized community that is beyond cultural tensions and competing desires. As he put it:

> [O]ur authority ... derives from the values of a larger—indeed, the largest possible—community of knowledgeable peers, the community that encompasses all others. The interests of this largest community contradict one of the central interests of local communities ... to maintain established knowledge. The interest of the larger community ... is to bridge gaps among knowledge communities and open them to change.
>
> (p. 650)

Since Bruffee worked within academia, he concluded that teachers can be both conservators of established knowledge and agents of change by "giving students access to the 'conversation of mankind'"[2] (p. 650). Similarly, we could argue that technical communicators can be both conservators of established scientific knowledge and change agents by giving previously excluded groups access to technologies through the documents and other media that we write and design.

Bruffee's argument about the role of writing teachers in collaborative learning reflects larger philosophic notions of social relations, knowledge, and power within an idealized community. His desire can even be seen as altruistic: creating and safeguarding a community that invites everyone to become a member. Despite this idealized goal, however, Bruffee's reasoning exemplifies a widely held contradiction that operates when we conjure the notion of community as a basis for explaining social relationships: that is, because the community has boundaries, some people must be excluded in order for the community to exist.

Who has the power to make that distinction between insiders and outsiders? In Bruffee's model, teachers like him had the power to invite people into the community and teach them its rules—or not. In the model put forward in this chapter, technical communicators also have the power to invite people into a community with/through technological knowledge and teach them the rules—or not. Someone has to make the distinction between insiders and outsiders, because if the community includes everyone, it ceases to be a community and becomes a totality.

Similar to Bruffee, Rheingold (1993) promotes a spirit of inclusion; he articulates a compelling argument that human+machine communities could "help citizens revitalize democracy," also warning that "they could be luring us into an attractively packaged substitute for democratic discourse" (Chapter 10). Regardless of whether these communities were democratic or consumerist, however, Rheingold believes that "most citizens of democratic societies, given access to clearly presented information about the state of the Net, will make wise decisions about how the Net ought to be governed" (Introduction). For Rheingold, open access to online communities would result in people making wise decisions about how to maintain their communities and cultures, leading to smart mobs and mobile virtual communities. His vision of a democratic human+machine community based on open access for all reflects the same desire for inclusion that Bruffee articulated in a pre-computer sense. As admirable as this desire might be, Rheingold's vision of human+machine democracy also masks mechanisms for inclusion and exclusion at work in the virtual world. Instead of Bruffee's model of teachers as gatekeepers, Rheingold's more contemporary model of inclusive community relies on economic and cultural gatekeepers. For example, people who cannot afford computer equipment and training are not included in the smart mob, or mobile virtual community. People that community trendsetters consider to be "uncool" are also likely to be excluded from the smart mob.

However, this idea of a universal community—and the desire for an all-inclusive community—is as illogical as it is compelling. In order to form a community, some people have to be included and others excluded. Community members know they are in the community (us), in contrast to who is not in the community (them). Without such boundaries, the community ceases to exist; the concept of a universal community, therefore, is not logical.

From a cultural perspective, any idea that is extremely compelling but illogical, like a universal community, calls for further exploration, because an important value is at risk beneath the "common sense" of this idea. We can start such inquiry with Williams' (1976) exploration of the etymology and cultural function of the word "community:"

> Community can be the warmly persuasive word to describe an existing set of relationships, or the warmly persuasive word to describe an alternative set of relationships. What is the most important, perhaps, is that unlike all other terms of social organization (*state, nation, society,* etc.) it seems never to be used unfavourably, and never to be given any positive opposing or distinguishing term.
>
> (p. 76)

To allow a positive opposing idea to the idea of community would be to invite disorder within the existing social order. This potential destabilization of the social/cultural order is a dangerous risk, so the actions we take to maintain existing communities also work to maintain social order. Because language and symbolic systems are important tools for carrying out cultural work, those people whose work primarily deals with language—such as technical communicators—are important cultural workers.

Barthes, in his essay "The Great Family of Man" (1972), describes how the need to maintain a stable idea of community plays out through language and images. He addresses the ideology expressed in a photo exhibition in Paris, "the aim of which was to show the universality of human actions in the daily life of all countries of the world" (p. 100). Arguing that even the universals of human life—birth and death—are given meaning through their cultural and historical contexts, Barthes finds that:

> the content and appeal of the pictures, the discourse which justifies them, aims to suppress the determining weight of history: we are held back at the surface of an identity, prevented precisely by sentimentality from penetrating into this ulterior zone of human behaviour where historical alienation introduces some "differences" which we shall here quite simply call "injustices."
>
> (p. 101)

Here, Barthes shows why our desire is so strong to stabilize the notion of a universal community. Like Bruffee's notion of a "conversation of mankind," the photo exhibition asserts the possibility—perhaps a cultural necessity— that humankind is progressing toward a universal community. Yet, Barthes warns that an appeal to this universal community masks injustices and potentially destabilizing inequalities among people in different circumstances and maintains the status quo.

The idea of community as critical to maintaining social order is important in stories we tell about the origins of human community—as preordained by God; as naturally organic; and as necessary for the survival of the species.[3] The fear here is that the formative act of inclusion/exclusion simultaneously casts some people as outsiders who pose a threat to the stable community, since those outsiders can and will form, or become their own opposing community with different values, desires, and goals. Positing the possibility of a universal community is less potentially destabilizing than examining our relationships with those that we place outside our communities.

Lyotard (1992) argues that this cultural silencing of injustices points to failure in uniting all people within a universal community. He asserts that the only way to construct a universal community is to deny local histories and culture, thereby "depriving peoples of their narrative legitimacy" to "make them take up the Idea of free citizenship ... as the only legitimacy" (p. 34). As much as forming a universal community seems like a natural and desirable thing to do, doing so masks cultural tensions, because the only way to have a universal community is to strip people of their local knowledge and coerce them into a totalizing "family of man." Such a project is at odds with the digital culture ethos that celebrates individual agency and the ability to accommodate difference (see Hunt, 1996; Peters and Swanson, 2004; Wood and Smith, 2004; Hodkinson, 2007; Postill, 2008). Instead of finding ways to empower people through their localized expertise and worldview, a universal community promotes the idea that knowledge is common across localized groups. Consider how, in the current culture in which we work as technical communicators, we often assume that we use rational, scientific methods that serve as universal, generalized ways to make knowledge. Yet, such a worldview can negate or impede other ways to make knowledge, and dismisses the reality that not all communities are powered by rational, scientific knowledge.

From a cultural perspective, the important question is this: Who gets to decide whose culture and knowledge will prevail, and whose will be silenced? Determining whose culture and knowledge will prevail will lead to decisions about which group of people has the power to make some things happen and to prevent other possible things from happening. For example, because technical communicators work with knowledge made through the dominant scientific system, we give voice to knowledge that will stabilize a technology-based culture and silence knowledge that comes, for example, from spiritual or emotional sensibilities. The work we do supports a human+machine culture, not a human+spirit culture, even though a spiritual culture produces knowledge that is valid among some groups of people, such as religious groups. Even in a virtual world built through technical knowledge, when we assert that virtual communities are open to everyone, we mask this cultural work of inclusion and exclusion—carried out largely through technical language—in a misguided attempt to (re)create the "family of man" in a virtual world. Like it or not, technical communicators are on the front lines of these decisions about inclusion and exclusion, especially in human+machine virtual worlds.

Modernism and What Follows

Because technical communicators are so instrumental in communicating this goal of social progress through technology, our work tends to legitimate knowledge that contributes to an ideal of universal emancipation through the application of these technologies. Lyotard (1992) describes the desire for a universal community as one of the "metanarratives" of modernity that works to legitimate some kinds of knowledge within a culture. These "grand narratives" do not stop "other stories ... from continuing to weave the fabric of everyday life" (p. 19), but they do appeal to what could be described as a fundamental desire within large social groups for the power to value some kinds of knowledge as acceptable, other kinds of knowledge as unacceptable. Social institutions and practices are built on and guided by these metanarratives.

Although a modernist goal of universal inclusion can be seen, on the surface, as altruistic and positive, this characterization is incomplete. Similar to Williams' (1976) warnings about the term "community" having only a positive form, we need to remain aware that any perspective that seems initially altruistic and universal also has an opposing aspect. Lyotard (1992) describes how technoscience has been working in the shadows to the point that modernity's universal goals have been destroyed:

> by the victory of capitalist technoscience over the other candidates for the universal finality of human history ... another means of destroying the project of modernity while giving the impression of completing it. The subject's mastery over the objects generated by contemporary science and technology does not bring greater freedom, more public education, or greater wealth or more even distributed. It brings an increased reliance on facts.
>
> (p. 18)

For Lyotard (1992), the logic of technoscience relies on its outcome of utility.[4] Within a technoscientific knowledge economy, utility signifies acceptance/ value/capital.[5]

As I have argued (2000), within our contemporary Western culture and institutions, technical communication is a technoscientific tool through which value is assigned to knowledge. Katz (1992) uses examples from Nazi Germany to illustrate this valuative function of technical communication, tracing how technical communication served as a tool to bring the project of modernity based on technoscience to its logical conclusion at Auschwitz by assigning relative values to people and machines. Analyzing a secret Reich business memo addressing "technical improvements to the vans being used in the early Nazi program of exterminating the Jews and other 'undesirables,'" Katz finds that the logic of this well-written memo was based on an "ethos of expediency" (p. 257). The memo's writer, identified only as Just, used "euphemisms and metaphors ... to denote, objectify, and conceal process and people" (p. 257), thereby negating human values through this Nazi project of language control and legitimating the technoscientific rationale of utility, success, or expediency. "Unlike honor or justice, which are based on higher, more abstract moral principles," Katz argues, "expediency is the only 'technical' ethic, perhaps the only ethic that 'pure rationality' knows" (p. 266). By closely reading and analyzing Hitler's writings on propaganda and control of the masses, Katz illustrates how language based on a technoscientific logic can be used not to join people into a universal community, but instead to evaluate and divide people, thereby identifying undesirable groups to be excluded and eliminated from the community. Similarly, when technical communicators attend only to the utility and expediency of our work, we risk falling into the ethical trap of rational inhumanity in the name of creating universal good. Taken to its logical extreme, the technoscientific ethic of utility/success/expediency brings the progressive modernist project of forming a universal community to its end by evaluating and dividing people into localized groups through the application of technical communication.

Postmodernism and What Follows

One characteristic of life in a postmodern world is being a member of a localized group (rather than a universal community). Inhabiting virtual worlds is another aspect of postmodern life. Baudrillard (1988) characterizes the postmodern as "the age of simulation ... substituting signs of the real for the real itself" (p. 167). Simulacra abound in digital culture, which is itself a simulation of physical culture. Even as we are expanding the physical and biological limits of our physical lives by creating online immersive virtual 3D worlds such as Second Life or OpenCroquet, these simulated environments continue to be based on physical and biological laws that we know from the "real" world. Those of us who inhabit digital worlds often claim that virtual communities are like "real" communities or are even better than "real" communities, reassuring ourselves that a virtual life is OK, that it is not detrimental to "real" life. Baudrillard warns, however, that to "simulate is to feign to have what one hasn't" (p. 167) and further, that "simulation threatens the difference between 'true' and 'false', between 'real' and 'imaginary'" (p. 168). Those of us living in Western cultures based in technoscientific knowledge economies increasingly find ourselves thrust into virtual worlds where we inhabit avatars and interact with other simulated beings. But how do we as technical communicators communicate in a community that includes avatars, bots, and human beings? What human values remain and what human+machine values emerge in simulated environments? And how do we negotiate the needs of localized and fragmented audiences in our designs?

People value human relations. We want to feel connected to other people. In the not-too-distant past, we had many face-to-face interactions with people, sometimes mediated by written documents. In the more recent past, we had many face-to-face interactions with people, but increasingly these were mediated by written documents or electronic devices such as telephones, telegraphs, phonographs, moving pictures, radios, or televisions. Currently, those of us living in first-world cultures have some face-to-face interactions with people, but even more interactions are mediated by either written hard-copy documents or by writing done on electronic devices. Since the 1980s, our interactions with people have become more and more mediated by electronic devices, especially the computer. As Baudrillard (1988) points out, "revolution separates each order from the next one" and we are in the order of the "hyperreal" (p. 121). To make these drastic changes seem like a natural evolution of human development, people will explain new, uncertain relationships in terms of earlier, accepted relationships. Baudrillard explains this process in these terms:

> The current revolutions index themselves on the immediately prior phase of the system. They arm themselves with a nostalgic resurrection of the real ... with simulacra of the [earlier] order ... All of these liberations offer ... the phantoms which the system has devoured in successive revolutions and which it subtly resuscitates as revolutionary fantasies.
>
> (p. 121)

Thus, we refer to computer screens of information as "pages" and directories of documents as "files" to refer back to and simulate a known reality of print documents. In virtual worlds, people explain their project as creating an all-inclusive community, masking the totalizing work of the techoscientific logic that also works to shape this nostalgic dream.

As people become more removed from one another in the physical world, we assure ourselves that the technological revolution enabling this alienation facilitates an idealized community, while also dismantling our physical community. This assertion comforts us, because we come to believe that an online virtual world such as Second Life is just like "real" life and is, therefore, OK. A challenge for technical communicators is to be aware that these nostalgic, metaphorical references have two kinds of power: they provide familiar concepts (or schema) to help users understand new information, but at the same time, these nostalgic references extend past social and power inequalities and injustices into the future. Communicators make choices that effect social relationships; the more aware we can be of the cultural implications of those choices, the wider the range of consequences we can foresee.

How People Make Their Own Ways

As we spend more time in virtual worlds and less time in real face-to-face contact with other people, we find ourselves in more intimate contact with institutions that seek to place us in manageable groups. For example, Gustafson (2002) finds that people who sign up for Web sites targeted to women want to connect with other people sharing their concerns. In doing so, however, they provide corporations with personal information that can then be used for marketing to these Web site members. People sign up to meet their personal needs, but in doing so, they also sign up to be managed as one of a group. Despite these institutional efforts to manage our actions, people continue to use their idiosyncratic knowledge to work around corporate intentions and accomplish their personal goals.

Jameson (1991) describes one characteristic of contemporary life in Western cultures based on technoscientific logic in these terms: "The 'reality' of groups ... must be related to the institutional collectivization of contemporary life" (p. 321). He argues that this collectivization of individuals could be observed in:

> the disappearance, from postmodern society, of the older kinds of solitude: ... the pathetic misfits and victims of anomie ... solitary rebels and existential antiheroes ... No current media topic illustrates this better than the "bag people" (also known, in media euphemism, as the "homeless"). No longer solitary freaks and eccentrics, they are a henceforth recognized and accredited sociological category, the object of scrutiny and concern of the appropriate experts, and clearly potentially organizable.
>
> (pp. 321–322)

Jameson asserts that people in a postmodern culture are either organized or organizable through language. And the language that can organize people by virtue of its valuative authority is technical (Yates, 1989; Longo, 2000). Jameson finds that the "ideological category that slowly moves into place to cover the results of such organization is the concept of the 'group' ... sharply differentiated ... from the concept of *class* ... [or] *status*" (p. 322). In Jameson's terms, when we appeal to an idea of community to justify the movement away from a physical life and toward a virtual life, we base this appeal on the economic and social situation in which we find ourselves—a situation in which the ethos of multinational corporations and technoscience profoundly shapes our lived experience and, therefore, what we will find persuasive. In the case of the idea of community, what we find persuasive is the nostalgia for some memory of community that we probably never actually experienced. But this nostalgic idea of community appeals to our desire to be connected with people despite cultural and institutional forces that work to make the face-to-face connections more difficult, replacing them with technology-mediated relations.

De Certeau (1984) explores effects of cultural and institutional forces on people's everyday lives, concluding that despite systemic influences working to organize people and their knowledge into what Jameson (1991) describes as "groups," people's everyday practices continue to work around these totalizing efforts. De Certeau describes a kind of "knowledge preceding that of the scientists" (p. 67) that laypersons and practitioners hold by way of their experience and memory. This knowledge can be idiosyncratic and unruly when compared to orderly, technoscientific categories of legitimated knowledge. Because it resides outside science, this disorderly, lay knowledge cannot be institutionally legitimated until it is "educated" into a scientific knowledge system. De Certeau describes the role of a technical communicator when he traced this process of educating lay knowledge into science: "[T]hey have to release it from it 'improper' language and invert into a 'proper' discourse the erroneous expression of 'marvels' that are already present in everyday ways of operating" (p. 67). In the face of this pressure to be educated and normalized into a technoscientific knowledge system, people can and do use their lay knowledge to create alternative knowledge systems or workarounds that exist in parallel with or opposition to the legitimated system, like jaywalking in the middle of a block rather than crossing at the corner with the electronic sign telling you when to walk. Many possible applications for Post-It Notes involve creating alternative communication systems to accommodate your desired ways of doing things versus procedures that have been built into a system for you to accommodate. Franznick (2008) provides some down-to-earth examples, such as putting a Post-It Note on the dishwasher to indicate when the dishes inside are clean or putting one on an office coffee pot to say when the coffee was made.

Technoscientific knowledge is built on a logic that favors rational deduction over imagination, intellect over dreams, logos over pathos, technique over art, intent over intuition, science over nature. This knowledge system seeks to order and categorize things and experiences for the purpose of controlling them (Aristotle, 1991; Foucault, 1994). Yet, despite the power of this technoscientific knowledge system to enable or disable possible actions, alternative knowledge systems also continue to exert power and control in people's lives. De Certeau (1984) describes how laypersons can use memory of what worked in past experiences and circumstances to effect change within a dominant knowledge system, despite an apparent lack of power or influence in the situation. Distinguishing between place-based strategic power of a dominant group and time-based tactical power of a non-dominant group, de Certeau identifies memory as the "'ultimate weapon' ... giving the maximum number of effects from the minimum force" (p. 82).

Spinuzzi (2003) articulates a concrete instance of the power of memory and circumstance in his description of workers creating their own alternative systems and documents to accommodate their needs when working with computer-based information systems. Recounting an instance of a user substituting information from her lived experience—stored on the memory aid of a Post-It Note—for information originally delivered from the system designers on a large map, Spinuzzi defines a common trope in user-centered design literature: the worker as victim. In this standard narrative, the user is "oppressed by an unjust tyranny and in need of rescue" (p. 1) by usability specialists who will educate these lay users into the system. Contrary to this standard narrative, Spinuzzi asserts that when a user finds a technology is not designed to facilitate her tasks, she does not wait helplessly for rescue by the experts. Instead, she "picks up available tools, adapts them in idiosyncratic ways, and makes do. Through these 'invisible' innovations ... she subverts the information system, inventing her own ways to turn it to her needs" (p. 2). She uses these tactical innovations to supplement her memory, as de Certeau (1984) describes, employing the tools at hand to record consequences of her experience for future use.

Spinuzzi (2003) points out that:

> most popular user-centered design methods assume that the goal of research is to inform centralized solutions; they assume that design solutions must spring from, or at least be ratified and promoted by, decision makers with specialized knowledge ... If individuals ... have developed an innovative way to get work done, these designers might examine that unofficial innovation primarily so that they can develop an official, approved, standardized version.
>
> (p. 3)

As de Certeau (1984) describes it, the information designers in this case "educated" unofficial knowledge into the official technoscience knowledge economy. In this scenario, Spinuzzi sets out an example of a layperson adapting an approved system by innovating her own solution to what she perceives as a shortcoming in the system as it was delivered. She relies on memory and circumstance to transgress legitimate use and transform the system for her own use. Spinuzzi further describes how information designers representing a dominant system react to this type of useful transgression by appropriating it and "educating" it into the system, thereby improving the utility/success of the system and protecting it from the threat of useful, but unacceptable practices falling outside the system. In this brief example of a usability situation, Spinuzzi illustrates profound systemic strategies and what de Certeau would call "tactical practices" at work to stabilize our culture's technoscientific knowledge/power economy. Technoscientific applications tend to identify each of us as a member of a manageable group in order to meet institutional and corporate goals. Yet people can choose to (mis)use our machines and tools in ways that meet our own personal needs, despite these efforts to manage our activities. In making these choices, we work incremental changes on our culture.

How Are Cultures and Activities Related?

If, as technical communicators, we make decisions based only on our understanding of activities and not of the cultural contexts in which these activities are embedded, we run the risk of proposing documents and systems that do not fit well with the organization where we work and our goals for the future. Utility and efficiency alone are not sufficient bases for decision making. We also need to understand how people in the organization will react, with all their histories, personal relationships, strengths, and limitations. We need to understand the cultural contexts as well as the technical aspects of our work.

Spinuzzi (2003) states that his study is not historical, nor is it cultural (p. 61). Instead, he explains, his study employs concepts from activity theory and genre theory to build a theoretical approach that he calls "genre tracing" (p. 22). By looking more closely at the distinction Spinuzzi makes in locating his own study, we can compare cultural studies with activity theory to see how cultural considerations can help technical communicators make appropriate decisions for their particular situations and contexts.

In defining activity theory, Nardi's starting point (1996) shares many basic theoretical building blocks with other theories: "Activity theory offers a set of perspectives on human activity and a set of concepts for describing that activity" (p. 8). Other theories may not focus so clearly on human activities, but any theory about people seeks to articulate tacit assumptions, values, beliefs, expectations, and logics that underpin our practices, professional actions, everyday activities, observable behaviors, and social groupings. In refining this definition, Kuutti (1996) states, "[A]ctivity theory is a philosophical and cross-disciplinary framework for studying different forms of human practices as development processes, with both individual and social levels interlinked at the same time" (p. 25). In this framework, an activity always includes artifacts that mediate the activity (p. 26). More specifically, an activity contains a subject and object whose relationship is mediated by artifacts/tools to achieve an outcome (p. 27). Tools can be "instruments, signs, procedures, machines, methods, laws, forms of work organization" (p. 26). Further, the primary relationship between the subject, object, and tools is mediated by community, rules, and division of labor. The relationship between the subject and community is mediated by rules; the relationship between object and community is mediated by the division of labor to achieve an outcome (p. 28). An activity is "the minimal meaningful context for understanding individual actions" see Figure 6.1.

Kaptelinin (1996a) explains how activities influence other activities and how change happens within the system under study:

> Because activities are not isolated units but are more like nodes in crossing hierarchies and networks, they are influenced by other activities and other changes in their environment ... Activity theory sees

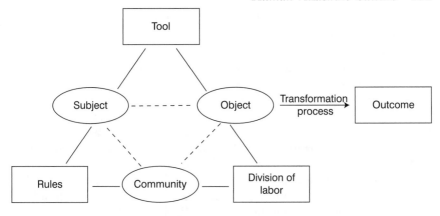

Figure 6.1 Basic structure of an activity (adapted from Kuutti, 1996)

contradictions as sources of development; activities are virtually always in the process of working through contradictions.

(p. 64)

He further explains that culture is not a focus of study when using the activity theory framework: "While culture, values, motivation, emotions, human personality, and personal meaning are embraced by the conceptual system of activity theory, the theory does not aim at giving a comprehensive description of all these phenomena" (p. 64). He describes the underlying assumption that the "human mind" is a generalizable unit and objective reality can be known within this framework: "The most fundamental principle of activity theory is that of the unity of consciousness and activity. 'Consciousness' in this expression means the human mind as a whole, and 'activity' means human interaction with the objective reality" (1996b, p. 107). From this explanation of activity theory, the assumption is that human actions can be understood through objective measurements because the human mind is similar enough across all cultures and times to apply measures of analysis and compare resultant data "apples-to-apples." This theoretical perspective accounts for community rules and division of labor to understand how a subject used a tool on an object to obtain an outcome through some transformative process.

For example, if a system administrator wanted to implement an electronic medical record system in a hospital, the subject of this activity would be the system administrator and the object would be the electronic medical record system. Considering this situation from an activity theory perspective, tools influencing this interaction would include traditional medical records systems, legal regulations concerning those records, and hospital computer systems. This primary relationship among the system administrator, the electronic medical record system, and the tools is mediated by rules, community, and division of labor, where rules can be standard procedures for recording, transcribing, and storing medical records; community can be the medical profession; and division of labor describes the relationship of medical transcriptionists to physicians, nurses, and legal staff. Activity theory would be useful for explaining work flow and how networks of people and machines interact within that flow.

What activity theory would not illuminate are the power differentials among medical transcriptionists, physicians, nurses, patients, legal staff, hospital administrators, insurance companies, medical researchers, pharmaceutical companies, and other institutional actors in the situation. Technical communicators need to understand these institutional tensions, in addition to a technologically efficient work flow, in order to know what work flows are possible and impossible in a complex social situation, and therefore, how to make appropriate choices in a particular situation.

In developing the method of "genre tracing" in his work, Spinuzzi (2003) adopts the model of elements set out by Kuutti (1996) and reproduced above. He then focuses on genre as a mediating tool or artifact and posits that when a researcher understands why people develop genres, he will also understand the "galaxy of assumptions, strategies, and ideological orientations" (p. 43) that underpin the generic artifact. He also assumes that genres are tangible representations of people's functional goals: "People develop genres so that they can accomplish activities" (p. 42). Therefore, a researcher can trace a genre (such as a medical record) and how people work with it through its life cycle and understand people's functional goals, because genre is "a sort of social memory ... Such genre habits ... provide us with ready-made strategies for interpreting ... the world as seen through the 'eyes' of that genre" (p. 43). Spinuzzi quotes Bakhtin (1981) to explain further how people's worldviews can be analyzed through language forms such as genre: "Cultural and literary traditions ... are preserved ... in the objective forms that culture itself assumes (including the forms of language ...) ... from there they enter literary works, sometimes almost completely bypassing the subjective individual memory of their creators" (p. 43). For Bakhtin and Spinuzzi, genre is a language form that can be identified and analyzed to determine people's functional goals, their strategies for achieving these goals, and their ideological orientations. Perhaps it is more accurate to say that genres permanently record a memory of these goals, strategies, and ideological assumptions within their structures.

From a cultural perspective, it is important to consider inclusion and exclusion, within this theoretical framework, by asking, "Whose goals, strategies, and ideologies are recorded? Whose are not recorded?" Like the genre tracing approach that Spinuzzi (2003) constructs with activity theory concepts, cultural studies is interested in the everyday practices of workers who are understood to have tactical power to change the tools and knowledge with which they work. Workers are not understood as "victims" waiting for "rescue" from "designer-heroes" in a modernist sense and their workarounds (in Spinuzzi's terms) or perruques (in de Certeau's terms,

1984) are analyzed as valid manifestations of the workers' tactical power to effect change in their work systems.

From this point of similarity in considering workers' tactical solutions to systemic limitations, cultural studies diverge from activity theory to ask more about the context within which the action takes place. For activity theory, the context includes a community, its rules, and its division of labor. For cultural studies, the context includes all these things *plus* questions about who has the power to make decisions, legitimate some kinds of knowledge and quash others, realize some possibilities and not others, give voice to some ideas and silence others, and record some stories and leave others to be forgotten. For example, in addition to recognizing and articulating rules at work within a community or genre, a cultural approach would also ask about who had power to shape those rules and legitimate some rules and not others; who benefits from the rules and the status quo that they work to stabilize; whose worldview does this set of community rules stabilize and whose is not included in that community; and whose worldview threatens to destabilize the community and who/what is threatened by it. And further, why is labor divided the way it is within that community and who benefits from that system; whose labor is valued more than others and why; what possible systems for dividing labor are not realized within this community, and what are results of that absence? These types of questions can help technical communicators envision innovative solutions that break out of "business as usual" and address new problems with new solutions. Such questions can help them, as well, understand more about their established and emerging relationships with technology in a human+machine culture.

Human+Machine Culture Within Its Context

Turning back to my relationship with my computer, I ask myself why I simultaneously love it and distrust the community it enables. What is it that I desire in this relationship; what is it that I fear? Assuming that I am a member in good standing of an academic community of researchers exploring questions about technical communication, rhetoric, and social studies of science/technology, I can also assume that my emotions about my relationship with my computer are shared to some degree by other people in that community. Simultaneously, as a member in good standing of a professional community of medical writers practicing that craft in a complex institutional setting, I assume that my reliance on my computer as an agent in my professional career is a feeling shared by other practitioners. The illogic and strength of these emotions about a machine I work with suggest that an inquiry into the complex relationship between technical communicators and technological systems is an apt object of inquiry for a cultural study.

Language and metaphor provide an entry point to understanding the human+machine culture that I both love and distrust. As Baake (2003) points out, scientists working on the edge of the known regularly employ metaphors to help bridge what is known with what is becoming known. In that transition period when a new idea or object is being explored and knowledge about it is taking shape, people who need to communicate about this emerging object are somewhat at a loss for words. They overcome this loss by employing similar ideas about what is already known (metaphors) as placeholders while they rearrange this old knowledge, add to it, and give it new language to solidify it into new, accepted scientific knowledge. This use of metaphor as a bridging concept is well established in the Greek form of the word, which has at its root the idea of bearing or carrying and in its prefix the idea of change, sharing, and pursuit (*Oxford English Dictionary*, 1989). As long ago as the fourth century SC, Aristotle (1991) taught that "all people carry on their conversations with metaphors; if one composes well, there will be an unfamiliar quality and it escapes notice and will be clear" (*Rhet.* III.2.6). If we use apt metaphors to describe unfamiliar concepts, the hearer or reader will not even notice that the concept is unfamiliar because it will be so easily understood through a metaphor. Thus, "Metaphor most brings about learning" (*Rhet.* III.10.2). By helping people to understand new things in terms of things that are already known, metaphors serve as bridges from the known to the unknown.

Looking at the history of language that was used to introduce electronic computers from military to general purpose uses after World War II, two metaphors were predominant in the popular literature: computer as brain and computer as robot. Applying the metaphor of "brain" to an electronic computer elevates this machine to the seat of humanity. In Cartesian terms, "I think, therefore I am" captures what it means to be human rather than being simply animal. Yet the "robot"[6] metaphor denigrates the electronic calculator to its place as a machine, but a machine with emotions that can threaten human existence. The "brain" metaphor tells us that the machine could accomplish logical calculations, but the "robot" metaphor warns that the machine is not entirely in human control.

If we experience both positive and negative emotions from our relations with computers and the virtual communities they enable, why do we continue to live in these communities and work as technical communicators to stabilize them? Gramsci (1992) asks a similar question about social classes in general and the "intellectual" subclass who "think of themselves as 'independent', autonomous, endowed with a character of their own" (p. 8): "What are the 'maximum' limits of acceptance of the term 'intellectual'"? In other words, why do we accept the aspects of social agents (e.g., technological, institutional) that affect us negatively and over which we have limited power to affect change? We do so because we desire the benefits we derive from these positive aspects more than we reject the negative effects. For example, we desire the benefits that result from technological developments—such as the ability to work on distributed teams with people that we never meet face-to-face—in order to accomplish our tasks, keep our jobs, and sustain our standard of living. We are generally willing to have what de Certeau (1984) calls our native "know-how" educated through technical communication into instrumental knowledge in order to function efficiently in this world of work. Gramsci describes the education of people's native knowledge into the knowledge that facilitates organized work, an education that takes place through technical communication in workplaces as readily as in schools:

> The school combated folklore, indeed every residue of traditional conceptions of the world. It taught a more modern outlook based essentially on an awareness of the simple and fundamental fact that there exist objective, intractable natural laws to which man must adapt himself if he is to master them in his turn ... [to] create that human order which historically best enables men to dominate the laws of nature ... which most facilitates their *work*.
>
> (p. 34)

Technical communication can be seen as a language tool that educates native knowledge (or superstition or folklore) into the instrumental knowledge of work so that the person with this instrumental knowledge can operate efficiently within the dominant community's rules and divisions of labor. In Spinuzzi's (2003) example cited earlier, when the system designers integrated the user's Post-It Notes approach into the computer system, they "educated" the user's native knowledge into instrumental knowledge that could be incorporated into the human+machine system.

In order for people to invest authority and power in the scientific knowledge system sustained through technical communication, we must believe in the leadership and moral authority we invest in that system. Gramsci (1992) set this out as one of two conditions for a community's ability to achieve a dominant position in relation to other groups: "the supremacy of a social group manifests itself in two ways, as 'domination' and as 'intellectual and moral leadership'" (p. 57). Despite the totalizing forces inherent in a concept of a scientific knowledge and power system sustained through technical communication, individuals do have the ability to shape the system, as they are shaped by it. De Certeau (1984) describes how people take timely, tactical actions in their everyday lives to effect change in a system. Spinuzzi (2003) describes these same everyday practices that workers take to modify technological systems to suit their local, specific needs. Gramsci also describes how each of us exerts power over some sphere of influence:

> Every man, in as much as he is active ... contributes to modifying the social environment in which he develops (to modify certain of its characteristics or to preserving others); ... he tends to establish 'norms', rules of living and of behaviour. One's circle of activity may be greater or smaller ... the representative power may be greater or smaller.
>
> (p. 265)

In a scientific knowledge economy, those people who have the power to establish and sustain a language system—and impose it through education—occupy a dominant position and exercise leadership. As the scribes of technology, technical communicators occupy this strategic position of authority and leadership to educate users' native knowledge into science and technology with the purpose of shaping that knowledge and the people who possess it into efficient workers within a community. Spinuzzi's study of information designers (2003) provides a clear description of technical communicators occupying a position of knowledge-making authority. Any time we explain a technical product or procedure, we exercise the authority to put forth one possible understanding of that subject for our readers/users, thereby informing and educating their native understanding and actions.

Human+machine culture represents both the hope of freedom from inhuman work and the fear that humans will not be able to control the machines they had made in their own image. The social organization that Gramsci (1992) describes supported a division of labor that managed people and machines in an industrial system to maximize efficiency and profit. The social organization that Capek (1928) describes supported a division of labor in which robot-machines took care of the routine, back-breaking work, thus freeing humans to engage in more creative and intellectual work. Philosophers in this period between world wars asked how people could contain these technologies and apply them for humane purposes rather than for human destruction. A few decades passed and the world was again at war. Once more we asked how we could contain the destructive potential of the machines we created and maximize the benefits of these technologies for more humane purposes.

As I sit at my computer and write technical documents that explain the chemical cascade of blood clotting or the benefits of a flexible heart stent, I know that I am helping to communicate information to physicians and patients that can potentially improve their lives. I also know that I am working to uphold a model of illness based more on medical science than on medical art. The mechanical model of the heart's functioning at the core of this knowledge system underlies the development of devices that can improve the quality of patients' lives and even save lives. At the same time, this model overrides other approaches to preventing or treating cardiovascular disease through nutrition, relaxation, even prayer. I belong to a community of people who have the power to educate other people's native knowledge into science and technology through my strategic positions as a credentialed professional within an academic institution and as a practitioner within the medical field. As I question my role in this human+machine culture, I realize that—as a technical writer—my words have the power to shape this culture, even as they are shaped by it.

Notes

1 Ultimately, Bruffee illustrated why this philosophical goal is impossible.
2 Here and throughout this chapter, I have left quotations intact, even those in which the use of "man" indicates men and women. In fact, there are numerous instances of this use of the masculine pronoun in this chapter, now generally considered to be sexist language. Although I find this use of the masculine term to include men and women to be inappropriate in current writing, it does reflect the times and philosophies explored in these quotes as historical artifacts.
3 See Longo (2003), "Tensions in the Community" for an extended exploration of these myths of community.
4 As he puts it: "Success is the only criterion of judgment technoscience will accept" (p. 18).
5 Lyotard finds that a society relying on technoscientific values will lead to "populicide:" "At 'Auschwitz' ... a whole people was physically destroyed" (p. 19) This event marking the logical end of technoscience "can be taken as a paradigmatic name for the tragic 'incompletion' of modernity" (p. 18).
6 This word's origin is in Capek's play (1928) about Rossum's Universal Robots.

References

Aristotle. (1991). *On rhetoric* (G. Kennedy, Trans.). New York: Oxford University Press.

Baake, K. (2003). *Metaphor and knowledge: The challenges of writing science*. Albany: SUNY Press.

Bakhtin, M. (1981). *The dialogic imagination: Four essays*. Austin, TX: University of Texas Press.

Barthes, R. (1972). *Mythologies*. New York: Noonday Press.

Baudrillard, J. (1988). *Selected writings* (M. Poster, Ed.). Stanford, CA: Stanford University Press.

Bruffee, K. (1984). Collaborative learning and the "conversation of mankind." *College English, 46*, 635–652.

Capek, K. (1928). *R.U.R. (Rossum's Universal Robots): A fantastic melodrama* (P. Selver, Trans.). Garden City, NY: Doubleday, Doran and Company.

de Certeau, M. (1984). *The practice of everyday life*. Berkeley, CA: University of California Press.

Foucault, M. (1994). *The order of things: An archaeology of the human sciences*. New York: Vintage Books.

Franznick, K. (2008). Workarounds. Retrieved June 5, 2008 from: http://www.workarounds.com.

Gramsci A. (1992). *Selections from the prison notebooks*. New York: International Publishers.

Gustafson, K. (2002). Join now, membership is free: Women's web sites and the coding of community. In M. Cansalvo & S. Paasonen (Eds.), *Women and everyday uses of the Internet: Agency and identity* (pp. 168–188). New York: Peter Lang.

Hodkinson, P. (2007). Interactive online journals and individualization. *New Media & Society, 9*(4), 625–650.

Hunt, K. (1996). Establishing a presence on the World Wide Web: A rhetorical approach. *Technical Communication, 43*(4), 376–387.

Jameson, F. (1991). *Postmodernism or, the cultural logic of late capitalism*. Durham, NC: Duke University Press.

Kaptelinin, V. (1996a). Activity theory: Implications for human-computer interaction. In B. Nardi (Ed.), *Context and consciousness: Activity theory and human-computer interaction* (pp. 103–116). Cambridge, MA: MIT Press.

——. (1996b). Computer-mediated activity: Functional organs in social and developmental contexts. In B. Nardi (Ed.), *Context and consciousness: Activity theory and human-computer interaction* (pp. 45–68). Cambridge, MA: MIT Press.

Katz, S. B. (1992). The ethic of expediency: Classical rhetoric, technology, and the Holocaust. *College English, 54*, 255–275.

Kuhn, T. (1962). *The structure of scientific revolutions*. Chicago, IL: University of Chicago Press.

Kuutti, K. (1996). Activity theory as a potential framework for human-computer interaction research. In B. Nardi (Ed.), *Context and consciousness: Activity theory and human-computer interaction* (pp. 17–44). Cambridge, MA: MIT Press.

Longo, B. (2000). *Spurious coin: A history of science, management, and technical writing*. Albany, NY: SUNY Press.

——. (2003). Tensions in the community: Myth, strategy, totalitarianism, terror. *Journal of Advanced Composition, 23*(2), 291–317.

Lyotard, J. (1992). *Postmodernism explained*. Minneapolis, MN, MA: University of Minnesota Press.

Nardi, B. A. (1996). Activity theory and human-computer interaction. In B. Nardi (Ed.), *Context and consciousness: Activity theory and human-computer interaction* (pp. 7–16). Cambridge, MA: MIT Press.

Oxford English Dictionary (1989). (2nd ed.) OED Online. Oxford University Press. Retrieved April 2, 2009 from: http://dictionary.oed.com/cgi/entry/00307429.

Peters, B., & Swanson, D. (2004). Queering the conflicts: What LGBT can teach us in the classroom and online. *Computers and Composition, 21*(3), 295–313.

Postill, J. (2008). Localizing the internet beyond communities and networks. *New Media & Society, 10*(3), 413–431.

Rheingold, H. (1993). The virtual community. Retrieved April 3, 2008 from http://www.rheingold.com/vc/book/intro.html.

Rorty, R. (1979). *Philosophy and the mirror of nature*. Princeton, NJ: Princeton University Press.

Spinuzzi, C. (2003). *Tracing genres through organizations: A sociocultural approach to information design*. Cambridge, MA: MIT Press.

Wood, A. F., & Smith, M. J. (2004). *Online communication: Linking technology, identity, and culture* (2nd ed.). Mahwah, NJ: Lawrence Erlbaum.

Williams, R. (1976). *Keywords: A vocabulary of culture and society*. New York: Oxford University Press.

——. (1983). *Culture and society, 1780–1950*. New York: Columbia University Press.

Yates, J. (1989). *Control through communication: The rise of system in American management*. Baltimore, MD: Johns Hopkins University Press.

7 Understanding Digital Literacy Across Cultures

Barry Thatcher

Digital literacy means accessing, understanding, and appropriately using digital media in specific communication situations. Digital literacy across cultures means understanding how this access, understanding, and use vary according to the broad rhetorical and cultural patterns of a target culture. For example, in recent work that I carried out for a United States–Mexico border environmental project, we used email, FTP, and Web/Internet technologies to communicate with stakeholders. The main deliverable for this project was a collaborative test plan that I initially composed, but submitted for review to a multitude of U.S. and Mexican stakeholders, including the U.S. Environmental Protection Agency (EPA) and its Mexican counterpart, SERMANAT. To help develop and review this test plan, the stakeholders needed to download the test plan document using FTP protocol over the Internet, comment on it using Microsoft Word's review function, and send their comments back to me via email. All stakeholders were required to be literate in these technologies; that is, to have and appropriately use these digital media in order to participate in the design of the technology test plan. In addition, the test team needed to use the digital media in a cross-cultural situation, something that proved difficult for many to do.

This difficulty in cross-cultural communication occurred mostly because many of the Mexican and U.S. collaborators used the digital media according to their own rhetorical and cultural traditions, not understanding how these traditions differed on the other side of the border. Consequently, some U.S. collaborators used email in situations or in certain stages of the document production that were appropriate for their own contexts, but inappropriate for Mexican contexts, and vice versa. To develop effective cross-cultural digital literacy, technical communicators need four competencies: first, they need to understand the rhetorical characteristics of the digital medium itself; second, they need to match those characteristics to the demands, constraints, purposes, and audience expectations of the situation in their culture; third, they need to assess how the situation varies in the target culture; and fourth, they need to adapt their communication strategies to the different rhetorical expectations for the target culture.

In my environmental border project, all of us on the test plan team needed to understand the most appropriate uses of the media in our work, something that can prove difficult in cross-border and multi-language communications. For example, we often used telephone or face-to-face communications for some purposes, but email and Web-based communications were used for others. Recent research has revealed useful findings for such an effort. For example, a significant body of research has documented the pros and cons of using email in organizational communication, showing how email is best for some communication situations such as information dissemination, but not as effective for others, such as delicate interpersonal communications (May and Mumby, 2005). Other recent research has shown that legal and intellectual property issues can be quite different with Web-based communications than with print-based communications (Symposium, 2000). Recent research also shows the communication suitability of blogs for specific situations, purposes, and audiences (Gurak and Antonijevic, 2008). And the research that connects the key communication attributes of digital media to specific types of situations has a long and rich history (Kaufer and Carley, 1993; Bolter and Grusin, 2000; Hawisher and Selfe, 2000).

However, one key weakness of much research and practice on digital literacy is that it fails to provide a global or cross-cultural framework for understanding how digital media function outside the United States or many Western European countries. Instead, these theories generally presuppose a broad framework of U.S. cultural values and organizational behavior that uniquely structure both the communicative situation and the relation of the digital media to that situation (see Thatcher, 2005). Not surprisingly, digital media simply do not fit all communicative and cultural traditions the same way. For example, in *The World is Flat*, Friedman argues that the Web creates a triple convergence that will flatten the world through information access, more horizontal ways to collaborate, and the opening up of new cultures (2006, pp. 176–181). Similar arguments have been developed (and critiqued) about email and hypertext (see, for example, Hawisher and Selfe, 2000). However, this triple convergence and other democratic arguments assume mostly U.S. and Western cultural values such as individualism, specific orientation, low-context communication patterns, and universalism.[1]

Unfortunately, this kind of ethnocentrism—assuming that another culture will simply use digital media the same way as your own—is actually quite common in much U.S. research and theory, a point I discuss more thoroughly elsewhere (Thatcher, 2005). This chapter addresses this kind of ethnocentrism with the practical goal of helping technical communicators adapt their approaches for cross-cultural contexts. The first section provides a case study that illustrates the critical need for a cross-cultural approach to digital literacy. The next section lays out a global framework for understanding how digital literacies relate to communicative traditions both in U.S. contexts and around the globe. The third section explores how technical communicators can adapt their digital literacies for cross-cultural contexts using five strategies that are common in U.S. technical communication practice. Finally, the article presents a case study of adapting a U.S.-based Web site to meet better the cultural and communicative traditions of Mexico.

Rhetorical Characteristics of Digital Literacy and the EPA Project

In my cross-border environmental work, I used to be continually frustrated because the EPA set up the document development cycle following U.S, not Mexican, cultural values. This cycle used email and FTP for initial planning stages, phone calls for the intermediate stages, and email and FTP for final stages of the document cycle. This review cycle works well in the United States because of its values of individualism, universalism, and specific orientation. This cycle, however, did not work well in Mexico, which tends to have more hierarchical and interpersonal values, thus implying different uses of digital technologies. I continually tried to bridge that cultural problem, but at times had limited success because of the rigidity of the cycles. I was fortunate enough to have on my team a Mexican national who was working for the EPA in our border area. Both of us knew full well that in Mexico, setting up the test plan needed to be done initially in face-to-face meetings, then we could use email and FTP to iron out the main differences, and finally a combination of face to face and email to finalize the details. However, the EPA guidelines for this contract would not allow us to conduct the face-to-face interviews until the test plan document was in good enough shape for review. We tried to work through these problems by "re-purposing" the emails. For example, when we were assigned to write the Spanish translation of the official email that explained and asked for participation in the review, we composed a very different email than the U.S. version.

As shown in Figure 7.1, the original email was issued from the project leader in Ohio. It typified U.S. cultural and communicative practices: note how it is short, reader friendly, and functional, based on what the single reader needed to do.

Both my Mexican EPA colleague and I knew the U.S. email version (even in Spanish) would not work in Mexican contexts, even though the audience in the United States was similar in knowledge, purposes, and attitudes to that of Mexico. When we communicated this concern to the EPA project team, I was asked by the EPA project leaders to develop a Spanish version that would be based more on the needs of the Mexican audience. When I wrote it, I introduced myself (Mexican term for giving my name, title, occupation, and location), clarified my relation to the EPA and the project, spelled out the authority relations among the members of the project team, and used a more formal tone. I sent it to my Mexican EPA colleague, who revised it even more in terms of tone, interpersonal relations, and authority, making it into what he thought was more appropriate for our Mexican audiences. The

ETV ESTE RFID Vendor participants,

Thank you for your interest in the ETV/ESTE Program Evaluation of RFID in Tracking Hazardous Waste Shipments across International Borders. A DRAFT test plan Quality Assurance Project Plan (QAPP) was prepared for verification field testing and is now available for your review and comment. In addition to describing all the elements of this Verification Program, this document includes information that was submitted by each vendor participating in the program (Section 3).

At the beginning of Section 3 is a summary table that introduces each vendor and summarizes basic system operating information. Information presented in the subsections includes the system description (with schematic diagram or photograph, if desired) and a description of the system approach for tracking HAZMAT and operating instructions (with schematic diagram or photograph, if desired).

Vendors should review and submit corrections to the summary table, as well as any additional information for inclusion in the subsection that highlights the vendor system. Your comments and input are very important to us.
The ESTE Test Plan/QAPP can be downloaded for review at the following Internet address:

ftp://ftp.xxyy.com/outgoing/DRAFT%20RFID%20Test%20Plan%20QAPP/

 Comments and additional information for the document must be received by January 18, 2008.

Questions and submittal information may be sent by email to xxxyy@xyy.com.

Happy New Year!

Jane Doe

Senior Program Manager
XXYY Research Group

Figure 7.1 Original email letter to project stakeholders

translated version of my EPA colleague's email revision appears in Figure 7.2.

As is evident, the two emails have distinct purposes: The U.S. email is to explain how the stakeholders can download the information, while the Mexican email reintroduces me and my EPA colleague, briefly describes how to review the document, and asks for continued collaboration. In essence, we tried to re-purpose the email based on the Mexican communicative traditions. However, even though my EPA colleagues and I know many of these Mexican colleagues and they were aware of the project before they received this email, we still did not get an adequate level of participation

Esteemed Directors:

Please receive a warm hello from Las Cruces, New Mexico. I would like to introduce myself—I am Dr. Barry Thatcher, and I am working with the EPA on a pilot project using Radio Frequency Identification technologies to track the transportation of hazardous materials between the warehouses in the United States and the maquiladoras in the northern border areas of Mexico. You can read more about RFID in the following website: http://es.wikipedia.org/wiki/RFID

For the pilot project, we plan to place RFID readers in a few maquilas in Ciudad Juárez and at the inspection point at the Santa Teresa, New Mexico International Port of Entry and attach RFID tags to the barrels and cartons of hazmat materials that are transported in tractor trailers. All of us working on the project—my project team as well as the EPA—believe that a reader placed at the Jeronimo, Mexico port of entry would give us many benefits.

Since we would like the full collaboration of our Mexican colleagues, we have archived a draft of the plan at the following web address: ftp://ftp.erg.com/outgoing/RFID%20Revised%20Test%20Plan/
We would very much like to ask you to help us develop this plan. You can download the draft, review it, and send you comments to Ms. Jane Doe at the following email address: jane.doe@xxyy.com.

The pilot project will have no cost for you; you only need to provide a small amount of space at the Jeronimo Port of Entry for the reader and help us install computer equipment inside the office at the Port. The private RFID vendors will provide all the necessary equipment for the project.

Dr. Juan Carlos, from the EPA, and I are ready to meet with you to discuss directly the plan and clarify what doubt or comment you may have. Please communicate directly with me.

I am at your orders.

Sincerely,

Dr. Barry L. Thatcher
bathatch@nmsu.edu

Figure 7.2 Translated email for Mexican stakeholders

and input from our Mexican colleagues. A month later, at a joint cross-border environmental forum, the EPA border director formally introduced me to the director of SERMNAT for our border area. He had been put in charge of our project from the Mexican side. In this oral context, the director laid out his review of the project, something he has been unable or unwilling to do via email. For many reasons, in this face-to-face situation, I did not ask him why he did not send his review to us via email. However, the EPA border director had known that his SERMNAT colleague would not do the email review, which is why he set up the oral meeting at the forum. Based on my 20-plus years of experience, I was able to understand quite well that the whole communicative cycle we had followed and its use of digital technologies did not match the communicative cycles in Mexico.

Cross-Cultural Framework for Digital Literacies

The cross-cultural framework for digital literacies that I will be presenting in this section actually originated with my experience in teaching technical communication in Spanish at a private university in Ecuador. As I began teaching, I simply transferred my U.S. communicative assumptions about writing to the Ecuadorian context, which, as my students quickly pointed out, did not work. Whenever I would assume that writing would best address a specific communicative situation, the Ecuadorian students would use orality, and vice versa. Whenever I assumed an audience based on a U.S. egalitarian, collaborative model (and one that relies more on writing), the Ecuadorian students presupposed a model based on hierarchical and interpersonal values (and one that relies more on orality). The same could be said about information needs, organizational strategies, and stylistic preferences. I simply assumed that written technical communications would serve the same purposes in Ecuador as in the United States and believed the only relevant cultural differences were document organizational strategies. (This approach, by the way, is precisely the expectations of EPA's document development cycle.) Yet, from that moment, it became clear to me that communication media have different communicative purposes that are tied to their broad cultural and communicative values.

To explore the relations of communication media and communicative situations, I developed a valid cross-cultural comparative framework that places the cultures on as equal standing as possible (see Thatcher, 2001; 2005). In this framework, communicators need to start by recognizing similarities based on shared contexts and then by considering differences within the framework of these similarities (Bhawuk and Triandis, 1996; Lucy, 1996). Or, seen another way, when "comparing apples and oranges," researchers should not start by looking at all the specific characteristics of the orange and then of the apple, because the apple will be seen in light of the orange, an ethnocentric approach. Instead, apples and oranges are both fruit, generally about the same size, and are used for similar purposes, and their textures are not remarkably different. We need to avoid an embedding of difference in a framework of similarities, because it works against analyzing a second culture using the cultural constructs of the first culture, such as seeing an apple only in light of the orange (Bhawuk and Triandis, 1996).

In the example of apples and oranges, both fruits share size, purpose, texture, and color. However, comparing cultures is naturally more difficult. What do all cultures share? Or what could be the basis of a shared framework for comparison? Following the work in Lucy (1996) and others

(Hofstede, 2004), I developed a framework to compare features of human life that all cultures share regardless of their value orientation. It is basically a functionalist view of common human thresholds that identifies what all humans constantly negotiate. In this framework, I chose to use the most important shared features or thresholds that commonly cause dilemmas in cross-cultural contexts (Hampden-Turner and Trompenaars, 2000). For this chapter, I have chosen to describe for you just three such values that are most connected to different uses of digital media. Among many common thresholds of interaction, all cultures share the dilemma of the "I" relating to others or to a group (I/Other). Second, all cultures make and enforce rules, but the reason for their creation and the flexibility of their enforcement varies (Norms/Rules). And third, all cultures negotiate public/private sense of space (Public/Private). All cultures usually exhibit a variety of approaches to these common human dilemmas, but most cultures have a ying-yang tension between two contradictory, yet complementary approaches, and one side of the ying-yang dyad usually predominates, thus defining its cultural integrity.

I/Other

All cultures share the I/other threshold of human interaction, that is, how a single person relates to others. Essentially, this value assesses the levels of dependence or independence among people. For some cultures, the most likely approach to the "I" relating to the group is individualistic, while in others it is collective. Individualism exists when people see themselves as primarily independent of others and define themselves, see the world through, and negotiate life based on individual identities and efforts. Most intercultural researchers agree that individualism is the strong default approach in the United States, Australia, South Africa, and other Western European-Protestant countries (Stewart and Bennett, 1991; Hamden-Turner and Trompenaars, 2000; Hofstede, 2004). One very common touchstone for individualism–collectivism is the use of senior citizen or retirement homes, with individualistic cultures having a much higher ratio of use than collective cultures where older people simply stay with their children or relatives. For example, Las Cruces, New Mexico with a population of about 100,000 inhabitants has more retirement homes than Ciudad Juárez, in Chihuahua just 40 miles south of the border into Mexico, which has a population of about two million inhabitants.

The communication patterns of individualism include a focus on the "I" rather than on the group, with the individual as the unit of analysis; a strong bifurcation between personal and objective communication strategies, which resolves interpersonal conflicts by going back to the uniqueness of the individual rather than to that person's political or social context (Stewart and Bennett, 1991); a dumbed-down readership level so as to uncomplicate the interpersonal dependence of communicators (Kras, 1989); and an emphasis on personal achievement, self-creation, and reader-friendly document design patterns (Hinds, 1987).

On the other hand, a very common approach to the I/Other threshold is collectivism, which predominates when people view themselves as highly dependent upon others and define themselves, see the world, and negotiate life based on social or family groups. Most intercultural researchers argue that collectivism is the most likely approach in Mexico, central and northern South America, Asia, and the Middle East (Stewart and Bennett, 1991; Hamden-Turner and Trompenaars, 2000; Hofstede, 2004). Some researchers have distinguished between more horizontal or vertical collective values, with Latin America usually exhibiting a vertical collective orientation, while countries in Asia usually reflect a more horizontal collectivity.

Collective communication patterns emphasize interpersonal relationships, social hierarchy, social leveraging, group identities, close personal space, and writer-friendly writing patterns (Hinds, 1987).[2] Collective communication patterns do not have a strong bifurcation between personal and objective strategies because they see the person in light of their social context, effectively combining the personal and social political. Thus, instead of resorting to the uniqueness of the individual to resolve interpersonal conflicts, collective communicators usually say something like "we don't get along because we come from very different social or political grounds." Instead of a dumbed-down readership level, collective communicators tend to complicate their interpersonal dependence as a way of stating the purpose of the communication and their involvement; this creates writer-friendly document design patterns (Hinds, 1987). As exemplified in the two EPA emails, the U.S. email demonstrates strong individualism focusing on one reader and that person's reading needs and processes, while the Mexican email is much more collective, focusing on interpersonal relationships, and especially on authority.

Norms/Rules

All cultures establish norms or rules, but their approaches and applications greatly vary. The two most common approaches are universal and particular. In universalist cultures, the default approach is to establish rules that define what is good and right regardless of the social standing of the individual. The ideal of a "level playing field" is an apt analogy for universalist cultures. In these cultures, many of which share common law legal traditions, laws are based on precedence and should have equal application from the one case to everybody. Not surprisingly, "family businesses" are possible, but not the norm, in universalist cultures because a family business cannot treat its employees "fairly" or hire according to universalist protocols. Universal communication patterns include strategies of fairness, justice, equality, and parallelism, and strong use of templates or branding. In addition, in universalist cultures, addressing a person in light of that person's background or ethnicity is often defined as stereotyping because in universalist cultures, this background information is irrelevant to the equal treatment of everybody. For example, in the United States it is illegal to ask for certain kinds of information in a job interview, such as ethnicity, social background, age, or gender.

In particularist cultures, the default approach is to apply rules and decisions depending on relations and context. Instead of "the level playing field," the particularist playing field is overtly structured, and thus, there is a specifically tailored set of rules for each social relationship. For example, in many particularist cultures, such as those in China or Ecuador, resumes frequently require a picture and commonly have space for marital, political, ethnic, and other personal information usually deemed illegal to include in universalist cultures such as the United States but that in particular cultures, are often the most critical decision-making criteria for hiring. In addition, hiring employees from within the family or close social groups is frequently the default approach, especially at the low- and mid-level, because the rules for treating each other are established by familial roles and trust is built in. Particular communication patterns include uniqueness in document design; emphasis of context and particular relationships; mention of exceptional circumstances; and consideration of social prestige and power relations. According to most intercultural researchers, universalism is the default approach in many Western European countries, the United States, Canada, and South Africa, while Latin American, Arab, and Asian cultures show the strongest particular approaches (Hampden-Turner and Trompenaars, 2000; Hofstede, 2004).

In the two EPA emails, it was interesting for me to note in hindsight that the Mexican email focuses almost exclusively on concrete, particular situations, including people involved and specific contexts of use. The U.S. version sounds almost like a user manual, universally describing the processes.

Public/Private and Degree of Involvement

A third common threshold of human interaction is degree of involvement across different spheres of life, usually involving a public/private divide and trust. Researchers have defined the two most likely approaches as diffuse or specific. Diffuse cultures are usually collective cultures; thus, involvement in friendships, social relations, and work environments often crosses boundaries—you work with your friends and close social acquaintances, thus sharing the relationship across these spheres. These acquaintances usually also cross over into your more private life, including religion, family, recreation, and business. Also, the hierarchy of the relationship may cross over into other spheres. And so, the boss at work may also be the boss on the tennis court, at school, and so forth. At the university, a student's professor, for example, is an authority not only on composition, but also on all aspects of life, and assumes the role of a holistic mentor. In addition, it takes a very long time for students to make friends in class, because with the making of friendship, there is an expectation that the friendship will move beyond the classroom and into different areas, such as the same social, work, or recreational activities.

Consequently, in diffuse cultures, there are high levels of mistrust between people of different social groups or families, making work or collaboration in a public sphere fraught with many conflicts. This is why some researchers have argued that democracy is so difficult to develop in more particular cultures such as Mexico and Latin America (see Thatcher, 2005).

On the other hand, specific cultures are based on the ease and public trust that individualism and universalism give people in separate spheres of life, with friendship belonging to one or two spheres only, with little or no cross-over of authority. For example, university professors are only authorities on particular topics; outside those topics, they are just other people. Specific orientation also relies on the reliable social structure of the level playing field, which allows them to quickly work or make friends with people in all kinds of spheres. Consequently, the specific orientation favors more public collaboration, something that is much more difficult in diffuse cultures. It is not surprising, therefore, that democracy has been relatively simpler to establish in specific cultures. In specific cultures, the hierarchies that are in place in business or education, for example, do not transfer as easily to the political realm, or vice versa. Thus, there is an easier transition to more democratic or egalitarian forums.

University students, for example, can often quickly make friends in the classroom so as to facilitate effective learning and group projects, but outside or beyond the classroom, these relationships rarely continue. One of my favorite examples of this diffuse/specific orientation is when I happen to meet a student outside of the classroom such as at the grocery store. In Ecuador and Mexico, it does not matter where I am, for I am always that student's professor. For example, about four years ago, I taught a qualitative research methods course to beginning professors at the Autonomous University of Ciudad Juárez. I still meet and work with these people frequently in new contexts, but today they still treat me as their professor. In the United States, my experience is different, but U.S. universities, as a whole, probably tend to be more diffuse than is common in other U.S. business and organizational contexts. Thus, when I meet a U.S. student at Wal-Mart, for example, that student is often torn between addressing me as his professor (diffuse) or just another acquaintance (specific). Regardless, the quickness in making friends is possible in specific cultures because of the strong correlation between specificity and individualism and universalism. Individualism provides the personal freedom and universalism the security for quickly making and then disposing of friendships, especially in business relations. This quickness, though, is impossible in diffuse and collective cultures, which use interpersonal relations to structure the crossing over of boundaries, rather than the laws and policies of universalism. Consequently, in specific cultures, there is little transfer of authority or social hierarchy across spheres. You have a boss at work, but she is your boss only at work; at the beach, she is just another acquaintance. Thus, you have school friends, work friends, beach friends, and bar friends, with little crossover. As I have documented elsewhere (Thatcher, 2005), this specific and diffuse dilemma created difficulties for some of my Ecuadorian students when they first begin using email because they did not understand how the diffuse relations could be communicated in that medium. As I will explain later, in this more "decontextual" medium, the diffuse symbols of authority and status were not transferring as quickly as in other media, thus frustrating my Ecuadorian students.

As many intercultural researchers have argued, the specific approach is most likely in the United States, Canada, and Western Europe, while the diffuse approach predominates in Asian, Latin American, and Arab countries (Stewart and Bennett, 1991; Hampden-Turner and Trompenaars, 2000; Hofstede, 2004). Diffuse communication patterns emphasize approaches that address the whole person in all aspects and dimensions, including social hierarchies. As a result, persuasion does not require salesmanship, but rather a long-term establishment of interconnected, interpersonal values. Consequently, diffuse patterns seem (to specific people) very indirect and to circle around the point, because diffuse communicators need to understand the whole person before getting to the point. Specific communication patterns easily section off people into different groups: students, faculty, staff, alumni, parents, and so on. Specific communications are also direct and inductive, stating the main point quickly and then supporting it.

In the two EPA emails, it quickly is apparent that the Mexican email focuses immediately on establishing a viable relationship so that the project can succeed, while the U.S. email focuses on getting to the point. The U.S. email does not need to develop the relationship to achieve its outcomes because the legal structure of the U.S. provides enough security to carry on with the project without worrying too much about the players in the project.

Connecting Digital Media to Three Thresholds Across Cultures

The ways these three values (I/Other, Rules, and Involvement) manifest themselves in a specific culture demonstrate how that culture will relate to or fit digital media. To understand the culture/digital media fit, it is important to lay out briefly the basic characteristics of orality versus writing and email.[3] Many scholars (see Kaufer and Carley, 1993) have argued that orality tends to encourage a rhetoric that is narrative in structure, emphasizing repetition and aids to memory. Since this medium relies on the presence of speaker and hearer, there is also a heightened dependence on the communication context for meaning and a greater propensity for concrete and visual imagery, influencing what Stewart and Bennett (1991) call "horizontal" or "perceptual" thinking rather than analytical thinking. On the other hand, writing has been associated with more analytical thinking patterns, distanced interpretation skills, and abstract and more conceptual cognitive relationships (Ong, 1987; Kaufer and Carley, 1993), reinforcing what Stewart and Bennett (1991) call deep and analytical thinking. The development of writing is also correlated with "more developed" forms of communities (Kaufer and Carley, 1993). These "developed" communities are based on abstract, rule of law approaches for regulating individual and community behavior.

The rhetorics of email and hypertext are more difficult to define, perhaps because they are newer media, often forming hybrid communication characteristics. According to Moran and Hawisher (1998), email tends to have a decided public/private duality. On the one hand, the communicator is isolated and alone when communicating, but the communications can be exceedingly public. Also, the technological issues of the ease of storage, retrievability, and speed encourage certain communicative characteristics. Moran and Hawisher argue that email fosters illusions of intimacy, perhaps because of its immediacy and ostensible privacy. Email is a more decontextual medium than orality, because it does not offer the contextual cues that orality or other media offer.

Hypertext is an electronic medium exemplified by Internet Web sites and has been distinguished from text communications by its lack of linearity—the interlinkings of information creates the Web metaphors. Hypertext is perhaps the most explicitly global medium because of the World Wide Web and Internet. The New Mexico State University Web site, for example, is a hypertext communication because it contains many thousands of texts, pictures, sound bites, files, documents, and other information all interrelated in complex, simultaneous ways. Hypertext integrates written text with graphics and sounds in ways that are impossible for orality and writing. Hypertext also is uniquely contextualized by its links to other Web sites, forming complex ideological and social relations with these sites (Kress, 1997).

I/Other and Media

The communication media fit, or map onto the three cultural values in distinct and important ways, thus influencing how and why each medium is used in distinct cultural traditions. First, one of the traditional arguments about orality (Ong, 1987) is that it reinforces cultural collectivity. Orality tends to be the mechanism for sharing traditions and maintaining face and relational solidarity. Orality, though, seems to have a much weaker role in individualist cultures, perhaps relegated to expressing personal opinions and beliefs, but certainly not the backbone of society, as orality can be in many collective cultures. On the other hand, writing seems to correlate very strongly with individualistic cultures, most notably those with strong Protestant foundations (see Hampden-Turner and Trompenaars, 2000).

Writing seems to represent the distance, isolation, and personal space of individualistic cultures. Often, writing (and written communications) become the backbone of the laws, rules, and regulations that allow individualistic cultures to flourish (Stewart and Bennett, 1991). Writing does not have the same influence in collective cultures. Shared traditions, relational solidarity, and maintaining face can be accomplished through writing, but the preferred and the most effective medium—is still orality.

The relation of the individual–collective variable to email and hypertext seems not as clear-cut as with orality and writing, perhaps pointing to new cultural values that might be a product of these newer remediations (Bolter and Grusin, 2000). Email seems to have the distance and isolation of individualistic cultures, but the illusions of intimacy, dynamism, and sense of community that are more prevalent in collective cultures. Interestingly, the Web metaphor for hypertext communication actually symbolizes the collective approach, with the person at the center orchestrating relational solidarity. Hypertext is also more integrated with audio-visual elements, which are more characteristic of orality and collective cultures. Thus, email and hypertext will relate or map onto the cultural systems differently. For example, the U.S. audience for our EPA email letter had no problem with its individualism; they were willing to respond to the document regardless of the lack of information about the author and larger community involved. The Mexican audiences, however, needed more community information, almost to the point that they refused this medium for this purpose and context, most likely because it was too awkward for their cultural and rhetorical system. However, I have learned that once a relationship is established with my Mexican colleagues, email is used extensively. It simply takes longer to establish the relationship, and despite the conveniences of email, it is usually important to establish the relations face-to-face.

Rules and Media

The relation of universalism and particularism to the communication media is a particularly important variable. In my research in South America, many of the South American personnel preferred orality, because it facilitated a particular, case-by-case approach to the applications of norms and procedures (Thatcher, 1999; 2000). This value was so entrenched that most of the South American writers had never worked from written policies and procedures. Conversely, the U.S. writers working in these South American contexts automatically correlated writing with universalism. Writing something down and accepting it meant universalizing it; it meant developing the distance to analyze and create objectivity and equal application. Not surprisingly, then, the U.S. personnel experienced great difficulties in developing oral policies and procedures based on personal relations and a case-by-case scenario (see Thatcher, 1999).

The ways that email relates to the universal and particular cultural values are of significant importance to technical communicators. Since writing is so closely related to univeralist precedence-setting values and orality and to particular, case-by-case norms, communicators need to carefully consider the influence of the electronic media, which tend to be situated theoretically between writing and orality (Moran and Hawisher, 1998; Kress, 1997). In the area of law, for example, the debate about whether email is "writing" is becoming critical given the boom of Internet commerce. In the United States, only recently has email been designated in critical legal precedents as legally binding (see Symposium, 2000) and only when the authentication of signatures is possible. Canada similarly recognizes email as "writing" for e-commerce and other contracts (Symposium, 2000). However, in a recent study of Latin American countries, only Colombia recognizes email as "writing" for legal contracts, and only when authentication is guaranteed; this legislation occurred in 1999. In this survey (Symposium), Brazil, Peru, Ecuador, Chile, Argentina, and Mexico did not—and have no plans to—consider email as writing. As the survey explains, there are many legal, cultural, economic, and technological reasons for not considering email as writing in Latin America. Thus, technical communicators obviously cannot assume the same purposes, exigencies, and audience with email in the areas of policies, laws, and other standardizing efforts in intercultural contexts.

Furthermore, hypertext writing is considered as "soft" by many U.S. legal scholars, as it lacks the legal contractual ability of traditional print communications. For example, is a link to another corporation's Web site cause for copyright infringement? (Symposium, 2000). Or is linking to certain Web sites and avoiding others a reason for collusion? The U.S. legal system is trying to articulate the logic of legal responsibility in Internet communications (Symposium, 2000). Many other countries are considering similar legislation to clarify the actual legal binding authority of Internet/hypertext communications. Questions that need to be addressed include these: What kinds of research designs can measure the universalizing or particularizing of media-participant relationships in hypertext and email communications? Or are both of these electronic media creating new conceptions of universal and particular categories, essentially re-mediating these terms?

Public/Private and Media

Concerning the specific and diffuse distinction, it seems clear that orality favors diffuseness, while writing encourages a specific orientation. Since orality is a richer medium in terms of non-verbal communication, it works better in diffuse cultures such as those in Latin America and Asia. As in the case of the three previous variables, however, diffuse and specific orientations are mixed with email and hypertext. Email can have very specific applications because of its great audience reach and isolation, but email communities also can function over time if the diffuse qualities can be learned by members of the community. In an earlier study of mine (Thatcher, 2005), I found that Ecuadorian students ended up using many emoticons and other more "diffuse" rhetorical strategies such as family status, job background, and location in order to communicate effectively via email. Hypertext also seems to find a comfortable home in diffuse cultures because of its ability to create a community due to all the non-verbal information.

As a quick summary, Table 7.1 outlines the fit between cultural values and digital media.

Adapting Digital Communications Across Cultures

Understanding the media/culture fit helps researcher and technical communicators understand how to adapt digital literacy approaches for specific communicative traditions. This section explores how to understand and adapt each medium using a common five-point communicative heuristic: purpose, audience, information, organization, and style. This system helps both in analyzing and then developing communications for a specific context. This five-point prompt also can serve as a universal frame for approaching cross-cultural technical communication. Often, if this kind of frame or approach is not used, a communicator might revise the style of a communication only to learn (often too late) that the purpose of the communication or audience does not fit the context.

Purpose

The first common strategy and analysis involves purpose, which simply means, what must the communication achieve without it failing? As shown in Table 7.1, the purposes associated with different media differ markedly. When I was teaching in Ecuador, my first mistake was to assume a universalist, precedent-setting purpose for writing; that is, the idea that writing should be the norm to regulate and normalize behavior. I quickly learned that in Ecuador, orality served that regulating purpose more effectively than writing (Thatcher, 1999). Further, orality strengthened the default Ecuadorian collective, particular, and diffuse orientations, while writing worked against those traditions. Similarly, in four organizations in Mexico, I observed that writing tended to have more notary-like purposes, which served to legitimize the source of information, but orality had fit well the precedent-setting purposes when explaining processes or how-to instructions (Thatcher, 2006).

As exemplified in the EPA emails, email can have different purposes in non-U.S. contexts, something that technical communicators need to consider. First, the collective features of email will map onto collective cultures more quickly and deeply than in individualistic cultures, and vice versa, the individualistic features of email will be more awkward in collective cultures

Table 7.1 Fit of media and cultural values

	I/Other	Rules/Norms	Involvement
Orality	Fits much more easily with and encourages collective approach; uneasy fit with individualism.	Strongly supports particular approach; works strongly against universalism.	Strongly encourages diffuse approach because of orality's richness; specific approach is difficult, but not impossible.
Writing	Fits better individualism, although writing can facilitate distance-based communities.	Strong connection to universalism; works against particularism.	Can encourage either diffuse or specific, but easier fit with specific; compelling arguments exist that writing encourages analytical thinking, which has strong ties to specific orientation.
Email	Fits both individual and collective orientations well or poorly, depending on context. Isolated emailer fits individual, while mass audience fits collective.	Fits both universal and particular. Mass dissemination of information strongly encourages universalism, while isolation might encourage particularism.	Fits much better specific orientation because diffuse, holistic attributes are much harder to communicate via email.
Hyper-text	Mixed: visual and audio elements encourage oral-collectivity, but mass media and isolation encourages individualism.	Mixed: mass dissemination might facilitate universalism; but blogging, for example, easily encourages individualism	Can fit much better diffuse orientation because the richness of hypertext (visual, audio, and verbal) more easily communicates diffuse attributes.

(Thatcher, 2005). Second, since writing is so closely related to univeralist, precedence-setting values and orality is related to particular, case-by-case norms, technical communicators need to consider carefully their purposes for using email, which tends to be situated theoretically between writing and orality (Moran and Hawisher, 1998; Kress, 1997). Finally, the lack of media richness in email will be more awkward for those in diffuse, rather than, specific cultures (Thatcher, 2005).

Hypertext relates to the cross-cultural values in different ways, further affecting communication purpose. First, hypertext has more media richness than writing and even email because of its ability to convey verbal, visual, and audio information. Thus, hypertext communications can easily reinforce collective as well as individualistic traditions. For example, in recent research (Thatcher, *et al.*, 2007), many traditional, collective elements of Chinese culture, including icons, colors, idioms, and paintings, combined rather forcefully in three Chinese university Web site communications to contribute to collective, rather than individualistic, purposes for university Web sites. U.S. and Canadian Web sites, on the other hand, used the visual, verbal, and audio to highlight Western individualism.

Audience

The broad communicative traditions encourage distinct assumptions about audiences for different digital media. First, in collective cultures, email and hypertext can have highly ambiguous relations to an audience. They can be taken as encouraging the collective orientation because of their oral-like features, or reinforcing a more suspicious relation, based on their written-like connection to legal and particularist contexts, or combinations of both. For example, in Mexico and many other parts of Latin America, civil law legal systems dominate. In perhaps paradoxical ways, civil law systems rely mostly on written evidence often matched to legal codes, with very little oral testimony, which is deemed too unreliable because of the highly particular relations. In common law systems such as the one in the United States, oral testimony is an accepted method of discovery and adjudication, perhaps because of universalism, while written precedence serves to guide all processes. As a result, in Mexico, writing has a strong colonial and legal purpose associated with it, so strong in fact that some scholars argue that attorneys and their written rhetoric conquered Mexico rather than the blood and warfare of the conquistadores (see Kellog, 1995; León-Portilla, 1996). In addition, email and hypertext could encourage universal, level playing field relations between author and audience, based on their written-like features, or they could encourage particularism, based on their connections to orality. Finally, email (not hypertext) does not have the holistic, nonverbal richness that is so necessary in building relationships in diffuse cultures and that is usually unnecessary in specific cultures. Thus, email is usually more of an effective means of initiating and building audience–author relations in specific cultures, and not as much so in diffuse cultures. Hypertext, however, is characterized by distance and isolation, which work against collective, particular, and diffuse audience–author relations.

A key example of how these differences might play out across cultures is distance learning. Most U.S. distance learning approaches presuppose student–teacher relations based on U.S. values of individualism, universalism, and specific orientation. These values encourage a more level playing field between teacher and students, assuming that teachers are valued more as content experts than as holistic mentors and that "distanced" interactions are possible because of the presupposed equality and specific nature of their relations. In cultures where collective, particular, and diffuse communications predominate, distance learning relations are different. The particular adaptations mean that online written materials are often viewed less like legal, precedent-setting guidelines and more like adaptable starting points that are continuously revised as the relationships evolve, including lessons and assignments. The diffuse approach relies on the richness of hypertext to highlight the holistic elements of both the students and teacher, bringing out non-instructional dimensions of life that are so critical to diffuse interactions. Finally, the common argument that hypertext will destabilize social hierarchies (Friedman, 2006) does not work as well in collective cultures where social hierarchies and role relations are often strongly in place. Thus, online instructors working in collective cultures usually reinforce clearly and explicitly these roles and relationships.

Information Needs

Since purpose and audience vary according to the cultural approaches, the information needed in the communications in each media varies as well. For example, in more collective cultures, there is a greater need for role-based and group information in all communications (Thatcher, 2005). This role-based information usually includes formal titles and positions within the group or organization. Collective cultures also tend to emphasize solidarity in relations, the common good of the group, and little need to focus on individuals. This difference was seen very prominently in a recent study of 27 public university Web sites in 12 countries (Thatcher, *et al.*, 2007). First, in most collective university Web sites, pictures or photographs were rarely of one individual; usually, they depicted a group of people in a specific context in which the roles (such as teacher or student) were clearly communicated. The Web sites of Mexico, Costa Rica, Colombia, Chile, Nepal, and China generally portrayed students in tight-knit groups, working together to accomplish projects. The language in the collective Web sites rarely focused on one individual and that person's needs; rather, the most common terminology was either the "we" or group names and affiliations. In more individualistic cultures, there were frequently pictures of a single person, and that person took up most of the space in the picture. It is important to point out that this analysis focused on what was happening, not on what was deemed best practices by university Web site developers or other university stakeholders

The kinds of information needed in email and hypertext communications also differ in universalist and particular cultures. For the more universalist cultures, Web sites and emails were often a vehicle for disseminating policies and procedures, while for the particularist cultures, Web sites were a vehicle for displaying specific relationships (Thatcher, *et al.*, 2007). Further, universalist Web sites always highlighted the diversity of their students and faculty so as to emphasize the level playing field. The pictures on each homepage often showed a group of students composed of many ethnicities, both male and female, and some age variation, a combination that in no way reflects the actual breakdown of students. This level playing field was also emphasized by the strong presence of policies and procedures manuals, which were usually one or two links away from the homepage, thus making them easily available for public use. And closely following universalism, these policies and procedures were based on equality, uniformity, and transparency. The uniformity, parallelism, and universal audience strategies allow for the widest readership possible, further emphasizing universalism.

On the other hand, countries that score high on diffuse values emphasize information that contextualizes the university in the community, including local news, impact of the university on the community, and relevance of the university's graduates to the overall well-being of the community (Thatcher, *et al.*, 2007). This was most notable in the Chinese Web sites, which drew complexly on icons of Chinese heritage to display the significance of the collective whole. Not surprisingly, many of these contextual and interpersonal details seem intrusive to readers from more specific cultures who want information specific to their problem at hand. As another particularist impulse, the Latin American, Nepalese, and Chinese universities displayed policies and procedures that were not uniform across groups; in fact, they emphasized the differences between each group. Further, these universities did not display the diversity of their students. For example, Kathmandu University in Nepal has both male and female students from a variety of classes in Nepal, but the pictures show only males, and most often professors.

One interesting variable that emerged with the specific and diffuse threshold was the amount of pictures of people and their poses in the pictures. The Nepalese universities, for example, had very few pictures of people, because, according to Marohang Limbu, a graduate student researcher, this public space was not the appropriate medium for something as private as a picture. Likewise, the more diffuse Web sites had relatively few pictures, and in almost no picture were the people smiling. On the other hand, the Web sites in the United States, Canada, Israel, and Ireland all had many pictures of people, and in most of the pictures, the people had big, bright, welcoming smiles.

This difference in smiles perfectly exemplifies differences between the specific and diffuse. In diffuse cultures, the wide open public space of a Web site is usually not comfortable with or open to smiles, which are reserved for more intimate and familiar groups. On the other hand, in specific cultures, the wide open public space is the perfect place to welcome specific relationship building, a strategy that has been particularly dominant in the United States since colonial times when developing good neighborly strategies was necessary for survival (Alcalde, 1991; Stewart and Bennett, 1991).

Organizational Strategies

Different purposes, audiences, and information needs often encourage different approaches to organizational strategies for digital communications. Just as much research in contrastive rhetoric (Connor, 1996) has shown different preferences for organizing academic English prose, so is digital information organized differently according to cultural values. For example, in the study of 27 university Web sites, it was observed that Latin American, Chinese, and Nepalese Web sites preferred non-parallel or non-templated organizing strategies, while all the U.S. and Canadian Web sites studied strongly preferred the parallel, templated approach to Web site design (Thatcher, *et al.*, 2007). This strong universal impulse ensured the equality of different sections of the Web site across the sites, and uniformity of the total Web itself. In addition, all U.S. and Canadian Web sites showed a strong preference for linear and parallel Web pages across the sites, making for a uniform and simple navigation. Instead of this templating, the Web site designs of universities in particular cultures tend to demonstrate considerable uniqueness across each page. For example, in a university study (Thatcher, *et. al*, 2007), rarely did the pages from particular cultures mirror each other. Sometimes, the format was similar, but some aesthetic feature was either added or altered in some way to preserve uniqueness. The universities in Latin America, in particular, also emphasized more aesthetic elements in their display of uniqueness, using art, symbols, or collages of scenes. Most departments in Latin American Web sites had their own unique logo and own unique way of presenting their information, which is indicative of a particular environment. Uniqueness, rather than the consistency of templating, was a common feature in Web sites from particular cultures.

Thus, all the advice given in U.S. Web site design textbooks that emphasize parallelism, uniformity, and consistency simply does not fit more particular cultures. McCool (2009) also found that contrary to much advice given in U.S. textbooks, using metaphors to organize Web sites can be effective in cross-cultural situations, because analytical Web site organizations are actually more culturally specific than metaphors, especially natural metaphors such as animals or birds. In diffuse cultures, metaphors or other global organizing strategies were frequently employed so as to increase a diffuse understanding and acceptance of the communication.

Style Preferences

Style, or the communicative stance or posture of digital communications, also varies according to different purposes, audiences, organizations, and information. For example, in cultures where individualism predominates, there is a strong preference for personal expressions of individual beliefs; rarely are those beliefs tied to an overriding holistic philosophy, and they are simply reduced to the individual (Stewart and Bennett, 1991). Thus, expressions such as "I believe," or "I feel" or "my opinion is" occur very frequently. On the other hand, in collective cultures, style tends to be more formal, which addresses the roles in social hierarchy, and are more group-oriented, stressing the "we" instead of the "I" orientation.

In universalist cultures, communicative styles tend to be less formal as an effort to downplay social hierarchies; in addition, they have more overt signposting of organizing strategies, and word choice and information structure are developed for the lowest common reading style ("fifth-grade reading level"). For example, in our study of 27 Web sites, we found that the universal orientation of the U.S. and Canadian Web sites was also strongly encouraged by their universal audience strategies. The vocabulary choice and syntax, technical content, and assumptions of knowledge about the university were designed for the lowest common denominator so that as many kinds of people as possible could understand the message. This reduction of the reading level has the important purpose of granting almost universal access to the information. In contrast, in particularist cultures, more attention is placed on the uniqueness and sophistication of the particular readers and context, rather than on "dumbing down" the style so as to make it more universal.

Finally, in specific cultures, the style tends to be much more direct and focused on the issue at hand. This usually manifests itself as direct topic sentences and thesis statements, which orient the reader to what follows. It also includes a lot of metadiscourse (Williams, 2008), which breaks down the information into specific categories with the goal of helping the reader process the information carefully. On the other hand, diffuse styles are indirect, because issues have to be understood holistically. Often, diffuse styles are much more artistic and unique, representing the uniqueness of the situation.

Case Study of Adapting Texas Tech University's Web Site to the Mexican Cultural Tradition

As a guide for digital literacy experts, the following case illustrates many of the adaptations needed for effective cross-cultural communication in digital media for university Web sites. This case is based on adapting Texas Tech University's Web site to meet the expectations of a Mexican communicative and cultural tradition. The analysis in this section follows the same format as before of considering purpose, audiences, information, organization, and style.

Since much of the information will come from the home page, Figure 7.1 displays the Texas Tech Web site's homepage as downloaded in December 2007.

Purpose

As is evident, this homepage very closely reflects the cultural values of individualism, universalism, and specific orientation. This is evident by the single person alone and sitting down, the use of links that separate people according to categories, and little overt mixing of people across spheres. One major purpose of this Web site is to direct an individual reader (e.g., student, parent, faculty) rapidly and equally to the right navigational paths to obtain information specific to that reader's needs and circumstances. If the reader is not able to access information quickly that is specific to individual needs, this Web site has failed. In a Mexican communicative tradition, in contrast, one major purpose of university Web sites is to encourage collective

Figure 7.1 Texas Tech University homepage (image used with the permission of Texas Tech University)

knowledge and community solidarity. Thus, a Web site developer adapting Texas Tech University's homepage for the Mexican communicative tradition might make the following changes:

Individual→ Collective. This adaptation requires much less focus on the individual reader wanting access as fast as possible to immediate needs, and more focus on the common knowledge needed by members of Texas Tech as a community to function effectively. This change would mean much more prominence of the history of the university, its foundation, and its role in current local, state, and national issues.

Universal→Particular. Here, the Web site developer would downplay the Web site as a vehicle for disseminating information so as to enhance universal application of policies and procedures; that developer would emphasize instead links to organizational structures, roles, and important relationships at the university. From this information, readers could understand how university relations work, such as student–teacher and administrator–faculty. For example, instead of telling the reader how to do something, it would direct readers to the right people through which they could accomplish their goals.

Specific→ Diffuse. This adaptation requires redesigning the links topically instead of choosing them according to the specific type of person or group of people (such as student, faculty, or community). These topics would include holistic views of the student body, the Texas Tech educational philosophy, Texas Tech campus, and Texas. Included in these links would be connections between the university and surrounding community and the role of education in the overall development of a person.

Audience

As designed, this home page assumes a reader very largely independent of—and equal to—the author and who processes universalized information at will. It is designed for the reader's specific needs at the moment. Adapting these U.S. values to fit better the expectations of audiences would include the following changes:

Individual→ Collective. Instead of the independence assumed by this Web site, the Web communicator could assume a natural codependence based on concrete roles and relations. Thus, much of the language of "you can do it" needs to be changed to reflect a sense that "you and the university (through faculty, staff, and administrators) can do it together."

Universal→Particular. The audience assumed in the Texas Tech Web site is one of a level playing field. Neither the author (university) nor its readers is more important than the other. In fact, the student-centered focus is an important hallmark of universalism, of treating everybody equally. Interestingly, the only role articulated on this home page is the president's link; because this link is so compelling in its cultural context, it is shown in Figure 7.2.

In a classic U.S. audience assumption, the photograph in this picture greatly downplays the distance between the president and his students and staff. This happens to the point that we can hardly recognize who is the actual president. In particular cultures, the hierarchy is almost always exceedingly clear, whether in photos, language, or organizational charts. For the Mexican communicative tradition, the Web designer would need to help readers understand clearly that they are to be treated according to their roles and relationships.

Specific→ Diffuse. Because of the independence of the audience–author relations created by the individual and universal values, this Web site also creates specific orientation, that is, each person is put into a specific category with little carry over into other categories. Thus, there might be a picture or reference to a professor in a classroom working with students, but never does Texas Tech show a professor outside the classroom, mentoring students in a different setting. The relations are based on their specific relations such as teacher–student. Adapting to the Mexican tradition would show teachers mentoring in non-classroom settings; further, it would show how the university and its graduate help the overall situation of the community.

Figure 7.2 Office of the Texas Tech University President's web page (image used with the permission of Texas Tech University)

Information

Not surprisingly, most of the information on the Texas Tech Web site closely reflects U.S. cultural values of individualism, universalism, and specific orientation. And much of this orientation would need to be adjusted to the Mexican communicative tradition.

Individual→ Collective. The verbal information that very frequently references the "you" as individual needs to be replaced with group information. The pictures of the lone individual or individuals with no apparent grouping need to be replaced with group shots that reflect social roles and hierarchy. The information on individual goals, objectives, and achievements needs to be replaced with how the university and its graduates are holistically influencing the groups around them. Individuals need to be seen in the light of the groups they are a part of.

Universal→Particular. The links need to portray organizational relationships, showing how the roles and relationships in the collective work. The pictures need to highlight the structure of the relationships, rather than downplaying it.

Specific→ Diffuse. The information needs to be placed in better context generally, showing a more holistic view. For example, rather than the lone student sitting down, a larger more global picture showing this student in relation to a building, other students, and Texas Tech would provide a more diffuse approach, meeting better the expectations of a Mexican audience. Further, overt links and more information are needed about the history of Texas Tech and its role in the community.

Organization

As the purpose, audiences, and information must change for the Mexican communicative tradition, so should the organization of material in the communication. As is evident, the organization of the homepage very closely reflects the cultural values of individualism, universalism, and specific orientation. First, it is organized according to an individual's goal to access as fast as possible information that is specific to that person's needs. Second, the organization is strongly templated: it uses the same color scheme and basic page design throughout the whole Web site. Third, the links slice up the human users into specific categories such as students, faculty, and visitors. Adapting Texas Tech's homepage for the Mexican communicative tradition would include the following:

Individual→ Collective. Two intercultural researchers, Stewart and Bennett (1991), explain how most laws and institutions in the United States assume the unit of reference to be the individual, rather than the group. In addition, the U.S. common law legal tradition works much better if the focus at hand is the individual, instead of the group; thus, it is not surprising that the Texas Tech Web site's organization revolves around the individual, not the group. Instead of the individual reader (most frequently the student) being the overall organizing idea, the university should come first. This means that information about the university, its history, and its current status should be prominent in the Web page's organization. Next, the Web page would be organized around groups of students and their roles and relations. Finally, the overall achievement of the university would be figured prominently in the homepage, instead of the individual achievement and aspirations of the lone student.

Universal→Particular. Following quite closely the universalist tendency of simple phrasing, Texas Tech's Web site is strongly templated. This means that an overarching design and motif carry throughout the whole Web site. Thus, an important adaptation for Mexican contexts would be in creating uniqueness, rather than consistency, across the Web sites. This uniqueness would draw on and reflect the local organization that is represented by the different pages. In most Mexican public university Web sites, for example, each major division, such as each different department, college, or institute has an entirely unique look to it.

Specific→ Diffuse. The first key adaptation is to reorganize the pages according to topics such as academics, organization, and instruction, instead of dividing people into different spheres. The second adaptation for moving from specific to diffuse means reducing the linear and listed information and making the Web pages more artistic, nuanced, and holistic, effectively and artistically merging the verbal, visual, and audio together. Since the original Texas Tech Web site is templated so heavily, the visual template frequently does not correlate strongly with the information. In addition, there are many lists and categorizations that heighten the specific rather than diffuse approach.

Style

The style also needs to reflect the changes in purpose, audience, information, and organization. Thus, the following adaptations are recommended.

Individual→ Collective. The style of the language and visuals needs to be more formal generally, which signals better the social relations in the hierarchy. For example, the picture of the president and students all forming the TTU symbol with their hands and smiling is highly informal. In addition, as explained next, the style needs to change the "I" focus to the "we" focus. Pictures need to show more group dynamics and relationships.

Universal→Particular. One oxymoron of the individual–universal relation is that universalism provides the level playing field for individualism to flourish. However, as Stewart and Bennett (1991) explain, individualism does not equal uniqueness. Universal cultures tend to breed people who are individualistic in the same way, while particular cultures breed uniqueness that is derived from a common identity. Thus, a key adaptation for the Mexican communicative situation would be to reduce the equal treatment of individuals and focus instead on their great uniqueness and particular situations and relationships of the students, groups, and organizations. Other adaptations include reducing the linearity and parallelism that reflect strongly the universalist tendencies, and focusing instead on multiple time frames and uniqueness.

Specific→ Diffuse. This requires contextualizing people, the university, and its organizations in their complex wholes first and then getting to the point.

As should be evident by now, my approach for adapting the Texas Tech Web site for Mexico is a radical localization (Hoft, 1995) that assumes much more than translation alone. All five elements—purpose, reader, information, organization, and style—need to be adapted so as to be effective. Perhaps, as I have found in other cross-cultural contexts such as the U.S.–Mexico border (Thatcher, 2006), it would actually be easier to start over instead of to redesign the site. However, adaptation is possible and necessary when working across cultures.

Epilogue

Perhaps the great persistent question throughout this chapter is why should technical communicators adapt their digital communications for cross-cultural contexts? This is a huge question, well beyond the scope here; however, a few of my reflections about this might help us start to explore it. As a rhetorician, my first response to the question is: it depends on the audience and context. In some contexts, such as the U.S.–Mexico border area, a high percentage of bilingual and bicultural people function well across cultures and rhetorical systems. Thus, it does not really matter which system is used; and hybridity between systems is often used strategically (Hampden-Turner and Trompenaars, 2000). For example, in many of my border meetings, some of my Mexican colleagues will speak English and draw from the more U.S. rhetorical system as a measure of goodwill; and not to be outdone, many of their U.S. counterparts will speak Spanish, drawing on the Mexican cultural and rhetorical systems. However, outside the border area or with those unfamiliar with U.S. or Mexican cultural and rhetorical systems, serious misunderstandings occur daily. These misunderstandings do have ethical, cultural, economic, and often environmental impacts (Stewart and Bennett, 1991), which can be mitigated by cross-cultural adaptations.

In addition to the U.S.–Latin American tension, which is the focus of this chapter, the different rhetorics of digital media are becoming critical in Europe. Politically, the European Union is currently made up of 27 countries, 23 languages, and a multiple currencies. Former "Eastern Europe" countries are now integrated in the European Union. Countries like Croatia and Bulgaria are applying for integration. Even Turkey is making all efforts to become "European." It's now almost 20 years since the Berlin Wall opened. From an economic point of view, the European countries still have differences, but this is changing dramatically. French industries are outsourcing to Romania because of low-wage and language (Romanian is a Latin language). Prague looks like a "Western" city with wonderful historical buildings and Slavic charm. Perhaps in the twenty-first century, it is no longer a matter of West/East in Europe, but of North/South, much like the U.S.–Latin American divide described in this chapter.

Cultural differences can matter, sometimes in significant ways. This chapter presents a method for addressing the literacy–cultural issues, one that moves beyond the now taboo approach of listing do's and don'ts for communicating across cultures. It provides a useful framework for understanding why digital communication patterns are grounded in specific cultural values, what these patterns actually mean in the cultural traditions, which patterns need to be adapted for a particular context, and how to adapt those patterns. For those inexperienced in the intercultural body of knowledge, moving away from the taboo approach can be very difficult, because so many assumptions about communications, such as clarity, directness, and persuasion, are not naturalized as the "right way," but seen in their broader cultural context. For example, parallelism and consistency are usually key components of a clear and well organized technical communication in the United States, but why? This chapter explains why—because of the larger cultural values of individualism, universalism, and specific orientation rely on and reinforce this preference for consistency. In Ecuador or Mexico, the definition of clarity often is based on artful articulations of social relations aimed at helping readers understand decision-making hierarchy. This definition of clarity, again, is based on the broader cultural context.

As this chapter describes, doing a cross-cultural comparison of digital literacy is complex, and it takes much practice and thought to do it without reverting to the taboo mentality, but it is possible. An effective cross-cultural analysis needs to take place within a fair, universalist framework, one that does not privilege one culture over another. This framework also should be based on establishing commonalities or a common human threshold, and then on exploring different responses to that threshold. These unique responses to the thresholds encourage a unique cultural approach of purpose, reader, information, organization, and style for each media. This kind of analysis does not reduce cultural complexity to simple individual differences, to mere differences in language (such as English or Spanish), nor to differences in organizing written prose. Rather, this analysis situates communication media together in the cultural context so the technical communicator can understand the breadth, type, and relevance of cultural differences in a cross-cultural context.

Notes

1 These terms will be described later in this chapter.
2 Writer-friendly patterns, according to Hinds, means writing that reflects the complexity of the author's thoughts with little effort to revise the writing to accommodate different levels of audience knowledge and attitudes.
3 Many other writing technologies could be included in this comparison, such as multimedia, databases, and software programming. However, these three are perhaps the most common technologies and represent well the argument of cultural fit.

References

Alcalde, J. (1991). Differential impact of American political and economic institutions on Latin America. In K. W. Thompson (Ed.), *The U.S. constitution and the constitutions of Latin America* (pp. 97–123). Lanham, MD: University Press of America.

Bhawuk, D. P., & Triandis, H. C. (1996). The role of culture theory in the study of culture and intercultural training. In Harry C. Landis & Rabi S. Bhagat (Eds.), *Handbook of intercultural training* (2nd ed.) (pp. 17–34). Thousand Oaks, CA: Sage Publications.

Bolter, J., & Grusin, R. (2000). *Remediation: Understanding new media*. Cambridge, MA: MIT Press.

Connor, U. (1996). *Contrastive rhetoric: Cross-cultural aspects of second-language writing*. Cambridge, MA: Cambridge University Press.

Friedman, T. (2006). *The world is flat: A brief history of the twenty-first century*. New York: Farrar Straus Giroux.

Gurak, L., & Antonijevic, S. (2008). The psychology of blogging. *American Behavioral Scientist, 52*(1), 60–68.

Hampden-Turner, C., & Trompenaars, F. (2000). *Building cross-cultural competence: How to create wealth from conflicting values*. New Haven, CT: Yale University Press.

Hawisher, G. E., & Selfe, C. L. (Eds). (2000). *Global literacies and the world-wide web*. New York: Routledge.

Hinds, J. (1987). Reader versus writer responsibility: A new typology. In U. Connor & R. Kaplan (Eds.), *Writing across languages: Analysis of 1.2 text* (pp. 141–152). Reading, MA: Addison-Wesley.

Hofstede, G. (2004). *Cultures and organizations: Software of the mind*. New York: McGraw Hill.

Hoft, N. (1995). *International technical communication: How to export information about high technology*. New York: John Wiley & Sons.

Kaufer, D. S., & Carley, K. M. (1993). *Communication at a distance: The influence of print on sociocultural organization and change*. Hillsdale, NJ: Lawrence Erlbaum.

Kellog, S. (1995). *Law and the transformation of Aztec culture, 1500–1700*. Norman, OK: University of Oklahoma Press.

Kras, E. (1989). *Management in two cultures*. Yarmouth, ME: Intercultural Press.

Kress, G. (1997). Visual and verbal modes of representation in electronically mediated communication: The potentials of new forms of text. In I. Snyder (Ed.), *Page to screen: Taking literacy into the electronic era* (pp. 53–79). New York: Routledge.

Léon-Portilla, M. (1996). *El destino de la palabra. De la oralidad y los códices mesoamericanos a la escritura alfabética*. Mexico City: El Colegio Nacional Fondo de Cultura Económica.

Lucy, J. (1996). The scope of linguistic relativity. In J. J. Gumperez and S. C. Levinson (Eds.), *Rethinking linguistic relativity* (pp. 37–69). Cambridge, MA: Cambridge University Press.

May, S., & Mumby, D. (2005). *Engaging organizational communication theory and research*. Newbury Park, CA: Sage Publications.

McCool, M. (2009). *Writing around the world*. New York: Continuum Press.

Moran, C., & Hawisher G. (1998). The rhetorics and languages of electronic mail. In I. Snyder (Ed.), *Page to screen: Taking literacy into the electronic era* (pp. 80–101). New York: Routledge.

Ong, W. (1987). *Oralidad y escritura: Tecnologías de la palabra* [Orality and writing: Technologies of the word] (A. Sherp, Trans). Mexico City: Fonda de la cultura Económica.

Stewart, E. C., & Bennett, M. J. (1991). *American cultural patterns: A cross-cultural perspective*. (Rev. ed.). Yarmouth, ME: Intercultural Press.

Symposium. (2000). Responding to the legal obstacles to electronic commerce in Latin America: General questionnaire. *Arizona Journal of International and Comparative Law, 17*, 1–66.

Thatcher, B. (1999). Cultural and communicative adaptations for South American audiences. *Technical Communication, 46*(2), 177–195.

——. (2000). L2 professional writing in a U.S. and South American context. *Journal of Second Language Writing, 9*(1), 41–69.

——.(2001). Issues of validity in intercultural professional communication research. *Journal of Business and Technical Communication, 15*, 458–489.

——. (2005). Situating L2 writing in global communication technologies. *Computers and Composition, 22*(3), 279–295.

——. (2006). Intercultural rhetoric, technology, and writing in Mexican maquilas. Special Technology Transfer Edition of *Technical Communication Quarterly, 15*(3), 383–405.

Thatcher, B., Barrantes, E., Dalzell, A., Dong, Q., Ford, C., Klein, S., Gallagher, R., Limbu, M., & Ramirez, L. (2007). Web site analysis across cultures. In K. St. Amant (Ed.), *Linguistic and cultural online communication issues in the global age* (pp. 124–142). Hershey, PA: IGI-Global

Williams, J. (2008). *Style: The basics of clarity and grace*. (3rd ed.). New York: Longman.

8 Addressing Audiences in a Digital Age

Ann M. Blakeslee

Scenario One: A technical communicator is sent a 300-page manual in PDF for one of her company's products. The manual is not meeting the needs of its readers because it is systems-based; currently, it provides an exhaustive treatment of the product and all of its functions. Upon reviewing the manual, the writer decides to make it task-based and to completely reorganize and rewrite it. As the writer contemplates how best to revise the manual, she thinks, first and foremost, about product users and what they would want from the manual. She knows that none of them would find the manual useful in its current form. She also knows that there are different groups of users, and each group will need different parts of the manual based on their varied uses of the product. Her restructuring results in a document that is better targeted at its readers

Scenario Two: A technical communication consultant is hired to conduct a usability test of a Web-based application that helps individuals design and select health insurance plans. The application had been designed for groups of users assembled in a single location. Recently, it was redesigned to accommodate users in different locations. The consultant is concerned with whether users can achieve success with the application and with whether they can still interact with one another now that they are no longer in the same place. She knows that some users will be highly skilled in accessing and using the application on the Internet, while others will be less proficient. In addition to providing recommendations for improving the application, the consultant has been asked to develop an administrator's guide in PDF. What results is a carefully structured, task-based guide with numerous screen shots and figures.

A concern with audience has always been a defining aspect of who we are and what we do in the field. In the workplace and in academia, we view considerations of our audiences as a central part of our work. We brandish expressions like "user advocate," "user-centered design," and "ease of use," with the understanding that one of our main goals is to write and design documents with the target audience in mind, often with the aim of making their work easier. Further, to accomplish these aims, we usually strive to think about our audience in very specific and particular ways. Technical communicators traditionally have tried to obtain as much specific information about their audience as possible in order to develop documents that support their audience's work.

The above scenarios reinforce the importance for technical communicators of continuing to give careful thought both to identifying their audiences and to accommodating their audiences' needs and interests. Yet, whether technical communicators need to adjust their strategies for users in this new age of digital literacy has yet to be firmly established. Like the two technical communicators in the scenarios, we now, almost exclusively, prepare documents to be delivered online, e.g., as Web-based help, product-based help, and PDFs. We are also, increasingly, developing the potential to integrate instructions into the product, make documents more interactive, and deliver dynamic custom documents to our readers (Albers, 2003). However, as a field we have not yet addressed the shift to digital documents in our examinations of audience with digital texts. We have not questioned traditional approaches to analyzing audiences and to carrying out audience adaptation. We also have not posed more specific kinds of questions about best practices for thinking about and addressing audiences effectively in this digital age. Put another way, we have yet to reexamine the notion of audience to determine if anything is changing or needs to change in response to the field's shift to digital communication.

This chapter focuses on these concerns and shows, through data from five case studies carried out in three different companies, how writers are continuing to view audiences in very particular ways (e.g., in terms of their specific needs for and uses of a product) and to rely on a framework of problem solving and contextualization to analyze and address their digital audiences. It also shows, through descriptions from the five case studies, that our approach to audience with digital texts needs to remain as complex and nuanced as in the past. The data I collected show practicing technical communicators addressing and targeting specific audiences who have particular uses for the product and the documentation. For example, writers tailor information to address different needs of particular audience segments (e.g., owners of accounting firms, those involved with payroll at such firms). This evidence suggests strongly that the field would be remiss if it were to advocate for a generic one-size-fits-all approach to digital audiences. The chapter then concludes by suggesting what technical communicators can do in terms of embracing, researching, and applying new perspectives on audience in this age of digital literacy.

Audiences in the Digital Age

Although scholars in technical communication have yet to engage in any systematic study of audience in a digital age, one speculation is that audiences of digital documents may be different from those of print documents. The thinking here is that technology potentially makes our writing accessible to a much broader audience than before—potentially to all Internet users or to anyone who can access an online document. Porter addresses this universal conception of digital audiences, saying that the Internet "may blow apart the entire notion of a selective audience" because of its broad, and even limitless, distribution potential (1998, p. 142). He captures the essence of the notion of a universal online audience when he discusses "the vastness and diversity of the potential audience(s) involved in the Internet and World Wide Web" (p. 152), which he contrasts with the more limited and constrained audiences of the past: "print notions of audience," he writes, "tend to be more exclusive constructs" (p. 142). Finally, he cautions that, "It is dangerous, especially in cyberspace writing, to presume that your writing will have a limited and well-defined audience" (p. 145).

One risk with such a broad conception of digital audiences is that technical communicators might assume that they need not—and even cannot—analyze, understand completely, or consider the audience much at all in their work. Any generic and universal notion of audience implies that because the digital environment makes literacy accessible to everyone, it is now much simpler to address the audience—and it is futile and of little or no use to identify, analyze, and tailor technical communication to a target audience.

Some scholars have begun to address this risk. For example, Longo (this volume) notes that with the new age of digital literacy has emerged a common notion that, given an often global audience for digital documents, along with a perceived "universality" of technical communication work in Internet and other virtual realms, the audience has become more generic and far simpler than in earlier decades. Longo also exposes the misconception that technology somehow homogenizes cultures into "one universal digital culture 'embodied' in one all-encompassing virtual community." She contends that the "idea of a universal community ... is as illogical as it is compelling." As she puts it, "In order to form a community, some people have to be included and others excluded ... Without boundaries, the community ceases to exist" (pp. 150–151).

An opposite conception of audiences of digital texts holds that while we cannot predict all potential readers for documentation on the Internet, we can predict and define, with reasonable accuracy, particular types of readers for specific product and instructional documents. In this chapter, I argue in favor of this latter conception of digital audiences in technical communication. While the universal audience encompasses anyone who can access an online document, audiences for instructional materials, for example, are generally more particular audiences that we can and should analyze and predict. Consonant with such a view, Kitalong contends that with the proliferation of technology comes a "proliferation of users, who are now more fully diversified than ever before in terms of the traditional audience-analysis categories of educational background, profession, age, gender, race, and economic status" (2004, p. 171). As I will illustrate next through the case studies I conducted, it is this diversity—and complexity—that invite a careful consideration of digital audiences by technical communicators.

Empirical Support for a Contextual Approach to Audience

To gain a better understanding of the audiences of online technical documents, and how technical communicators are approaching their audiences in this new digital age, I conducted five case studies at three different companies with practicing technical communicators who have written both print and digital documents. My findings show the writers primarily focusing on the second, more particular conception of audience and clearly suggest that we still need to approach audiences as contextual, unique, and particular, just as we have been doing all along. Comments made by my participants show how writers continue to target documents at specific audiences that may use their products in very particular ways. Such evidence also points to the need to tease out the unique and complex characteristics of modern digital audiences.

My five case studies focused on writers in three companies who are all engaged in composing digital documents.[1] The companies were located in a mid-sized city in the Midwest. I collected artifacts from a significant project that the writers recently completed (e.g., drafts, planning notes, edited texts, final documents), reviewed these artifacts, and then interviewed the writers about their experiences and processes in undertaking the projects. The interviews focused primarily on how the writers characterized, approached, analyzed, and addressed their audiences for the projects. I also explored their perceptions of how their audiences, and their approaches to audience more generally, might have changed due to their now almost exclusive use of digital media.

Case Study Descriptions

Cases One and Two: Tax-Soft. The writers for my initial two case studies work at Tax-Soft,[2] a company that develops support tools for tax and accounting professionals. Tax-Soft is part of a unit of a large multinational conglomerate that has over 50,000 employees worldwide. The office where I conducted my two case studies has 575 employees altogether, with 19 full-time technical communicators. Overall, product documentation at Tax-Soft is delivered as HTML-based help, either on a product CD or posted on a server that users of the product can access. In some cases, PDF manuals are also shipped with the product.

My initial case study at Tax-Soft focused on the experiences and perceptions of Carrie, a technical writer who develops documentation and training materials for a product that helps accountants and tax preparers manage their businesses. Carrie's audience, as she put it, "is people who own or work in an accounting firm, which means at times I might be talking to the partner in charge, or I might be talking to a clerical or staff person who's just keying in data entry, and anything in between." The documentation she writes includes a Web help system with context-sensitive help and PDF guides that are accessible from links in the help.

Amanda, the focus of my second case study, is the lead writer for products that support payroll activities in accounting and tax preparation businesses. Amanda writes online help, training guides, and a number of other documents, including "the getting started, the tutorials, the user bulletins, and the installation guides." She said that she also reviews documents that other writers create, and she engages in other company projects as time permits.

Cases Three and Four: Secure Net. Secure Net, the site of my next two case studies, is another multinational company, but with a focus on network security. The company has about 300 employees worldwide, with 70 employees, including four full-time technical communicators, in the office where I conducted my study. My initial case at Secure Net focused on Julie, who writes user manuals for a product targeted at service providers. These, and most other manuals produced at the company, are posted as PDF files on the company's support site. Julie works mostly on the user guide for the product, which, she said, "is the guide for the Web user interface." She also prepares release notes that address new features of a release.

My second case at Secure Net focused on Susan and Kate, two technical communicators who write documentation for a product targeted at regular businesses. Both writers document updates to the product that accompany new releases. Kate, a team leader, said, "We also improve the documentation itself, making sure it conforms to the style guide." Susan also creates guides focused on preparing to use the product, including how to install it. I interviewed both writers at once since they worked together on the project I considered.

Case Five: TC Consult. TC Consult, where I conducted my final case study, characterizes itself as a user-centered design firm that "works to improve the quality and usability of products, Web sites, and services" (words found on the company Web site) in a variety of industries. It offers consulting services and has offices in four U.S. cities. Its main office, out of which my participant works, employs 12 professionals, including seven user-experience consultants. Barbara, who occupied the user experience role at the time of my study, has also occupied numerous other roles at the company, including roles in sales and project management. She said that when she undertook the project we discussed for my case, her "role was that of a user researcher or user experience professional." The project we discussed involved the testing of a Web-based planning application for medical benefits. It had several deliverables, including a report, an administrator's guide, and a white paper. Barbara said that projects such as this generally lead to reports that present problems, and also, when requested, recommendations for addressing them.

Study Findings: Heuristics and Strategies for Learning About and Addressing Audiences

The findings from the five case studies, as a whole, support a problem-solving and contextualized approach to audience in digital environments in technical communication. In particular, they suggest that while technical communicators may not know their exact audiences, the complexity of the product and the typical environments in which the product is used provide them with guidance in understanding their prospective readers. Digital audience adaptation, therefore, requires a problem-solving approach that allows writers to identify and analyze their audiences and to learn about their audiences' contexts and uses for the documentation. The digital environment gives writers various mechanisms, or heuristics,[3] for this learning—in other words, it provides them with alternative methods for understanding user needs and a means to solicit user feedback during both early and later phases of learning and research; it also helps them respond to and interact with users. As a result, writers are becoming more responsive to readers; they can now respond immediately to their readers' needs. They can also target documents to specific users and situations, and they can adapt documents more easily for their different audiences. In this section, I focus on these mechanisms and possibilities, showing, in particular, the strategies and heuristics writers can use, and are using now, to learn about and address their digital audiences.

Writers have always needed heuristics and strategies for learning about their audiences and addressing them effectively. My findings support the continued use of such heuristics and suggest some specific ones for learning about and addressing digital audiences. Some of these even depend on or are facilitated by digital technologies. Specific heuristics addressed by my participants include these:

- targeting specific users and situations as a way to respond to and address audience needs;
- developing personas;
- interacting with users;
- obtaining and responding to user feedback.

Responding to and Addressing Audience Needs by Targeting Specific Readers and Situations

User needs were a primary concern for all writers in my cases. Most of the projects they described came about because of a perceived need to improve documentation for the user. This was true for both of my cases at Secure Net. According to Julie:

> She [Julie's manager] and our product management staff had wanted to improve [the documentation] based on users. They were thinking

the users weren't able to use it because there was so much text that was verbose ... It wasn't chunked out properly so that it was easy to find information. All of the information was buried in paragraphs. PM [product management] had done a survey of all of the customers and the documentation had received some reviews that weren't the greatest—it was hard to understand, hard to find things. So we really had to think more from the perspective of the audience.

Kate added:

> We've definitely been focusing on improving our online help so that it is more useful and helpful to users. It's really come a long way. When I first started, the online help was not searchable and there was no table of contents. It was just context sensitive help based on the page you were on. We're now concerned with making sure that they can find the help that they need. I just don't think that that was really a priority.

For Julie and Kate, and for the other writers in my cases, technology is helping to address their users' needs. In digital environments, for example, writers can now target individual audience segments, and even isolated audience members. Technology facilitates this accommodation of documents by allowing writers to accommodate specific needs of distinct segments or members of their audiences. The writers in my cases all talked about tailoring documents to specific audiences, such as targeting and limiting dissemination to particular groups of users. They realized that different audiences might want different help or documentation depending on their particular uses of the product.

The writers from both cases at Tax Soft also addressed using technology to improve their documentation—in particular, they use it to structure and disseminate their documents so that users can access and go directly to the parts pertaining to them. Amanda talked about the potential in this regard:

> I'd say with things moving more digital, perhaps it makes it easier in the sense that technology makes it easier for us to figure out what people are licensed for. When they log on, we know who they are, what products they have, so maybe we can talk to them more directly. ... Maybe we can focus them in the right direction and rein them in and figure out through context where they should probably be pointed. I'm not saying we can do this right now, but it's the direction we would like to move.

Amanda sees technology as a tool for addressing the varied needs and skill levels of all her readers. She imagines a system that will recognize readers and take them directly to the documentation they need based on their roles and work contexts.

According to Amanda, such a strategy for targeting users essentially makes writing more, and not less, complex: "It certainly doesn't simplify writing the help. In fact, our help is going to become more difficult to write because we have so many audiences." What she talked about is consistent with a concern Johnson-Eilola expresses with bridging the gap between obtaining information about the product and its users and structuring that information in ways that meet the needs of those users in their particular contexts (1996, p. 260). For Amanda, technology provides a mechanism for accomplishing this better.

Carrie, from my second case at Tax Soft, expressed similar ideas in regard to using technology to target specific users:

> Most of my time is spent on product doc. The audience for it as I said is people who own or work in an accounting firm, which means at times I might be talking to the partner in charge, or I might be talking to a clerical or staff person who's just keying in data entry—and anything in between. The doc set for this product includes a Web help system with context sensitive help and a number of PDF guides that are accessible from links in the help. So we have a getting started guide and a number of smaller, tinier very specific PDFs for very specific areas of the program. We call these walk-throughs. These are more task-oriented while the help is more comprehensive, covering everything you might ever need to know about the program.

Carrie also mentioned a Web service her company offers that clients can use in very specific ways. She indicated that she and other writers at the company document this service, which provides another example of the ways in which digital media can facilitate the exchange and use of information for targeted users and purposes:

> Web services are another way for the accountant to interact with their clients to upload documents, information, so that they can transfer data not necessarily in real time, 24/7. For example, a client might have their own portal that they can log into and upload their tax information for the year. The accountant can access that, do what he needs to do, and send it back. The company provides the portals. We document them. They exist on our company's servers.

The very nature of digital media facilitates the kind of targeting that Amanda and Carrie describe. For example, Bernhardt has discussed how the qualities of electronic text "can lead to multiple versions, to individually adapted texts," and how readers may be able to individualize and structure text for their own uses (1993, pp. 173, 174). He also addresses how the nonlinear organizational patterns that are a trademark of digital documents enhance the possibilities of tailoring information to different audiences

(p. 164; see also Beaufort, 2008, p. 225). Barbara, from my case at TC Consult, also talked about how the nonlinear qualities of online texts facilitate accommodating audiences: "... we have more flexibility in layering information to accommodate and to invite them into reading more." Barbara addressed, as well, how different digital media and genres also make it easier to accommodate different learning styles and preferences: "And there are also media available to get the information across to all of the different information consuming styles that people have." Thanks to technology, therefore, documents and information can now be designed for, and targeted much more easily at, particular readers with particular roles and functions.

Developing Personas

Just as in the past, to target specific users, writers need effective heuristics for learning about and understanding their users' needs. One heuristic that many writers are now using is called personas. Barbara described personas in this way:

> These are more than user profiles ... which were descriptions of a person. These take it one step further—and put a face and a name and life description on them so that developers can really feel who they're developing for. You know, Joe, whose job is really as a librarian, but this is his experience—who goes home and never touches a computer but uses one all day.

Barbara also stressed the value of basing personas on more than speculation:

> You can do a user profile or persona on speculation, but part of what we do is go and talk to people we think fall into these categories and get more data to justify or validate their assumptions of these people. We pay attention to if the people match or if they're an outlier and part of a group our client doesn't know about.

Barbara's comments suggest that such an approach, if used well, can provide the kind of information about readers that writers are seeking. It can uncover details about the tasks readers need to perform, along with additional information about the contexts where they'll perform them, which hopefully will lead to a better user experience overall, both with the product and with the documentation.

Barbara also believes that this is the direction the field is now heading in regard to audience:

> [I] do think the information about personas is where this is going. For some of our studies we write interview summaries, which is source information for building a persona. The personas become the

same people/group we want represented when we do our studies and, ultimately, documentation. People would also want to consider these for the products they create. They might realize they might need to create different documents for different groups. You don't know what you don't know so it is possible to miss an important audience.

Her final comment suggests the importance of learning about all of the audiences for a product. According to Barbara, "The whole purpose of this is to make this more multi-dimensional to developers and writers. If they don't do this, they're developing for someone like him or her." By extension, we can expect that if writers think of their digital audiences only in abstract or universal terms—if they oversimplify their tasks with audience analysis—they may well risk doing the same thing.

Interacting With Readers

Another valuable heuristic for learning about and understanding reader needs is interaction, especially with actual readers. All of the writers in my cases expressed a preference for talking directly with readers as a means of obtaining detailed and context-specific information about them. However, while this was a common practice for Barbara and her coworkers at TC Consult, it was more of an ideal for the writers at both Tax Soft and Secure Net, who said that their companies typically prevent them from having direct contact with their customers. Julie, for example, explained her situation at Secure Net in this way:

> We don't have any contact with customers whatsoever, unfortunately. Everything that we get comes second-hand from PM (Product Management), development, sales, QA (quality assurance, which does the testing) ... So we have to kind of figure out where the features should be, what we need to document, what the users need to know ... [We have to figure out] the contextual information. How they would be configuring it; what would be the steps they would use to configure it. Is there anything before or after the configuration that they need to do?

Noteworthy in Julie's comments is her emphasis on context and contextual information in relation to her readers. Her comments point to the value and worth of contextualizing audiences, at least to the extent possible. Her comments also show, however, how addressing audiences can become a guessing game, with writers having to depend on individuals other than their readers to provide the contextual clues they need.

Another example came from Amanda, one of the writers at Tax Soft, who said, "So if I was able to, I'd have this [interaction with my readers] with every project; that's the way it's supposed to be done." She also addressed an implication of not interacting with readers: "It's very difficult having no contact with them ahead of time; we have to deal with it after the fact and so basically we have to find out from other people that we failed in order to succeed later." This can create a situation, Amanda said, in which writers end up guessing instead of really knowing what their readers need.

As an alternative to talking to actual users, Amanda talks instead to other employees at her company. She stressed in her comments that her very first concern in writing is with determining who her readers are and what tasks they need to perform:

> That is usually the first question we ask—who are we writing for, who is using this. I've asked my analysts more than once … is it just an accountant who's using this? … [Also] who is doing a particular task because there are about a million tasks that can be performed using our software—some of it is going to be done by an accountant, some by an administrator, some by someone whom they've hired to enter data … It depends what part of the program I'm writing for; what particular dialogue I'm working with. So basically I depend on my analysts to answer those questions.

Another strategy Amanda uses is less direct but still effective: "I'll sometimes resort to support call logs to perhaps get a feel for who is using that area of the program and therefore the depth of their knowledge." Amanda's comments reinforce the complexity of her digital audiences, all of which have different needs, understandings of the program and of technology more generally, and understandings of accounting and accounting business practices.

When I asked the writers and their managers what typically prevents them from having contact with their readers, I was given a variety of reasons. Sandy, the manager of the technical communication department at Tax Soft, emphasized that privacy and time are the key reasons at her company:

> Probably the biggest reason is a tradition of respecting our customers' privacy and their time. We limit all contact (even sales calls) to those who have raised their hands (e.g., if they raised an issue about doc on a survey, I can contact them with questions about that, but I am discouraged from "bugging" them with cold calls about our doc). Our users are very conscious of billable hours vs. non-billable ones. So … we have a tradition here (right or wrong) of pretty much staying out of their way.

Sandy said that often they "use other methods to determine what's on our users' minds (such as our online bulletin board system, their calls into Support or searches on our knowledge base, small focus groups, etc.)."

Carrie, also from Tax Soft, added that "writers are not subject-matter experts in our company, and, as such, it would not be appropriate to step into that relationship with our users." She said that others in the organization—

e.g., support, sales, customer service, and consulting staff—"have the relevant background in tax, accounting, and software development to manage those relationships with our users." Amanda, from my other case at Tax Soft, acknowledged that most of her information about her readers comes from the analysts, "who are the ones that have contact with the users" and who are supposed to "give us the information we need." She acknowledged, however, that even these individuals sometimes use alternative methods to obtain customer input: "They get feedback via phone, email, and bulletin board from 'product partners'—accountants who test the products and say what they need."

At Secure Net, there were additional reasons given for the writers not having direct contact with users. Susan attributes it to it not being part of the writers' job. Her supervisor, Char, said it's simply not feasible:

> [Our] customers/users are so widespread (worldwide) that it isn't feasible for us to travel to customer sites. Each network where our products are used is also so different … Generally even our engineers here don't meet with customers … For the most part, they also rely on sales and support engineers to funnel back any feedback or issues they cannot solve themselves.

Char also mentioned alternative information sources, including "bugs that the Support Center or the engineers file." She added, "We've also asked the Training Department and the Support Center to let us know when they see trends in customer questions." In the absence of that, she said, "we just do the best we can."

In contrast to the writers at Tax Soft and Secure Net, Barbara generally has access to readers, primarily because of her consulting role. She stressed that knowing the audience is one of her first concerns when she starts a project:

> One of my first concerns about an audience is that no one knows who it is. That's an impossible situation to be in. We need to get somebody at the client, a stakeholder, to agree who the audiences are. We're not going to make it up ourselves, so if they didn't have it at first, we need to work with them to develop a process to get one, to define who the audiences are.

Once the client identifies the audience, Barbara then solicits information directly from that audience. For example, she described talking to "people who may represent different job roles or use different parts of what we're writing about and ask questions about how they get the job done and what their background is." She also described a process her company uses for Web projects:

If a company comes to us with a huge Web site that's grown unwieldy and wants to redesign it … we interview representatives of the audiences who will be most important in using the site and learn what they want to look up and do with the information on the site and then we design a new structure for the site … So in this case, yes, absolutely, it is user driven.

According to Barbara, interaction with both users and clients is central to all these projects.

Obtaining and responding to reader feedback

Finally, since direct interactions with readers is often impossible, the writers identified another valuable heuristic for learning about readers: reader feedback, or responses to the product or documentation. The digital environment gives writers more effective mechanisms than ever for obtaining this feedback. It also helps writers interact with and respond to readers: they can even respond immediately to readers' needs. And, of course, writers can use reader feedback both to enhance their understanding of readers and to improve documents.

The writers from both Tax Soft and Secure Net discussed various tools for obtaining reader feedback. At Tax Soft, both writers mentioned a tool called Bugzilla that is used frequently in development environments, and that allows customers to report problems. Julie pointed out that, "It tracks all of these issues, gives them numbers, and allows people to comment on them." Kate noted how employees of the company also use it:

People file bugs, not just users, but our sales engineers, our customer support, and then our engineers themselves and product management. So if they're having trouble doing something and they didn't find it in the documentation, they usually file a bug (it's an online software product where they basically report a problem). And we get an email every time someone files a bug, so you see what it is, and we wonder if it could be solved if we documented that.

Kate described how the reports can lead to new or revised documentation. Her comments suggest that such tools provide another mechanism for learning about and addressing the needs of users:

So, we also write documentation to fix bugs. When we're delivering out deliverables for a release, we also work on closing out bugs, so a lot of times if it's a specific thing that's missing in the documentation or if it's something someone wants us to add, we definitely want to address those before delivering our final product.

Tools like Bugzilla also support another change that the digital environment is bringing about, which is that readers potentially become closer to each other and to the writer. Readers may even contribute to the development or evolution of a document; digital media can facilitate interactions and even collaborations between readers and authors.

At Tax Soft, the writers also learn about readers from the feedback they provide, in this case through call logs provided by User Support. They also make use of a bulletin board and chat room set up to facilitate problem solving. As Amanda noted:

> There's a bulletin board for users that's moderated by development. We can look at that too. We can take a peek at the users talking to each other. The whole thing is there for them to help each other with problems, so sometimes you can see how they're solving problems among themselves.

The feedback from the bulletin board is less direct in that the writers have to monitor it for issues and problems. Since the exchanges are usually between users, the writers learn from how the users discuss and solve their problems. This is also true of the chat room, which Carrie described in this way:

> We also have an internal chat room type thing where users can talk to each other unmoderated, and we can read these ... So if the users are being very frank about a feature or lack thereof, that's a very good indication of where to put our effort.

Carrie pointed to another strategy of obtaining information directly from the support staff:

> there's another source, which is hearing things through support—what support is dealing with, what specific types of users are struggling with, frustrated with, can't find. That helps inform which topics I need to beef up. Sometimes I get clues from seeing what the training department is doing too. ... And because training is a subset of doc, it lets me see what topics they're presenting to users in the space of a three-hour class. That tells me what's important.

Whatever its source, reader feedback is another heuristic writers use to obtain information about and direct feedback from their audience. It provides yet another perspective on and source of information about audience.

Digital literacy has also enhanced writers' ability to respond quickly and easily to the needs and concerns of their readers. Digital documents are much more fluid and dynamic—they can be edited, added to, and even replaced simply in the time it takes a writer to input changes or upload a new document (Bernhardt, 1993, pp. 172–173). Gone are the days of having to wait for the next product release or print run. Also, inputting changes electronically is much less expensive than printing a supplement or reprinting an entire document.

The writers in this study are enthusiastic about this ability to respond to users and update documents so easily. As Amanda said, "It's a big deal. It's pretty exciting to be able to go in, abracadabra, and correct information." She also enjoys not having to wait for a new release: "We don't have to wait for the next release date or patch or anything like that. We can update it just like that." She added that the ability to update quickly is the main reason her company is considering putting all of its help on the Web: "We're also looking at the option of putting all of our online help on the Web rather than [having it] hard coded so that we can update anything at a moment's notice." Amanda concluded by noting the following:

> For the guides, the updating is not every day, but sometimes someone will find an error in there and we can fix that. It's not a constant everyday kind of thing. And there are changes in the program ... It used to be a much bigger deal to get those things updated. It's simplified in some respects. We like it better because we hate it when our information is out of date.

Information Writers Need About Audiences

My case studies, along with my consideration of other scholarship in the field, also revealed that writers need and want to know the following toward their goal of achieving a more nuanced and contextualized understanding of their audiences:

- how readers will read and interact with their documents;
- how and in what contexts readers will use their documents;
- hhat expectations readers will bring to their digital documents.

How Readers Will Read and Interact with Documents

The writers in all my cases expressed a concern with how their readers would interact with and read their digital documents. They mentioned several features of digital documents that impact how readers use them. Susan, for example, at Secure Net, likes the "many ways in which users can use digital media." Her colleague, Kate, noted the ways in which users can jump around in digital documents versus the linear approach to reading reinforced by print. As a result, Susan said, "We have to be sensitive to the different ways in which audiences are using our documentation and try to anticipate in advance." Barbara also captured a sense of these features:

> Well, definitely there's no linear approach to using information when you can put it in a digital format. There's no linear way to organize it. There's still linear use because people will hop from thing to thing to

thing looking for what they need. You can imagine multiple branches through it, and they're not using a TOC and index.

Barbara also emphasized the importance of search in such cases, "because that's the one that cuts through all of the other ways to organize if you design for good searching."

These comments reinforce observations in recent scholarship on how the features of digital documents can make the processes of using and reading them different and potentially more complex for audience members. As Bazerman and Rogers (2008, p. 172) and Bernhardt (1993, p. 173) argue, we may need to develop a fuller understanding of how readers may approach and interact with digital documents. In particular, we may need to develop new skills for writing and reading digital texts and for selecting from all of the available information in them.

As early as 1993, Bernhardt addressed the need to consider how readers interact with digital text (p. 151). Several of his observations about such texts are especially useful when considering instructional documents, for example, how readers often are engaged in other actions as they read text on a screen and how reading can become "a second-level activity, resorted to when the higher-level task activity hits a snag" (p. 153). It becomes, in essence, "situationally integrated with other activities" (p. 153). Readers, in these cases, become "doers or seekers" and reading becomes something that, according to Bernhardt, "is driven by a pragmatic situation" (p. 153). Johnson also addresses how documentation can even draw a reader's attention away from the activity at hand (1998, p. 146).

Because of these possibilities, care needs to taken in writing digital documents so that information is easily accessible to readers and reading itself does not become intrusive. Barbara, from my case study at TC Consult, said that it's important, therefore, to minimize the work readers must do:

> I guess the things we wrote for this product—rewriting the onscreen and full help—in both cases it was making it so people didn't have to read very much to do their job … In our online help systems we try to make it easy for people to navigate from topic to topic to get what they're looking for.

She added, "We come up with ways to provide instruction that don't require reading. In this case, some of the recommendations made things much more intuitive to the user." She also mentioned pictures and examples as two effective ways to minimize text: "Sometimes showing how to do something by example is better than just telling what the rule is. And you can choose examples that appeal to particular audiences so that they can identify with the information."

Numerous scholars have also addressed how readers may interact with digital texts and the implications of this for writing such texts. Bernhardt, for example, addresses how readers of digital texts often interact physically with the text: "Readers become participants, control outcomes, and shape the text itself" (1993, p. 154). He adds, "Screen readers are actively engaged with screen text, as they key in information, or capture text from one file and move it somewhere else, or annotate or add to existing information in a file" (p. 156). He also mentions readers having to make constant decisions about where to go and what to do, all contributing to unique readings of a text (p. 156).

Nelson talks about how readers' choices in regard to "*when* and *if*" they read something blurs the boundaries between authoring and reading, allowing readers to become more like authors (2008, p. 440). She notes how "Bolter's and Landow's argument is that the nonlinear nature of hypertext empowers the reader, whose choices create a unique text" (p. 440); she adds how this possibility creates the opportunity for enhanced reading and learning but also disorientation (p. 440). Finally, Wysocki, addressing similar issues, talks about the added responsibility placed on readers for constructing meaning from digital texts (2008, pp. 606–607). She discusses how hypertext "encourages multiple, unclosed readings," and concludes that readers need new strategies for reading such texts (pp. 606–607). This latter point suggests the value of writers thinking about the strategies their readers bring to such texts.

The potential for collaboration and even coauthoring that these scholars describe is a significant change for authors of digital texts, particularly as they think about their audiences. Writing has, and is still becoming, more social, collaborative, and intertextual, and it both invites and enables the active participation of the audience. The potential of the latter is much greater with digital documents. Audience members can become closer to the writer and can even become documentation collaborators. Wysocki points to the potentially collaborative nature of some digital texts, noting that "applications like blogs and flickr encourage readers to see writing not as individual effort or even finalized but as intertextual and social, always collaborative to some degree and ongoing" (p. 607). Beaufort similarly talks about how readers of hypertext may become coauthors with writers and notes how this potential "presents additional organizational possibilities and problems for writers" (2008, p. 225). While the writers from my case studies did not address these possibilities for collaboration explicitly, such potential certainly suggests a productive focus for future research.

How and in What Contexts Readers Will Use Documents

To target users more precisely with their digital documents, writers also need to grasp the specific uses readers have for their documents as well as the contexts in which those uses will occur. The writers from my cases were all concerned with their specific readers, the contexts in which their readers work, and the particular tasks they need to perform. Their comments suggest a fine tuning and targeting that need to be based on specific information, not on abstractions or assumptions. In other words, there needs to be a shift from developing documentation based on what writers think their readers need, to developing it based on how those readers will actually use the information to complete a task.

The writers I interviewed provided several examples of this need. At Secure Net, for example, usability testing provided both the writers and the developers with concrete information about users of their products and experiences those users were having. As Kate put it,

> I think it definitely brought to light the fact that our product wasn't necessarily intuitive to users, and I think it also kind of showed how sometimes developers work on separate pieces of a product but they don't always see how it fits together. And that's one of the things we saw after the first usability study was that ... just because it made sense to them [the developers], didn't necessarily mean it made sense to anybody else.

Kate added that it was "the first time we were getting real feedback." She said the goal was to improve their online help "so that it is more useful and helpful to users." To do that, she said, "we really looked at how it was organized and asked a lot of questions about how our users use it." She concluded, "I think that at some point in both products we sat down and wrote the guides in a way that followed along with how the user uses the product." Her colleague Susan added, "I have to be able to teach the reader but also within the context of how they're using the software."

At Tax Soft, both writers also expressed a concern with connecting tasks with readers and then targeting the documentation accordingly. Commenting on their process for this, Amanda said, "We've started thinking a lot more task-based. Who is doing a particular task because there are about a million tasks that can be performed using our software." Carrie talked about reconfiguring documentation so that readers can more easily obtain what they need. She described a shift from writing documentation that is comprehensive, to writing different documents for different readers:

> So what started out as an effort to make sure we covered all the bases is now more an effort at how to get started using the product aimed at decision makers who would be purchasing or setting up the product. That's a different audience from the 1.0 version of the getting started guide. It's slimmed down and more targeted toward the things you would need to do to take a product out of the box and configure it as fitting for your firm. The other day-to-day type stuff—data entry and what not—is [now] in the walk-throughs, and no one needs to read those unless they do those things in the firm.

Finally, Barbara, from TC Consult, described the process she and her coworkers use to obtain the information that's needed to tailor documents:

> If we don't have anything written already by someone else then we need to talk to people who may represent different job roles or who may use different parts of what we're studying or writing about and ask questions about how they get the job done and what their background is and what they do and don't like about the current thing, whatever it is.

Where and how readers would be using their documents was on the minds of all of the writers I interviewed.

Scholars' recommendations have been consistent with such contextualized views of audience. For example, Faber and Johnson-Eilola emphasize in their work the importance of "understanding users in real contexts" (2002, p. 139). They argue that technical communicators should engage more in actual knowledge work, and they advocate understanding users' needs with the aim of "constructing creative solutions for users" (p. 139). Elsewhere they discuss how technical communicators especially value in themselves their "ability to design strategies for addressing specific situations for particular users" (2003, p. 229).

Johnson-Eilola also argues that users' true contexts are often invisible and, as a result, not sufficiently addressed (1996, pp. 246–247). He warns that users' tasks can become fragmented and decontextualized when we fail to consider the broader contexts and purposes of their work (p. 250). What technical communicators need to do, according to Johnson-Eilola, is produce documentation that is more attuned to users' needs (p. 259). He cautions that we oversimplify all of this with treatments of straightforward audience analysis when it really entails much more (p. 260). While these challenges cannot be addressed easily, the strategies and heuristics that the writers from all of my cases discussed at least offer mechanisms for accomplishing this.

Johnson similarly advocates adopting a user-centered approach to documentation, which he defines as "a thorough form of audience analysis that is aimed at designing documentation that fits what a user *actually* does, not necessarily what we *think* he or she should do" (1998, p. 136). This approach "envisions the user as situated in a particular time and place: the user is not using the documentation to learn software abstractly, but rather is learning the computer application for a specific purpose" (p. 129). The focus, then, is on the tasks and actions readers perform within their particular work contexts, which is precisely the focus that the writers from my cases were adopting (p. 131). Johnson also addresses the challenges involved in "creating customized documentation for specific, localized contexts" (p. 148). In other words, doing so is a complex task that involves a good bit of effort on the part of the writers.

Finally, other scholars reinforce the importance of understanding the very specific needs and experiences of users within their particular work contexts. Mirel emphasizes complex problem solving as a significant component of audience analysis (1992; 1998; 2002; 2004). She stresses repeatedly, and with ample empirical support, the importance of considering work-in-context and the decision making and problem solving that accompanies it. Borland (2002) captures this as well, suggesting a shift in the needs of users and what technical communicators should be doing to address those needs:

> A new "documentation" can emerge, a documentation that communicates domain information and strategies for solving complex problems. Technical communicators no longer concentrate on form and content for new computer or program users, but on domain problems and more particularly on complex tasks in those domains. ... The task then is to help users set up their problems and tasks. (p. 193)

All writers in my cases are concerned with the more targeted approaches that these scholars describe. They also believe that such approaches can result in improved documentation. For example, Julie, from Secure Net, described improvements that have benefited both the customer and her company:

> Prior to 4.0, our sales engineers really didn't want to show the customers the documentation because it was so awful ... It was so ungainly that they didn't want to point the users to it unless they knew very specifically themselves where the information was. After we did the whole conversion, hearing from our product manager, he was really proud of the documentation, and he said, "you know, before this the sales guides didn't want to show the documentation to the users, but now I think we should market this. I think we should have a presentation that shows the documentation to the sales guides".

Carrie, from Tax Soft, explained how their documentation has become a point of pride for her company:

> If the user is satisfied with it, that's what matters ... if they have to solve a problem, we've done our job if they can solve it in the least amount of time possible without relying on support ... So I like to think that that effort spent making the information findable pays off for the user. And we have actually received good marks before on the docs, which is astonishing because journals that review products usually never mention docs. So, a shameless plug.

Julie's and Carrie's comments suggest that such achievements also can help technical communicators demonstrate their value to their organizations.

Expectations Readers Will Bring to Documents

It is clear from my findings that digital media have improved the delivery of information to users and have increased access to that information. Such changes also can lead to changes in the expectations that readers bring to digital documents. Writers need to understand the expectations their readers bring to texts, and then plan for and try to meet them—or, in some cases, consider ways to change them. Barbara addressed how such expectations have become important in her work at TC Consult:

> It's more up-to-date on the Web—and that's perhaps one of the biggest changes with digital for the user. They'd like to think they can find the most information there. That's often part of our studies—how frequently they'd like to see it updated, how up-to-date they'd like to see it ... Companies like to see that so they can match it.

Barbara also sees the potential ramifications for writers, and for companies, if they fail to meet audience expectations. If users expect information to be up-to-date and it isn't, for example, they may become frustrated. All of this, I would argue, suggests yet another layer of understanding that writers need to acquire in relation to their digital audiences.

One consideration is that user expectations and preferences also can run the other way. For example, readers might miss and prefer using print manuals, which means that writers may have to help readers with the transition from print to digital media. Amanda suggested challenges that companies may face—and that her company, Tax Soft, is facing—as they move to digital documents:

> The only other thing about it becoming digital is that I think it raises more questions for us now than it answers. There are so many more things that I think we'd like to do, and can do, that can make things better for the users—make it more accurate, help us to provide more help with less effort ... We're trying to avoid the number of things they have to print out and make things more accessible more quickly. On the other hand, people like to print out, so we don't want to go too far that way either. I think we're working on training our users to use help differently instead of getting that big giant PDF or hard copy guide that's dead the moment it hits the table or comes off the press. We're training them to become more savvy technically—getting their program updates and their help online.

Depending on the product and its documentation, this transition for readers to digital documentation may be gradual, which again underscores the importance of writers understanding the expectations of their audiences. Writers should know not only what information readers will need, but also how readers are likely to respond to it. Determining reader preferences and expectations can help writers decide how best to deliver the information.

Cultivating a Contextualized Understanding of Audience

As my five case studies reveal, writers rely on a variety of heuristics and strategies to learn about and address their digital audiences in specific, situational, and contextual ways. Their actions and approaches also suggest, conversely, that ignoring audience, or oversimplifying approaches to audience—because writers think audiences of digital texts are too amorphous—simply will not work. In this final section, I explore what practitioners and scholars can do to embrace, research, and apply the perspectives on audiences explored in this chapter to their own practice in this new age of digital literacy.

Embracing Perspectives on, and Characteristics of, Audiences

The writers who were part of my cases, as well as scholars in the field, have shown us how digital writing is increasingly social, collaborative, dynamic, and fluid. These characteristics have significant implications for thinking about the audiences of digital documents. They have implications, for example, for how audiences perceive the documents, how they read and interact with them, how they use them, and what expectations they bring to them. Audiences, as we have seen, can even play an active role in the creation and revision of such documents. All of these are factors that writers benefit from thinking through during every stage of composing, but especially during early analysis of their audiences.

Embracing the implications of digital literacy for the notion of audience, more generally, as well as the characteristics of digital audiences, more specifically, means acknowledging that digital audiences are complex. It also means understanding that the processes writers should use to understand and address their digital audiences must be similarly complex. Abstractions and generalizations simply are not sufficient for addressing our audiences effectively in digital environments. What writers need, instead, is a full, accurate—and contextualized—understanding of their audiences. One way to acquire this, which was addressed by all writers from my cases, is to interact directly with members of our audiences.

I have addressed the value of interacting with audiences in previous work (Blakeslee, 2001), as has Spilka (1990). I show how scientists rely heavily on interactions with members of their audiences as they formulate and present claims and draft their scientific articles. Although my study was not situated in a digital environment, this work illustrates the value of interaction in developing rich conceptions of audience. Similarly, Spilka talks about using interaction as a tool for fulfilling rhetorical goals even prior to the process of drafting documentation; interactions can facilitate informing, persuading, and instructing readers, and also obtaining audience adherence by helping readers feel good about a document, even before anything is written (pp. 58–59). These works reinforce interaction as an effective strategy for both understanding and addressing audiences.

The findings from my cases suggest that interaction remains an important heuristic for understanding digital audiences. When interacting with readers is not possible, writers should seek to obtain as much information as they can from whatever other sources they have available to them. For the writers in my study, the most common source of information related to readers was usually other individuals in their organizations—e.g., product managers for the writers at Secure Net and analysts for the writers at Tax Soft. Many of these individuals, in turn, have methodical and reliable processes for collecting and analyzing user data. Although not always perfect—these groups can be subject to biases that can influence how they collect and analyze their data—these sources at least can give writers foundational information on which they can build. Writers, like those from my cases, can rely as well on a variety of other creative means for learning about their readers, such as trade magazines, Web sites, conference proceedings, white papers, training materials, and so on.

As an example, Amanda, from Tax Soft, uses bulletin boards and call logs to obtain information about readers. Kate and Susan, from Secure Net, use spec sheets. Kate explained that this foundational knowledge can facilitate further efforts to learn about readers: "We get most of our information from those and then we ask questions of the developers. And occasionally we'll ask questions of sale engineers and product management as well since they have that direct line with how customers are using the product." She added, "When the developer writes a spec sheet, they'll add … the expected use cases." And Julie, also at Secure Net, mentioned white papers, marketing material, and training documents:

> We take marketing material, white papers, [and] just informational papers that the sales guides would develop … We also go to product training whenever we can and that provides just another layer of information. … The first training I went to, it was given by a sales engineer, and he had a lot of user anecdotes.

When interaction is possible, as it can be for Barbara at TC Consult, the outcomes can be that much richer. Heuristics, such as personas, can also lead writers to fuller and more contextualized conceptions of their readers.

Researching Audiences

Technical communicators also need to continue to conduct research on both writing and reading in digital environments. We need to pose questions that will help us develop understandings of how writing is composed for and presented in digital environments and how it functions in those environments, in addition to greater appreciation of the complexities of rhetorical contexts and needs of digital audiences. The field has begun to show some interest in this work. For example, in 2004, the Society for Technical Communication (STC) issued a request for proposals (RFP) on three pressing issues in the field, and one of these was "addressing mixed audiences." Also, at the Milwaukee Symposium in 2000, 18 representatives from both industry and academia (Mirel and Spilka, 2002) generated a useful list of research questions; many of these questions began to address concerns with digital audiences. In Appendix A, I categorize some pertinent questions, generated by that group, which offer productive starting points for future research on digital audiences. The categories include questions about users and their preferences, context and contextualization, media and the shift from print to digital, and multiple audiences, writing, and technology.

While the questions posed by the participants in the Milwaukee Symposium provide a valuable starting point, we can pose additional, even more specific, kinds of questions as we begin to explore how writers analyze and accommodate their digital audiences. Technical communicators have not, for example, researched systematically or thoroughly actual heuristics or "best practices" for audience accommodation in either print or digital realms. Instead, most of our research has focused on audience analysis. Valuable, as well, would be new research about digital literacy that considers both writers and readers in actual work contexts. Such studies, like the one reported in this chapter, can lead to a better understanding of what writers of digital documents already do to understand and address their audiences, as well as of how readers actually use and respond to these documents. And considering the latter can help writers identify which audience accommodation practices succeed and which do not, from the perspective of readers.

To begin addressing our research needs in relation to audience, I have generated my own set of questions that supports the more particular view of audience and the framework of problem solving and contextualization that the writers in my study addressed (see Appendix B). I base the categories on the same heuristics, strategies, and categories of knowledge generated by my findings. I begin and frame my list with two overarching questions:

- What are best practices for identifying and understanding digital audiences and best strategies for addressing them?
- How can and should writers of digital texts plan and design with audiences in mind?

Research focused on these questions, like the study reported in this chapter, will lead to a better understanding of what writers of digital documents already do, and can do, to understand and address their audiences. It can also test the effectiveness of writers' decisions by revealing how readers may use and respond to these documents.

Finally, technical communicators need, as well, to examine audience considerations in the development and use of new technologies and genres, such as Web 2.0, wikis, and blogs. To the extent that technical communication begins making use of such technologies and genres, we will need to develop different, more interactive conceptions of audience that account, for example, for how these technologies and genres may bring documentation into products themselves, make documentation more dynamic and customizable, and facilitate collaboration between writers and readers (see Albers, 2003). From all this research, we can move beyond speculation and guesswork and develop a more coherent, substantial, and comprehensive approach to thinking about and addressing digital audiences.

Applying What Our Research Reveals About Audiences

Finally, technical communication research is of little value unless we apply what we learn about digital audiences to our everyday practice. One potential outcome of research is that it may help us identify additional heuristics and strategies for understanding and addressing digital audiences. It may also provide guidance for using those heuristics and strategies in different situations and settings.

What the literature and my findings suggest right now is that digital audiences have very specific needs and that they function in complex rhetorical contexts. Digital readers are individuals who perform complex tasks in technologically rich settings. They need sufficient support from our documentation to perform those tasks successfully. In turn, we need to determine how best to provide this support, which entails acquiring an understanding of their tasks, of the situations and environments in which they perform them, of the contingencies they may encounter, and so on. Such analysis will help us develop a contextualized understanding of our digital audiences, and then we can make use of that understanding as we develop documentation. We also need to take advantage of the features of digital media that facilitate addressing audiences in much more nuanced and sophisticated ways.

Audience in this new age of digital literacy is not something anyone can simplify or treat only as an abstraction. Digital audiences are complex, requiring processes of analysis and accommodation that embrace and take full account of this complexity. The case studies reported in this chapter provide just a glimpse at that complexity and at strategies writers are using to comprehend and address it. The field needs to continue expanding its perspectives on digital audience by pursuing work that sheds additional light on its complexity.

Acknowledgments

I would like to thank Rachel Spilka for her careful readings of and thoughtful responses to my chapter. Her insights were extremely helpful as I wrote and revised the chapter. I would also like to thank all of my research participants for the time they devoted to the project and for their interest in it. I learned a great deal from the experiences they all shared. Finally, I would like to thank my three practitioner reviewers for their close readings of the manuscript and their insightful and valuable feedback.

Notes

1 My research received human subjects approval from the IRB at my home institution as well as approval from management at each of the three companies.
2 All company and participant names are pseudonyms; also, all quotations that I present from case study participants were personal communications that I either heard during in-person interviews or received from participant emails addressed directly to me during this study.
3 I define heuristic in this chapter as a mechanism or approach that aids learning or problem solving in relation to one's audiences
4 All of these questions are from Mirel, B., & R. Spilka (Eds.) (2002). Appendix: Proposed research agenda for technical communication. *Reshaping technical communication: New directions and challenges for the 21st century* (pp. 197–201). Mahwah, NJ: Lawrence Erlbaum.

References

Albers, M. (2003). Multidimensional audience analysis for dynamic information. *Journal of Technical Writing and Communication, 33*, 263–279.

Bazerman, C., & Rogers, P. (2008). Writing and secular knowledge within modern European institutions. In C. Bazerman (Ed.), *Handbook of research on writing: History, society, school, individual, text* (pp. 157–175). Mahwah, NJ: Lawrence Erlbaum.

Beaufort, A. (2008). Writing in the professions. In C. Bazerman (Ed.), *Handbook of research on writing: History, society, school, individual, text* (pp. 221–235). Mahwah, NJ: Lawrence Erlbaum.

Bernhardt, S. A. (1993). The shape of text to come: The texture of print on screens. *College Composition and Communication, 44*, 151–175.

Blakeslee, A. M. (2001). *Interacting with audiences: Social influences on the production of scientific writing.* Mahwah, NJ: Lawrence Erlbaum.

Borland, R. (2002). Tales of brave Ulysses. In B. Mirel & R. Spilka (Eds.), *Reshaping technical communication: New directions and challenges for the 21st century* (pp. 189–195). Mahwah, NJ: Lawrence Erlbaum.

Faber, B., & Johnson-Eilola, J. (2002). Migrations: Strategic thinking about the future(s) of technical communication. In B. Mirel & R. Spilka (Eds.), *Reshaping technical communication: New directions and challenges for the 21st century* (pp. 135–163). Mahwah, NJ: Lawrence Erlbaum.

Johnson, R. R. (1998). *User-centered technology: A rhetorical theory for computers and other mundane artifacts.* Albany, NY: State University of New York Press.

Johnson-Eilola, J. (1996). Relocating the value of work: Technical communication in a post-industrial age. *Technical Communication Quarterly, 5*, 245–270.

Kitalong, K. S. (2004). Who are the users? Media representations as audience-analysis teaching tools. In T. Bridgeford, K. S. Kitalong, & D. Selfe (Eds.), *Innovative approaches to teaching technical communication* (pp. 168–182). Logan, UT: Utah State University Press.

Mirel, B. (1992). Analyzing audiences for software manuals: A survey of instructional needs for "real world tasks." *Technical Communication Quarterly, 1*, 13–38.

——. (1998). "Applied constructivism" for user documentation: Alternatives to conventional task orientation. *Journal of Business and Technical Communication, 12*, 7–49.

——. (2002). Advancing a vision of usability. In B. Mirel & R. Spilka (Eds.), *Reshaping technical communication: New directions and challenges for the 21st century* (pp. 165–187). Mahwah, NJ: Lawrence Erlbaum.

——. (2004). *Interaction design for complex problem solving: Developing useful and usable software.* Boston, MA: Elsevier.

Mirel, B., & Spilka, R. (Eds.) (2002). *Reshaping technical communication: New directions and challenges for the 21st century.* Mahwah, NJ: Lawrence Erlbaum.

Nelson, N. (2008). The reading-writing nexus in discourse research. In C. Bazerman (Ed.), *Handbook of research on writing: History, society, school, individual, text* (pp. 435–450). Mahwah, NJ: Lawrence Erlbaum.

Porter, J. E. (1998). *Rhetorical ethics and internetworked writing.* Westport, CT: Ablex.

Spilka, R. (1990). Orality and literacy in the workplace: Process- and text-based strategies for multiple-audience adaptation. *Journal of Business and Technical Communication, 4*, 44–67.

Wysocki, A. F. (2008). Seeing the screen: Research into visual and digital writing practices. In C. Bazerman (Ed.), *Handbook of research on writing: History, society, school, individual, text* (pp. 599–611). Mahwah, NJ: Lawrence Erlbaum.

Appendix A

Research Questions Pertaining to Audience from the 2000 Milwaukee Symposium:

Starting Points for Research on Audience[4]

Questions about Users and Their Preferences

- Who is online? What do they use? (p. 199)
- How does the difference between initial learning, intermediate learning, advanced learning, and reference affect the choice of help systems and media of delivery? (p. 199)
- How do people search? (p. 200)
- How do people choose? (p. 200)
- What are strategies for facilitating experiences online? (p. 201)

Questions Pertaining to Context and Contextualization

- How do you determine if someone needs to know information and who needs to know it? (p. 199)
- What do people do in the context of where they're working? What are work flows of various professions? What are some patterns within subject matter domains? (p. 199)
- Which media (text, graphics, video, animation, audio, multimedia) best fit which audience segments (age, gender, culture, experience) in which task domains with which product categories? (p. 199)
- Which help systems and mechanisms of technical communication (paper, Help, CBT, demonstrations, assistants, wizards, Internet support sites, interfaces) best fit which audience segments in which task domains with what product categories? (p. 199)
- How do you instructionally support online decision making? (p. 200)
- How do you help people search complex arrays so that they can make good decisions? (p. 200)
- How should data be designed to support complex retrieval and problem solving? (p. 200)

Questions about the Media and about Print-Digital

- Which media (text, graphics, video, animation, audio, multimedia) best fit which audience segments (age, gender, culture, experience) in which task domains with which product categories? (p. 199) [this question appears in the context category as well]
- What is the best way to integrate multimedia and improve the aesthetic and cognitive experience of users? (p. 200)
- What are problems in applying paper-based design criteria for online products? (p. 200)

Questions about Multiple Audiences, Writing, and Technology

- What is best for a multiple audience? How can something be used broadly by different specific audiences? (p. 200)
- How can you apply principles of minimalism effectively to new contexts? (p. 201)
- What is the value of an interface? What makes a difference to this value? (p. 201)
- What has to be done to make communication more accessible to include more groups? Do design choices make a difference? (p. 201)

Appendix B

Additional Research Questions Pertaining to Audiences of Digital Documents

Overarching Questions

- What are best practices for identifying and understanding digital audiences and best strategies for addressing them?
- How can and should writers of digital texts plan and design with audiences in mind?

Questions about Targeting Specific Users and Situations

- How can writers use technology to target specific readers and/or to address particular uses of a product?
- How are writers currently using technology to target readers?
- How do readers approach and respond to documents that are targeted at them specifically, or that are written with their specific uses of a product in mind?
- How effective and successful are documents that are tailored to and targeted at specific readers?
- How are readers using digital documents more generally? To what extent are they individualizing and structuring them for their own purposes?
- How are digital media and genres being used by technical communicators to accommodate the different learning styles and preferences of readers?
- In what ways is layering being used to accommodate different skill levels and uses that readers have and bring to digital documents?

Questions about Personas

- How do writers develop personas? What information do writers use to develop them, and how do they acquire that information? What are effective strategies for doing this?
- In what ways do/can writers use personas?
- What kinds of contextual information about readers do personas provide? What do personas reveal about the tasks readers need to perform and the contexts in which they will perform them?
- How effective are personas for capturing characteristics of readers and their actual work contexts? Is the contextual information sufficient?
- How effective are personas in helping writers understand their readers generally? Are they sufficient? In what ways are they limited?

Questions about Interacting with Users

- How can technical communicators overcome organizational and project constraints that prevent them from interacting with actual readers?
- When interaction is not possible, what other strategies can and do technical communicators use to acquire information about their readers?

Which of these strategies are most effective, and/or what factors can influence their effectiveness?

- What are the implications for writers of not having interactions with actual readers?
- Do writers make compromises when they are not able to interact with their readers? What are those?
- How do writers develop an understanding of readers when they are not able to interact with them?
- How do writers conceptualize readers when they do/do not interact with them? Or, more generally, how do writers learn and think about their audiences?
- How do writers make use of audience information in developing digital documents?

Questions about Obtaining and Responding to User Feedback

- In what ways is technology facilitating reader feedback?
- What mechanisms/tools are now available for providing/obtaining feedback?
- How are writers making use of these mechanisms/tools? In other words, how are writers using the heuristic of reader feedback to obtain information about and input from their readers? How are they using it to learn about and understand their readers?
- In what ways are writers responding to reader feedback? What are they doing with it? How are they using it?
- How are documents changing as a result of reader feedback?
- In what ways is the digital environment facilitating the involvement of readers in the development of documentation?
- In what specific ways, and at what points, are readers contributing to the documentation development process?
- How has the ability to update and revise documents quickly and easily changed documentation for readers?

Questions about How Readers Read and Interact with Digital Documents

- In what ways are readers using digital documents? How do they interact with digital documents?
- How is reading different with digital documents?
- What are the implications of a nonlinear format for the design of documents for readers?
- What are effective strategies for making information in nonlinear documents accessible to readers?
- What features of digital documents do readers prefer and for what reasons?
- How do readers read and select information in digital documents? How do they navigate through them? What kinds of strategies and navigational devices do they find most useful?

- How do readers integrate the reading of digital documents with other activities? What other activities do they perform while reading?
- What roles do readers take on while reading digital documents? What are their goals for reading and how do they achieve those?
- In what ways do readers interact physically with the text and how does this affect the reading process? In what ways are readers more active in reading digital documents?
- What challenges do readers face in reading digital documents?
- Is learning enhanced with digital documents? If so, in what ways?
- In what ways are the boundaries between reading and authoring blurred with digital documents?
- How are digital documents—and various digital genres and media—changing the nature and scope of writing? What are the implications of these changes for writers and readers?
- How are reading and writing more social and collaborative with digital documents?
- What are the implications for writers of readers becoming coauthors and/or collaborators on digital documents?

Questions about How and in What Contexts Readers Use Digital Documents (see previous category as well)

- How do/can writers learn about readers' contexts and uses of documents?
- How do/can writers obtain an understanding of readers' specific purposes in using particular documents?
- How can writers best acquire the specific information they need to target documents effectively to their readers? How do they learn about the very specific needs, experiences, and purposes of their readers?
- How can writers best take account of their readers' broader purposes and contexts? What has changed in regard to how readers use documents? What are the implications of these changes for writers?

Questions about the Expectations Readers Bring to Digital Documents

- In what ways have digital media changed how information is delivered to readers?
- How have digital media changed readers' access to information?
- What expectations do readers bring to digital documents?
- What do readers do when their expectations for digital documents are not met?
- How can writers learn what expectations readers are bringing to their documents?
- How can writers determine if their readers' preferences and expectations have been met?

9 Beyond Ethical Frames of Technical Relations

Digital Being in the Workplace World

Steven B. Katz and Vicki W. Rhodes

As a matter of ethical policy, a nonprofit corporation in the health industry publicly refers to its clients as "individuals with developmental challenges," and in external communications would never refer to them "handicapped" or "disabled people," which it considers to be a demeaning form of labeling. However, in internal email communication, these clients may be routinely referred to as "handicapped" or "disabled" for the sake of efficiency and expediency (the external phrases are much longer). Is this organization hypocritical? Does it violate its own ethical standards and those of society at large when in its internal communication it uses politically incorrect terminology? Or is it possible that there is a way of understanding these opposing positions of communication as appropriate and compatible, a way of ethically "framing" these digital situations?

Organizations seldom consider their relationship to technology as ethical frames of reference. Professionals often view and use technology to communicate as if it were value-free. How often do you hear about the many technological resources available at our fingertips? "Need an expert? Press a button. That's the Human Network Effect" (E-network, 2009). It's fast, easy, more efficient, and productive. Whether it is a quick and simple search on the Internet that yields hundreds of hits, instant news alerts on our smartphones, or networked data recording systems, we are perpetually linked to technology, information, and each other. But in the midst of this digital abundance, how often do you or your organization evaluate the way you think about, interact through, and exist with technological advances? This chapter aims to examine the ethics of digital communication, and to reveal facets of "technical relations" that may ultimately enable you to move beyond limited, compartmentalized, and even conflicting ethical perspectives in the work world, and to see them in ways that could actually improve every aspect of your business. To stay competitive, as well as avoid potential crises, organizations and the professionals within them must both acknowledge and actively engage in multiple ethical frames of technical relations.

The digital revolution is fundamentally changing the nature of the workplace, and indeed the world. But are current communication ethics theories and practices adequate for such a revolution? Although innovations in usability, information design, online social networking, and virtual reality are becoming common, technical communication has been slow to recognize the ethical frames inherent in the evolution of communication technologies. In this chapter, we attempt to identify these ethical frames, and how they define human–machine relations. What are these relations? How are they shifting in digital communication? What are some professional implications of the digital relationships of machines and the humans who increasingly depend on and exist alongside them in all walks of life? After briefly surveying ethical frames of technical relations, and examining through a case study the changing ethical interfaces of human-machine interactions in digital communication environments, we offer ways in which organizations can apply these frames for specific purposes. We conclude by suggesting a new ethical frame that can more fully reveal the complex, dynamic interrelations between humans and technologies, and help professional workplaces better adapt to them to improve business as well as the relationships that result.

Most treatments of ethics in technical communication approach the subject from the point of view of particular philosophers, such as Plato or Kant; different philosophical systems, such as Utilitarianism or the Ethics of Care; or specific ethical situations, such as the space shuttle explosions or the tobacco industry scams (e.g., see Dombrowski, 2000 for examples of these). All of these approaches are both valid and extremely valuable in studying human relations; however, they leave several dimensions of technical relations hidden, and so cannot fully account for the shaping of human values in the workplace world.

For the purpose of this chapter on digital communication and ethics, we will define ethical frames as a set of philosophical assumptions, ideological perceptions, and normative values underlying and/or guiding how people relate to and exist with technology. These ethical frames are not merely brought into the workplace by employers and employees, or the values of society, or the ideologies of culture. Rather, these frames are also the result of the interaction of humans, machines, social structures, and ideologies created in and through specific technological and managerial procedures and channels. In delineating the ethical frames of technical relations that define human–machine interactions, we therefore recognize the socially dynamic and constructed nature of ethics; indeed because we do, we hold that technology both instantiates and helps construct social and moral values.

In this chapter, we are not so much privileging technology, or decrying a new "technology determinism" that threatens to take over human life, as we are focusing in on the significant role we believe technology plays in social and cultural dynamics—particularly in the workplace. Winner (1999) contends that technical artifacts possess values, either extrinsic or intrinsic; but if they do not, technology is fundamental in shaping our interactions. As Ellul (1964) and Barrett (1978) cogently argued long ago, technology is not only machines, nor even simply techniques or procedures, but also "technics"—a complete, historical value system in and of itself that "distinguish the long-term processes of transformation from spectacular but fleeting technical innovations" (Stiegler, 1998, p. 21). Aside from the central role that technology plays in creating ethical frames, digital communication technology is the latest context for an emerging ethical frame that is profoundly affecting the workplace. Before revealing the new ethical frame, we examine the import of ethical frames in which technical relations are embedded and enacted, and through which people, procedures, media, and machines for all intents and purposes digitally become one and the same.

Six Ethical Frames of Technical Relations

In the workplace, as in philosophy, practices revolved around the notion of technology as a means, a tool, a machine, or a particular action to achieve an end, the accomplishment of a specific task, or the production of an object. But other frames exist that have not been brought to the surface or even fully delineated in ethical discussions. Starting with the assumption of means–ends relationships that have defined most thinking about technology, we can identify six "ethical frames of technical relations": 0)[1] technology as an illusory means and a false end (false frame); 1) technology as a tool—a means to an end (tool frame); 2) technology as both means and end (means–end frame); 3) technology as autonomous—not only its own end, but its own *raison d'être*, one that is seen to subsume other values and relations (autonomous frame); 4) technology as a mode of thinking (thought frame); and 5) technology as a mode of being (being frame). These ethical frames can be considered diachronic *and* synchronic: they grow from and enfold one another, and while the frames develop historically, they also overlap, encompass, subsume (but not supplant or replace) each other, and operate simultaneously (see Figure 9.1).

An important purpose of this chapter is to begin to unfold and define the boundaries of these different ethical frames "at work" in contemporary digital communication, and to delineate their effects in a study of uncertainty in the email exchanges of a nonprofit organization. The "real" sixth frame will be revealed at the end of this chapter, replacing the false frame.

False Frame

As Stiegler (1998) discusses,[2] the misunderstanding of technology arises from the supposed split between *techne* (art) and *episteme* (knowledge) begun by the ancient Greek philosopher Plato, and both propagated and modulated by his student, Aristotle. For Plato (1956), who believed that Ideal Forms existed outside the realm of physical reality and the senses, technology, like any material instrument or object, is not a valid way of knowing, and of little consequence in ascertaining Truth. In this extreme ethical position, technology does not facilitate the discovery of Knowledge[3]. Technology, including digital technology, is neither a valid means nor a noble end, but only produces the semblance of Knowledge. Plato believed that

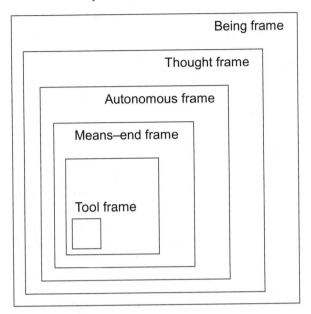

Figure 9.1 Unfolding ethical frames

the technology of writing itself was false (both as a means and an end): it does not lead to (or even accurately record) Knowledge, and is not itself new Knowledge, but only an imitation of Knowledge (actually, an imitation of an imitation of Knowledge). Contemporary constituents of this position might include skeptics of television, video games, or rock music, who believe these activities are not sources of redeeming values, but rather at best, simply worthless entertainment, and at worst, wasteful and even sinful physical indulgence.

Tool Frame

According to Stiegler (1998), this false distinction between *techne* and *episteme* also gives rise to the instrumental belief in technology as a tool, as a means to an end. For example in the *Nicomachean Ethics*, Aristotle allowed that *techne* is concerned with production, but that the "final cause" of production, the determination of the end, cannot be in the technology. Rather, the final cause of production resides ultimately in the producer who is necessarily human and not only uses technology to create, but also exercises judgment as the final arbiter of the object's end—its purpose.[4] Thus, in the tool frame, technology is a means to another end, any end.

Obviously, in this tool frame, communication ethics must focus primarily on how well the producer uses the tool (i.e., craftsmanship). For example, in technical communication, think of the purpose of instructions, or technical manuals, or online help menus; these tools operate as mechanisms and systems to help their users meet their work goals, and ultimately enable companies to achieve specific ends. How can we use digital communication to increase profits? Is the technology performing at maximum efficiency to satisfy demand? Can internal organization be technically improved to enhance the company's bottom line? In the tool frame, the end is taken as a given outside technology and not questioned in relation to it.

Means–End Frame

Some professionals and scholars regard technology not merely as a means, but also as an end. That is, technology can never only be a tool, but is also a producer, a determiner of ends. In the means–end frame of technical relations, both the means *and ends* are technological; that is, contra Aristotle (1984b), the technology itself (or its values), and not necessarily the human agent as in the tool frame, determines the ends as well as the means: technology itself appears to be "the final cause" (Stiegler, 1998). Thus, in this frame, the evaluation of the quality of the document, tool, mechanism, or process occurs in relation to the technology as the means and the end.

If the technology defines both the means and the end, the object of virtue becomes finding and maintaining the proper alignment between the means and end not only for purpose of production and profits (ends in themselves), but also for the purpose of meeting technical requirements of the technology. In this frame, then, the primary ethical issue is whether the technical end justifies the technical means (the question may or may not be examined of whether the end itself is justified beyond being technically advantageous, useful, or expedient). In the work world, questions in the means–end frame might take the form of: Can we streamline email correspondence as a way to make internal communication more efficient? Could we update the company Web site to generate and handle more online traffic?

Autonomous Frame

It is perhaps only one short step away from the means–end frame in which technology is or determines both the means and the end, to the autonomous frame, in which technology is not only a producer of its own means and ends, but also a producer of its own moral codes (productivity, speed, efficiency) In the autonomous frame, technology is perceived as a self-contained ethical entity. Societies whose economic goals are the accumulation of material things, wealth, and power, require and reinforce the complementary ethical values of productivity, speed, and efficiency as ends as well as means, and hence, the autonomy of technology in those societies (Habermas, 1970). The development of science as well as technology becomes the driving force of economic progress, which tautologically then drives further scientific and technological progress. People become subservient to the values and principles of the technology, which in turn further reinforce those technical values. Thus, as Ellul (1964) insists, technology becomes its own *raison d'être*—its reason for being.

In the autonomous frame, the values of technology—not always those that directly or even indirectly benefit humans—can become the values of the organization as a system. The object of virtue in the autonomous frame now becomes more than just finding and maintaining the proper alignment of the means and end for the purpose of production and profits (the means frame), or for the purpose of meeting the technical requirements of technology itself (the means–end frame); it also becomes a way to facilitate the primary value systems of the organization that have become technical.

Have you ever noticed how some systems or procedures at work—say, a time-tracking system, registration process, or evaluation procedure—are more adapted to themselves, more focused on their own efficiency and operation, than on the human being who is the ostensible object or user? In fact, much usability research, or what used to be called human factors engineering, can be considered an attempt to circumvent the almost self-perpetuating, self-referential, even solipsistic nature of technology and technological systems—to bring them back out into the human world, to make them "user friendly." The autonomous frame is seen most easily as a closed system, such as content management systems, which allows system-related communications, but restricts communication to specific and defined data permitted in the database; as with other "non-technical" values humans might consider important, in the autonomous frame, all other data is excluded as irrelevant. These questions therefore may emerge as moral imperatives in this ethical frame: Are managers, workers, and your organization as a whole implementing and following all technical procedures according to the machine's specifications or the system's values? What techniques or changes in organization, managers, or workers might facilitate the efficient functioning of the machine or the application of the procedures within your company? Do you have procedures or programs in your organization that are geared toward desired technological outcomes rather than how people must use them?

Thought Frame

Just as the autonomous frame can be understood to derive from the means–end frame, the thought frame can be understood to derive from the autonomous frame. In the ethical frame of technical relations as a mode of thought, the autonomous system of values based on means–ends relations becomes a form of strategic reasoning, a dominant rational mode of thought. For the early Habermas (1970), in industrial and post-industrial societies the value system of thinking and communicating as rational calculation replaces the "traditional values" of a society with technical values. He analyzes in depth the transformation of social and communication values, charting the symbolic values common in "traditional institutional frameworks" (such as those of religion) that are not so much supplemented as supplanted by the technical values of "purposive-rational frameworks."[5] So, for example, as an extension of the autonomous frame (means–ends relations as value system) into a rational mode of communication and thought, "technical rules" replace "social norms"; "context-free language" replaces "intersubjectively shared ordinary language"; "skills and qualifications" replace "role internalization"; "growth of production" replaces "individuation"; and "inefficacy" and "failure in reality" replace "punishment" (Habermas, 1970, p. 93).

For us, the thinking machine as model *par excellence* is the high-speed computer. Significantly named, *Fast Company* magazine features an article by Thompson (2006) about the invention of new memory devices and software that are literal, physical extensions of the rational mind into an external hard drive: autonomous technology—not only machines, but also faith and belief in technical values which together constitute technological systems—becomes the basis of human thought. While working on a document, we have all typed in words about whose spelling we are uncertain, hoping that the spell-check will recognize and either verify or correct them so that we can keep working as quickly as possible. The reliance on external software for mental work, while a valid topic, is not the issue here; rather, it is the underlying value system of autonomous technology that is absorbed into consciousness and alters the process of writing according to its own mechanics (many writers, including the authors of this chapter, now entirely draft and revise directly on the computer as a matter of course, learning and incorporating new technologies of doing so as they go along). The whole "process" (note the computer metaphor) of writing takes place in and through the machine, is changed by it, and the technology is valued because of it. So, too, thought through the auspices of technological invention (while writing this sentence, we are resisting the squiggly green insistence of our computers' grammar-checker that the last clause is a sentence fragment and needs to be corrected).

One example of the thought frame is evidenced in the information-processing model of communication—the way we think and talk about thinking and talking—in industry and science (see Katz, 2008; Mebust and Katz, 2008). Like thought in cognitive psychology generally, the information-processing model entails conceptualizing human communication in computer terms. At work, do you refer to people, things, and actions with words like information, function, connection, transmission, input, output, processing, short-term and long-term memory, and noise in the system? These terms and others like them stem from technological systems, yet in both the workplace and the everyday world, we have absorbed them as mental constructs of our own thought and communication—so much so that we can hardly think or talk without them. Technological diction like this reflects the faulty mode of risk communication in both government and corporate entities (see Katz and Miller, 1996; Katz, 2008). These mental constructs as technologies become closed technological systems of thought (as well as or opposed to closed technological systems of values in the autonomous frame). In light of this ethical frame of technical relations as a mode of thought, does your organization refer to people as having "hard-wired" propensities toward certain "skill sets?" Does your organization conceptualize or refer to communication as a transmission of information from sender to receiver? Does it regard emotional response in the workplace as noise in the system?

Being Frame

If autonomous technology as a value system and social standard can evoke rational calculation as a mode of thought, then rational calculation may precipitate another ethical frame of technical relations: technology as a mode of being. For Heidegger (1977), rational calculation becomes a modern form of consciousness, our way of relating to the world and to each other. "Modern technology," by which he means not only machines, but also thought itself, is also a way of ordering nature and our relation to and knowledge of it—"a way of revealing" (p. 12). Heidegger calls the technological way of knowing and being "Enframing." He maintains that it is not entrapment, but our way of encountering the world; he suggests, however, that there is a negative dimension of Enframing: it is a further extension of means–end relations, of strategic action that "challenges" and "puts to nature the unreasonable demand that it supply energy that can be extracted and stored as such" (p. 14). Heidegger believes that this technological ordering of nature and our knowledge of it, this demand, turns everything into what he calls a "standing-reserve" (p. 17). For our purposes, another way of putting it would be that all the other ethical frames of technical relations we have discussed, from tool frame to thought frame, lead to means-end relations as our primary way of *being* in the world.

It is obvious that much of professional communication has embraced Enframing as the basis of communication: the technical artifact or document is something standing in reserve, ready for use by technology, as technology. In this being frame, not only machines, but humans as well are Enframed, and considered a standing-reserve—not only for use by the organization, but also by the machines to which we must adapt. Enframing as a form of technical consciousness is common in organizational goals and structures, where people as well as things are "resources"—present as a standing-reserve, ready for use. Probably the most explicit example of this frame in the work world is the conveniently, if ambiguously, labeled office of "Human Resources"—the name denoting both the resources available to humans, and the humans available as resources to the company. Thus, as Heidegger (1977) notes, there are two dangers in Enframing. The first is that not only does it turn humans into objects (the result of other means–end relations),"but rather, exclusively as standing-reserve" (we will return to this later); and second, that within Enframing, while we think we rule over nature and control destiny through technology, our consciousness itself has become this particular kind of rational ordering that begins in means–end relations: "Where this ordering holds sway, it drives out every other possibility of revealing" (p. 27).

At work, people, as well as technology, are means to achieve strategic organizational ends, of course, but in this ethical frame of technical relations as being, these means are no longer simply tool, means–end, autonomous, or even thought frame, but our conscious existence in the world. So powerful is this particular ethical frame that we no longer recognize that we are in it. Evidence of this phenomenon abounds in the work world, where offices are labeled by position instead of by employee name, suggesting that personnel are temporary and can be replaced easily by others; or by employee benefits plans, as a facet of Human Resources, whose ultimate purpose cynically may be seen to provide a way for organizations to maintain a reserve of employees. In the technical form of consciousness, everything is a standing-reserve.

Not only is standing-reserve the perspective of the organization, but also of the employees, who see themselves as temporary, changeable, transient—and mobile. Employees view themselves, think of themselves, and live as resources, even outside of the organization. The digital and technical has become the personal (e.g., Blackberry devices, Facebook), and extend around the wired world. We exist everywhere with technology as a technology; we stand with resources as a reserve. This being frame may generate questions such as these: Do you take your laptop on picnics or to the beach so that you can work on vacation, or check emails every night before you go to bed? Do you wear a Bluetooth through the grocery store and during movies? Acknowledging the mundane, important, and practical reasons that inhere in many of our thoughts, decisions, and actions, this is the way we live today; it is our technical mode of being, in which all other ethical frames of technical relations exist, and to which they lead (see Table 9.1).

Our Digital Being

As we have discussed, Enframing is a technical form of consciousness. As an ethical frame of being in the world, it is not only natural to us, but also transparent and invisible. This is nowhere more literally apparent than in digital media. As a kind of consciousness, a contemporary mode of being, digital media is a simulation that has replaced "the real," and the virtual reality of media has become as real as, or more real for us than the tangible world (see Baudrillard, 1994) (one only has to think here of the ubiquity of television, Internet, video and virtual games, social networks, etc., to see this phenomena at work). Debord (1990; 1994) asserts that media not only represents and shapes, but also replaces and becomes our social and economic reality (media creates social structures, influences policies, makes money). He chastised the function of mass media that renders this reality a ubiquitous and powerful "spectacle." Insofar as digital media cloaks its

Table 9.1 Six ethical frames of technical relations

Ethical Frames	Short Descriptions	Possible Examples
0. False Frame	Technology as nothing valuable	Entertainment, indulgence
1. Tool Frame	Technology as a means	Calculator, hammer
2. Means-End Frame	Technology as both means and end	Web site for Internet sales
3. Autonomous Frame	Technology as value system	Content management systems
4. Thought Frame	Technology as rational calculation	Technical terminology applied universally
5. Being Frame	Technology as consciousness	Electronic devices, virtual networks as daily routines

ideology and construction in myths of transparency and objectivity (see Bolter and Gromala, 2003), those myths become a source of the medium's rhetorical power to define the contemporary digital technical frame that shapes human being.

As a development of the ethical frame of technical relations as being, digital being can be understood to encompass all the other frames as compartmentalized perspectives that reveal different views of ethical relations in technology (see Figure 9.2). In the being frame, all ethical frames exist as part of a larger dynamic, and are necessary for specific purposes within the being frame. The being frame affords equal attention to each of the other compartmentalized frames as a part of the whole.

In light of our discussion of Enframing, we can conceptualize how digital media converts objects into virtual objects that are the epitome of standing-reserve, or rather, into non-objects whose only existence is as standing-reserve. Digital being, like digital technology, can be considered an extension of Enframing, which cloaks the ethical frame of technical relations in a transparency that allows us to forget that much of our life and work exists as technics. Digital being has enabled us to forget that our values, our thinking, and our work are heavily defined by our technology, and that much of our life now exists outside our flesh, essentially in digital bodies. In the work world, professionals have become accustomed to spell-check and grammar-check systems that replace errors—automatically, if so enabled. Without technological assistance, employees, especially new ones, now more frequently struggle with writing and spelling, as our digital machines have literally replaced our "mental storage" of "information" (the model itself technologically conceived) with more rapid and efficient instruments in a rational system. Such instruments, like computers and PDAs, now harbor in their plastic-metal bodies knowledge that was once the non-automated property and responsibility of humans.

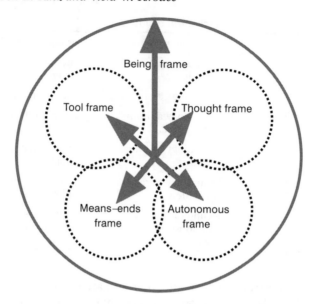

Figure 9.2 Digital being in the being frame

Digital Enframing leads to an increase in rational order, and thus the ethical frame of technical relations as literal being will only intensify. Already we are seeing not only a philosophical but also a physical merging of flesh and machine. In medicine we see the drive to develop artificial organs implanted within the body, and the quickening development of sophisticated prosthetics external to the body, not only to replace limbs or sustain life, but also increasingly to supplement and augment (both physically and aesthetically) the human body (e.g., see Smith and Morra, 2006). Digital "prosthetics" are now evolving beyond the medical realm as removable apparatuses that enhance technological existence. For example, we use Bluetooth devices on and off the job to link us continuously to our jobs and relations through a global satellite system. The physical converging of human and machine, which your business is participating in and perpetuating, is going on right now in artistic and scientific experiments, in our science fiction fantasies and our pharmacologies, and in our media and medical realities (see Cartwright, 1995; Lury, 1998; Hayles, 1999). The body is conceptually and physically becoming digital technology (see De Kerckhove, 1995; Benthien, 2002, especially pp. 221–234). Technologies, particularly digital technologies and the media environments they spawn, are seemingly penetrating every aspect of work and leisure. Our purpose here is not to critique digital media, nor to praise it. Instead, like Aristotle, we try to describe what it is. Whether we like it or not, digital communication has become an extension of ourselves, increasingly projecting our consciousness outward so that our image becomes the medium of our existence and the object of our gaze.

So pervasive and necessary are the uses of digital technology in the workplace, that organizations and the people in them can be understood to exist almost literally in the digital realm—not just in virtual worlds in which humans themselves are recreated as avatars, but also in the physical and work world where our social and business interactions are carried out via email, video, podcasts, smart phones, Web sites and webinars, social media, listservs, wikis, and blogs. To paraphrase Negroponte (1995), we are indeed "becoming digital." As an ever-expanding range of technologies continues to sweep over culture and into the organizations that constitute and support that culture, it is crucial that practitioners and scholars begin to understand and address the ethical dimensions and effects of the digital technologies upon which technical, organizational, and personal communication now depend. One way to do that is through the ethical frames of technical relations we have been describing—the tool, means–ends, autonomous, thought, and being frames—which are compartmentalized and hidden, but also integrated. When they are unpacked and made opaque, they can reveal different ethical dimensions of technical relations that also combine to more fully reflect our digital being. In the next section, we look specifically at one of the most widely used and integral forms of digital communication today: email.

Email Relations: Findings on the Framing of Ethics in the Workplace

Ethical frames of technical relations usually exist in the modern workplace as individual philosophies that govern both organizational and employee values and actions. A pilot study by Rhodes (2008) uncovers evidence, through an analysis of employees' emails, of various compartmentalized frames at work in a southeastern nonprofit organization. The findings in the pilot study provide us with a case that allows a tangible examination of ethical frames though examples in the digital work world.

In many work environments, as well as in our personal lives, email is replacing not only the telephone, but face-to-face (f2f) communication as well (see Wellman and Haythornthwaite, 2002). Devoid of f2f interaction, employees increasingly "meet" each other solely through digital interfaces as they maneuver through their work tasks and environments. They make judgments and decisions about others based on what they "see" on their computer screen, and so in essence, the employees become their emails. Many computer-mediated communication studies (e.g., Pratt, *et al.*, 1999) note the medium's limited bandwidth, or number of "communication channels." But while the medium may be lean in terms of bandwidth, and therefore not be the optimal choice for communication, in work environments, the use of email to communicate even to someone across the hall has more or less become established practice.

In the past, email, like other media, has been viewed as a tool, a neutral conduit for transmitting messages, both in academic and professional realms (e.g., see Nissembaum and Price, 2004). While most professionals in corporate America today likely will admit that digital communication inevitably conveys glimpses of individual personalities in the course of "transmission," many companies still operate within ethical frames that attempt to separate the person from the technology. The majority of studies on email continue to approach it as a tool for transferring information within the organization—as a means–end system for accomplishing technological work, accepting and adopting the value(s) of email itself as an autonomous system—instead of also as a projection and extension of self. Email thus represents a technical mode of being, encompassing both task-based purpose and personal expression in technological relations. Rhodes' study sought to capture a more comprehensive picture of employees' email relations through the application of communication theory and rhetorical analysis, which we will now present as a case study to explore ethical frames in digital communication.

Pilot Study Description

The pilot study, conducted by Rhodes (2008) at a nonprofit in the southeast United States,[6] sought to look holistically at digital relations by examining the email of 42 employees (183 emails in total) during a period of temporary change in the organization.[7] The study explored how employees sought information, expressed uncertainty, and "enacted uncertainty reduction techniques" through electronic communication for two months before and two months during the Executive Director's medical leave. This leave required that job responsibilities and organizational roles be temporarily restructured, causing significant situational uncertainty for the organization's employees.

The email data collected during the four-month period were coded first for source origination and, drawing from prior research by Miller and Jablin (1991) and Miller (1996), coded next for information-seeking tactics (indirect/disguising conversation, overt/direct, testing, and third party) and information types (appraisal, normative, referent, and social). Then the data were classified by parts of speech and grouped by themes that appear to suggest employee values in the diction. The modality, or level of certainty, of the individual words within those categories revealed employee attitudes and degrees of confidence. Latour and Woolgar (1986) offer a construct of five "statement types" that denote various levels of modality along a spectrum, which for the purposes of Rhodes' pilot study were adapted to analyze individual words used in email.

The organization Rhodes chose for the study is a nonprofit partnership of several entities that exchange information regularly as a necessary part of daily operations. Examining this conglomeration of organizations is fitting for our investigation of ethical frames in the digital workplace for two reasons: first, nonprofits are increasingly fulfilling moral and ethical roles in secular society; second, email is the preferred and primary method of communication and digital exchange in this organization as it is in many other workplaces. In this nonprofit, almost all communications with the Executive Director are channeled first through email; even if a f2f meeting has been arranged (usually via email), most exchanges are conducted via email in the interim between these official meetings.

Email as a Tool and an End

To explore the digital relations of employees who communicate predominantly via email, Rhodes' pilot study used an extended application of Uncertainty Reduction Theory (URT), a well-known communication theory introduced by Berger and Calabrese in 1975. Briefly, their theory asserts that "individuals in uncertain situations are likely to feel discomfort, and information-seeking is a viable solution to that discomfort" (Boyle, *et. al*, 2004, p. 157). And one mode for gathering such information, especially in today's work world, is email. Information technology has become a primary means of managing and reducing uncertainty in the workplace (Dewett and Jones, 2001), but ethics is seldom a consideration in these studies, and the ethics of technology even less so. In fact, URT is a prime example of traditional communication theory that perpetuates compartmentalized ethical frames (note its categories of information, mentioned previously), which, independently, fail to grasp the complete picture of technological being that is increasingly becoming our reality. According to perspectives in URT research, which reflect those in the workplace, operationally, a person can be separated from an email message (even when studying affective uncertainty) so that only the professional and task-related elements remain.

Employing URT principles, the pilot study unearthed communication patterns in employee emails such as the "type of tactics" used and the "type of information" sought. These findings indicate employees' reinforcement of compartmentalized frames through their chosen "tactics" (strategic action = means–end), and chosen words. Overall, participants in the study sought referent (task-related) information 58.16% of the time, and employed overt (direct questioning) tactics 85.2% of the time when seeking information via email. These majorities suggest that the organization and its employees participate in frames that both regard and utilize email as simply a means to an end—a tool to accomplish work goals (tool frame). When the writing of the email itself becomes a primary activity of the business—in an information economy, a product of the business, rather than simply the conduct of business—email becomes both the means and the end. The writers/readers of such email find themselves situated in a frame of technical relations where in a sense they become a conduit of the business of email.

In the pilot study, referent information was sought more often than appraisal, normative, or social information. The results thus suggest that employees sought information to accomplish work-related objectives, and used email as a professional tool. The preference of overt tactics over indirect, third-party, and testing tactics, implies that these employees viewed email primarily as a dedicated organizational channel for asking questions and gathering information. Employees' deliberate use of email for work-related goals also indicated that the organization's culture maintains the view of digital communication as a work tool. However, even at this nonprofit, email is not only a means, but also an end, as evidenced by policies within the organization outlining guidelines and restrictions for the use of email, such as tagging messages that are not directly related to organizational objectives.[8]

Many employers today continue to perpetuate compartmentalized ethical frames that capture only a part of our technological being. Probably the most prevalent of these is the tool frame, classifying humans and machines and their interaction as tools for accomplishing work goals. The view of technology as separate from human, and email as a means to achieve technological ends, reiterates the framing of technology not only as a tool, but also as a means–end. These ethical frames, accepted and supported within the organization in Rhodes' pilot study, as in the professional realm at large, may not be sufficient to account for, describe, or support the rich (and seemingly ethically relative) content of communicative values and emotions in the nonprofit, or in the wider world of work. URT certainly helps shed light on the complexity of workplace communication, but illuminates only specific frames, and thus only a portion of the experience of the technical relations involved.

Email as Values and Thought

Taking into account the perspective that emails are also extensions of self, Rhodes (2008) added a rhetorical analysis to supplement URT's framing. This part of the pilot study sought to address the complexity of digital communication by assessing words according to denotative meaning, connotative meaning, and modality, in an attempt to portray a more holistic picture of email in the professional environment and of the people existing within it. Email is one of technology's adaptations of written texts, and therefore (contrary to Plato's view that technology and writing are false forms of communication) reflects thought and emotion like traditional texts; but as with conventional written texts, the "primary acts of email are reading and writing, which limit the transmission of meaning to the limits of these particular processes" (Pratt, 1996). As people interact with each other and select particular words that convey thoughts, they reveal the nature of their relationships and attitudes, though limited by the medium. Differences in language choice and the implications of such choices suggest how people engage one another and how they exist within their ethical frames of digital relations.

Email, which exists both as tool and as technological expression, both as means and as end, is also its own source of values as an ideology. As Habermas (1970) might suggest, and Moses and Katz (2006) demonstrate, when the values of the company become the values generated by or inherent in email, writers and readers find themselves situated in the autonomous frame. As Moses and Katz suggest in their research on email, communication via email does indeed conform to the values of a rational-purposive rather than the traditional institutional framework. (Modifications and parodies of standard spelling, the proliferation of new abbreviations, or the use of emoticons are all in large measure the result of electronic communication; instant messaging and text-messaging as well as email, are just the surface evidence of this change). Not only is the line between work and play erased in email, but the play itself is technologically expressed, made possible and occurs via an electronic medium with its own ideology and rules that have little to do with personal expression and much to do with technology and profit. In the pilot study, a rhetorical categorization of the diction in emails by grammatical parts of speech revealed employees' stances, attitudes, actions, patterns, and values as portrayed through such language. For example, a survey of nouns used in the employees' email correspondence included words like appointments, approval, deadline, department, email, expenses, information, items, outcome, and schedules, which again indicated that in the organization, email is used primarily, and arguably only, for work-related tasks.

Modern organizations perpetuate the autonomous frame by valuing email that is strictly and artificially restricted to work content only, whereby email becomes a system of communication based solely on strategic means–end relations embedded in technologies that engulf the entire organization. Within the context of an organization—or perhaps more accurately, as the context of the organization—email thus becomes a technological source of social values as well, at least as these pertain to communication, but also and often spilling out into other facets affecting the way people relate and do business. In this way, email not only shapes expectations and norms of behavior, but becomes those expectations and norms. (Imagine hiring an employee who did not know how—or refused—to use email as a part of the job!)

The distinction between the autonomous frame and the thought frame is the focus on autonomous values versus technological modes of thinking. Thus, in the autonomous frame, the company assumes the values of the technology, in this case email, but does not necessarily adopt them as "mental constructs," but in the thought frame, technology dictates not only the organization's philosophies, but also the way employers and employees think. That is, the rational modes of thought underlying email technology become those of the organization and everyone in it. URT theory used in

Rhodes' study reveals, and itself illustrates in its principles and methods, the thought frame operating through the tool, means–end, and autonomous frames. The assumption that email is a communication "channel" for rationally seeking information and performing the work of technology (tool and end) that can and should be regulated and studied as a system closed to other values (autonomous frame), demonstrates the thought frame operating in the nonprofit that is fulfilled by both the organization and its employees. Additionally, the rational values, derived from technology and its use, have become so integrated into the mental constructs of those parties that even the concept of "information" and the "tactics" for seeking it are innately part of how we participate in and describe our relationships, and thus our communication theory; purposively, rationally, we have stepped into the thought frame.

Email as a Way of Being

Other findings from the rhetorical analysis indicated a different ethical frame than the tool frame or means–ends frame (as identified by the URT analysis), or than the autonomous frame or thought frame (revealed by the rhetorical analysis of parts of speech). Analysis of the modality of the words, based on an adaptation of Latour and Woolgar's (1986) statement types, revealed employee priorities and levels of uncertainty—that is, their emotional states—that more fully reflect their states of being. For example, during the Executive Director's leave (the last two months of the data collection time period), employees' emails showed a 2.3% increase in their level of uncertainty, and a 3.0% decrease in their level of certainty, both of which were reflected in the modality of the adverbs. These shifts suggest an increase in expression of uncertainty during periods of organizational change, constituting emotional self-expression rather than neutral message transmission (tool frame), a fulfillment of organizational work goals (means–end frame), technological values and norms (autonomous frame), or wholly rational modes of thought (the thought frame).

Another finding that uncovers a fuller ethical relationship in the nonprofit, and seems to imply the being frame, is the contrast between how newcomers and incumbent employees seek information. Unlike Morrison's (2002) research that contends that neophytes seek referent and evaluative information from supervisors, but relational and normative information from peers, Rhodes' data supports the claim that veteran employees seek relational and normative information from supervisors, but referent and evaluative information from peers. Rhodes' findings suggest that email is also a tool for affirming relationships. Perhaps like electronic match-making services or social networks, as a primary media resource in a technological system, email and the employees who use it to express emotion, foster personal relationships, or satisfy other needs and purposes become "standing reserve," in a rationally prescribed system (the way they seek, express, foster, or satisfy are ordered by the requirements of the technology).

Looking at emails, and indeed all digital communication according to compartmentalized frames via URT or rhetorical methods, enhances the breadth of understanding of digital technology. A compilation of ethical frames allows us to discover facets of communication that are ignored when only one frame is used, or when frames are used independently of each other. For example, URT theory assumes and confirms that uncertainty exists, but not specifically why or to what extent. Uncertainty Reduction Theory alone is insufficient to grasp the complexity of human–machine relations, because as the term "reduction" implies, it is based on a somewhat instrumental view of humans in relation to technology, and emotion as a standing reserve. If emails are people expressed digitally, then rhetorical analysis helps satisfy another gap that remains from the solitary use of approaches that are based in the tool, means–end, and autonomous frames. In the pilot study, URT principles address issues in these three ethical frames of technical relations, but only when these ethical frames, inherent in URT theory itself, are made opaque by rhetorical analysis. And while the rhetorical analysis aims to capture the nuances in email communication that reveal the ethical frames of technological relations as modes of thought and being, their value is perhaps most useful when seen in the context of ethical frames revealed by URT. In other words, URT helps to scientifically frame technical relations, while rhetorical analysis focuses on the values and emotions of individual speakers and audiences within digital media as part of the rhetorical situation.

To resolve our ethical blind spots and understand the nature of technical relations more fully, we need to be able to see simultaneously all the ethical frames, how they operate, and how they interact. The complexity of digital communication cannot be adequately described or evaluated with isolated ethical frames; however, all of them taken together may begin to provide a more accurate representation and analysis of digital being in a technological age.

Digital Being in the Workplace World

In the being frame, people, machines, and nature are components of the "standing-reserve," each with access to this reserve via a rationally prescribed order to achieve a technological end. As we and our organizations are swept up in the flickering bustle of digital existence, we forget that technical relations encompass each and all of the ethical frames of technology (tool, means–end, autonomous, thought, and being). Acknowledging compartmentalized frames is a necessary place to start, but we need to be able to appropriately apply these frames to technological situations. Because the frames are diachronic, synchronic, and overlap, they can be applied in tandem to reveal different relationships, that is, different dimensions of technological being that might coexist, but that differ in their significance according to context, audience, and purpose. In your own analysis of your company's consideration of certain ethical frames, it is crucial that all the ethical frames remain active in the background. and that we remain conscious of them, so that employers and employees are able to see them all at once, and apply them as needed. We will now explore why this is important.

Traditionally, organizations at best use only a few, compartmentalized frames, which limits their ethical view of the digital environment. Although individual frames are useful for gaining a focused perspective, given the far-reaching and instantaneous nature of digital communication, each frame and all frames should be evaluated, and reevaluated, regularly and together, to determine which technical relation is active or dominant, and if it is still the most "useful" or "appropriate" for the situation or audience. Digital communication in the organization studied by Rhodes seems to operate within the being frame, using compartmentalized frames for specific purposes while acknowledging the whole. For instance, in light of the organization's varied audiences, and in accordance with the better tenets of political correctness, certain terms for those with developmental challenges, like "disabled people", are considered to be a detrimental form of labeling. However, while this ethical and political position is realized and substantiated by those within the organization, such terms are consciously used in internal communication (conversation, email). In this example, technological values (efficiency, expediency) are placed above social norms (tact, political correctness) in internal correspondence, but the reverse is true for external communication. The organization is able to apply the ethical frame that is most appropriate for the situation because it is aware of all of them: in internal communication, technology is autonomous, but in external communication, it is a tool (whereby the individuals remain free of the label that would turn them into merely an end). To stay *technologically* correct and market relevant, the organization must maintain a perspective that considers all of the compartmentalized ethical frames and keeps them active, even when only one is applied at a time. In this example, failure to keep all the frames active could result in internal language that violates social codes being used inappropriately in external communication, creating a severe public relations crisis. On the other hand, using the elongated, external language for internal communication violates "technical rules" of the organization.[9]

The ethical frames of technical relations seem to be adjusted according to audience and purpose, which continually change. This is more than audience adaptation, but perhaps less than heresy: it is an actual shifting of ethical frames based on technical relations. If these frames are relative at the cultural level, it appears that technical relations in the work world extend to the local organizational and even personal level as well. The multiplicity of ethical frames is necessary for companies to succeed in a digital environment— necessary not because it is "right," or because these ethical frames enable them to achieve different organizational goals, important as these may be. In our time, an organization's relevance, and indeed survival, may depend on its ability to consider all ethical frames actively in context, and to flexibly shift between them to create or adapt to different technical relations.

Human–Machine Sanctity

Should all relations be technical? While the ethical frame of technical relations as a mode of being currently allows the most holistic perspective, the application of it in the professional realm automatically reframes being into technical compartments that ultimately have their origins in tool and means–end relations. Certainly, ethical frames of technical relations should not obviate moral codes to the detriment of human beings. That they sometimes (often?) do point to the need for a new ethical frame, one that could benefit both business and humanity. Because in a digital environment we are merging with our machines, we need an ethical frame based not on means-ends relations, as are all the others we have discussed. We need a larger ethical frame, one that encompasses each of the compartmentalized frames (tool, means–ends, autonomous, thought, and being) as well as the relationships and interactions among them, but that also goes outside and beyond technical relations to characterize our digital existence.

We now reveal the sixth ethical frame (see Figure 9.3).

Buber (1970) may help us to understand the emerging configuration of human and machine, and perhaps suggest an alternate, ethical frame of

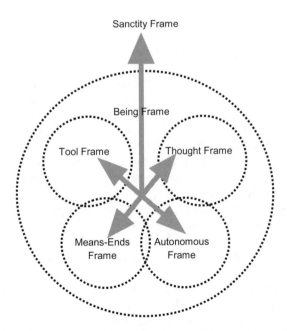

Figure 9.3 Moving beyond digital being: human–machine sanctity

relation. For Buber, the most basic and sacred relationship is the "I–Thou" relation that is based not on means–end, or strategic action, which for Buber is the "I-It" relation. On the contrary, the "I–Thou" relation is a configuration based on reciprocity and mutual respect. Perhaps it is time to begin to reveal the machine as a "You," an entity with whom "We" might develop a relationship that moves beyond means–end in all its ethical manifestations (all the frames we have discussed) toward an ethical frame of sanctity based on reciprocal relations. In this frame, both humans and technology (often merged) would no longer be an "It," a "thing" completely objectified, a means to end, and thus rendered as a standing-reserve. Rather, outside technical consciousness, an "It" might become a "You," a subject that is intimately related to "I." Contrary to Heidegger's Enframing that reveals encounter as standing-reserve, for Buber (1970), "All life is actual encounter" because all things are defined in a mutual relation that is whole (p. 62).

If we are ever able to push through technical consciousness to one of reciprocity, we may arrive at this new and as yet not clearly defined ethical frame. This sanctity frame represents an alternative to technical being even in a digital age; it is a *non*-technical frame that offers us another relationship with technology (and with each other), one that is not based on means–end, but instead on mutual respect. As Buber knew, this kind of non-technical relation is an ideal (even the notion of sanctity as a frame is a limitation we may never be able to escape). And yet, as we will discuss, it is realizable at least in part, and immediately benefits the business world.

Implications of Sanctity in the Workplace

Several ethical implications for technology and digital communication emerge from our study. One example in the modern workplace is that organizations rely on but impose restrictions, either explicitly or implicitly, on the use of email. In the interest of efficient operations, organizations outline expectations and guidelines for email communication aimed at limiting the level of an employee's personal expression. Professionals are expected to disassociate themselves from communication in order to convey only task-based, "neutral" messages. But is this truly possible? Is this a fair ethical standard? Is this separation of person and machine the only feasible way to get things done in the work world? Are people, machines, and nature just standing-reserve, each with access to this reserve prescribed by a rational order to achieve a strategic end? The ethical frames of technical relations we have discussed in this essay would lead us to think so.

The sanctity frame, however, recognizes the relationship between personal and professional being because it recognizes the new relationship between humans and machines as whole entities. Neither is just an object, a resource, or a standing reserve, just a means to an end at different levels of technical relations. The compartmentalized ethical frames of technical relations that we have been describing damage the whole by targeting and using portions—of humans, machines, or nature—and turning those portions into standing-reserve by disregarding the rest of its being. (As a mode of being, technical frames objectify the entire being, as well as nature, consciousness, and machine.) But human-machine sanctity would address the same entities with reciprocity, where nothing would be simply targeted, objectified, reduced to a mere resource, used. Because human–machine sanctity, ideally, would be based on non-technical relations—not on means–end, but on reverence and caring for the whole—it would directly improve relations within your organization: between employer and employee (each held in mutual respect), between employee and machine (in the treatment of equipment), between company and clients (as equal partners in "customer relations"), and between company and nature (in the conservation of energy and search for "renewable resources"). By its very nature, human–machine sanctity might achieve the same goals as ethical frames of technical relations in the digital workplace, and yet improve both means and ends by extending beyond them. In other words, through a consideration of the whole and reciprocity of its parts, the values of the ethical frames, such as means, ease, efficiency, speed, productivity, profits as well as the thought, and being frames themselves, might be achieved and transcended.

A workplace example that perhaps comes closest to arriving at the ideal of the sanctity frame in digital communication is found in cause-related marketing (CRM). CRM is the "public association of a for-profit company with a nonprofit organization, intended to promote the company's product or service and to raise money for the nonprofit" (Foundation Center, 2009). What is important to note here is that there is not simply one "end" (say, selling products), but multiple ends, and not all of them *relations* technical (e.g., cancer research, human health, the betterment of society, the greater human good). With CRM, the for-profit company not only attracts clients and increases its profits through sales; the nonprofit also expands its donor base and receives funding to support its mission. (Many safeguards are in place to guard against the inauthentic use of CRM.) Several studies show that "consumers carefully consider a company's reputation when making purchasing decisions and that a company's community involvement boosts employee morale and loyalty" (Foundation Center, 2009). If this is the case, the cooperative relationship embodied in CRM might extend to other aspects of the organizations involved, such as employee relations, machine maintenance, cultural awareness, and environmental responsibility.

What are the different relationships between humans and machines created in your company, and what ethical frames are they based on? Are the frames all means-end relations—that is, frames that we hope we have demonstrated, if viewed in isolation, are no longer completely helpful to the ethics of digital communication technologies, and the conditions they create in the workplace today? How do these frames affect your organization, your employees, your customers? Are the ethical frames beginning to reveal a new relationship evolving between humans and digital technology that cannot

Table 9.2 An ethical audit: heuristic for evaluating relations in your organization

Ethical Frames	Effects on Employees	Effects on Managers	Effects on Company	Effects on Clients	Effects on Machines	Effects on Nature	Possible Resolution
False Frame							
Tool Frame							
Means-End Frame							
Autonomous Frame							
Thought Frame							
Being Frame							
Sanctity Frame							

be fully encapsulated in any or all of these technical relations? To help you conduct an "ethical audit" within your organization, we include a heuristic for evaluating the ethical frames at work in your organization, and their effects on various stakeholders (see Table 9.2)

Technology and digital communication, like email, are more than means for achieving goals, and organizations must both understand reach beyond technical relations in digital environments.

Ideally, with improved staff spirits and strengthened commitment to the company, in the sanctity frame, employees who are treated as whole human beings will in turn consider the organization's best interest along with their own, resulting in actions like taking better care of equipment, being frugal with company materials, and treating coworkers with respect. The overall condition of the employees as well as the organization, and subsequently society at large, could be enriched. Failure to acknowledge and address the expanding dimensions of our technological being and the associated ethical dynamics and implications does not negate their existence, but instead may leave crucial aspects of workplace communication unrecognized. The result might be organizations that are unprepared and ill-equipped to succeed in a world in which, beyond ethical frames of technical relations, humans, machines, and nature are increasingly coming to be seen as wholly interrelated, integrated, and interdependent.

Acknowledgments

We would like to thank Dr. Teresa Fishman, Director of Academic Integrity at Clemson University, for her discussions in the initial stages of this project. We'd also like to express our gratitude to Doctors Sean Williams (English) and Daryl Wiesman (Communication Studies) at Clemson University for their invaluable guidance and assistance with the pilot study upon which a part of this essay is based.

Notes

1 The zero here is not an error. Because Plato considered technology to be neither a reliable means nor a true end, this first position of technology as a *faux* frame is really a non-frame; hence our numbering of it as zero, which perfectly describes its place in the chronological sequence. We know that zero is not commonly used in numbering, but suggest that its use here is not only justified but also suggestive and even liberating.

2 Although our approaches and especially our conclusions are quite different from Stiegler's (1998), our definitions and exploration of ethical frames are informed by his discussion of the history of technics in the early part of his book.

3 We use the captialized "Knowledge" to denote Plato's belief in absolute "Truth".

4 Aristotle (1984a) calls ethical reasoning about the end *phronesis*, prudence (*Nicomachean Ethics*).

5 As Habermas (1970) explains, "traditional institutional frameworks" are those social structures in which traditional political, ethical, and religious values, be they

monarchical or democratic, fascist or communistic, reign; within the traditional institutional framework, the technical-economic values at work in the society form the "purposive-rational subsystem." The decisive period comes when the society, based on the development of science and technology, industrializes to the point where the purposive-rational subsystem of technical-economic values supplants traditional values and becomes the institutional framework; in a society governed by the purposive-rational system, the traditional institutional framework becomes the repressed or exotic subsystem (for a diagram of this transformational relation, see Moses and Katz, 2006).

6 Per agreement with the company, the actual identity of the organization as well as the participants studied with IRB approval must be kept confidential.

7 Because of the small sample size in this pilot study, results are not necessarily statistically significant, but rather are treated as indicators.

8 In this nonprofit organization, a specific if unstated rule mandates that any correspondence sent within the workplace that is not directly related to organizational (read email) goals must, in the subject line, at the beginning, in all caps, followed by a colon, before the descriptive subject line, include "EXTRA:" so that employees receiving the message may efficiently elect to delete it or set a filter on their email system that automatically discards such correspondence. These rules do allow non-work emails in this nonprofit, but only within restricted parameters, and a violation of these rules may result in a reprimand. However, the emphasis on efficiency of sorting emails also indicates the operation of a technical rule in purposive-rational systems, as noted by Habermas (1970)—that the ultimate repercussion of a failure to follow the rule is not "punishment," but rather of "inefficacy" or "failure in reality" (p. 93). We explore email in the autonomous and thought frames in the next section.

9 The operation in language of technical rules similar to those described by Habermas (1970) were studied by Marcuse (1964). Katz uses the example of the semantic differences between "poverty level families," where families are identified or fused with their economic level, vs. "families at poverty level," where through the simple preposition "at," the families as entities are allowed to retain something of an existence independent of an economic report or chart. In the nonprofit organization we study, even "people with disabilities" is preferred over "disabled people." The point in this chapter is that, understood in different ethical frames, there will be times when the former is not only preferred but also more correct by any number of technical standards, depending on the ethical frame. Indeed, ethical principles themselves, such as expediency, can be understood, for better or worse, to operate in similar ways (see Katz 1992, 1993). The relativity of ethics makes the study of ethical frames that much more important.

References

Aristotle. (1984a). *Nicomachean ethics* (W. D. Ross; rev. J. O. Urmson, Trans.). In J. Barnes (Ed), *The complete works of Aristotle* (Vol. 2) (pp. 1729–1867). Princeton, NJ: Princeton University Press.

——. (1984b). *Rhetoric*. (W. R. Roberts, Trans.). In J. Barnes (Ed), *The complete works of Aristotle* (Vol. 2) (pp. 2153–2269). Princeton, NJ: Princeton University Press.

Barrett, W. (1978). *The illusion of technique: The search for meaning in a technological civilization*. New York: Anchor Books.

Baudrillard, J. (1994). *Simulacra and simulation* (S. Faria Glaser, Trans.). Ann Arbor, MI: University of Michigan Press.

Benthien, C. (2002). *Skin: On the cultural border between self and the world*. New York: Columbia University Press.

Berger, C. R., & Calabrese, R. J. (1975). Some explorations in initial interaction and beyond: Toward a developmental theory of interpersonal communication. *Human Communication Research, 1*, 99–112.

Bolter, J. D., & Gromala, D. (2003). *Windows and mirrors: Interaction design, digital art, and the myth of transparency*. Cambridge, MA: MIT Press.

Boyle, M. P., Schmierbach, M., Armstrong, C. L., McLeod, D. M., Shah, D. V., & Pan, Z. (2004). Information seeking and emotional reactions to the September 11 terrorist attacks. *Journalism & Mass Communication Quarterly, 81*(1), 155–167.

Buber, M. (1970). *I and thou* (W. Kaufman, Trans.). New York: Scribner's.

Cartwright, L. (1995). *Screening the body: Tracing medicine's visual culture*. Minneapolis, MN: University of Minnesota Press.

Debord, G. (1990). *Comments on the society of the spectacle* (M. Imrie, Trans.). London: Verso.

——. (1994). *The society of the spectacle* (D. Nicholson-Smith, Trans.). New York: Zone Books.

De Kerckhove, D. (1995). *The skin of culture: Investigating the new electronic reality* (C. Dewdney, Ed.). Toronto: Summerville House Publishing.

Dewett, T., & Jones, G. R. (2001). The role of information technology in the organization: A review, model, and assessment. *Journal of Management, 27*(3), 313–346.

Dombrowski, P. (2000). *Ethics in technical communication*. Boston, MA: Allyn & Bacon.

Ellul, J. (1964). *The technological society* (J. Wilkinson, Trans.). New York: Knopf.

Foundation Center (2009). What is cause-related marketing? Retrieved April 3, 2009 from: http://foundationcenter.org/getstarted/faqs/html/cause_marketing.html.

Habermas, J. (1970). Technology and science as "ideology" (J. Shapiro, Trans.). *Toward a rational society: Student protest, science, and politics*. Boston, MA: Beacon Press.

Hayles, N. K. (1999). *How we became post-modern: Virtual bodies in cybernetics, literature, and informatics*. Chicago, IL: University of Chicago Press.

Heidegger, M. (1977). *The question concerning technology and other essays* (W. Lovitt, Trans.). New York: Harper and Row.

Katz, S. B. (1992). The ethic of expediency: Classical rhetoric, technology, and the Holocaust. *College English, 54*, 255–275.

——. (1993). Aristotle's rhetoric, Hitler's program, and the ideological problem of praxis, power, and professional discourse. *Journal of Business and Technical Communication, 7*, 37–62.

——. (2008). Biotechnology and global miscommunication with the public: Rhetorical assumptions, stylistic acts, ethical implications. In H. Grady & G. Hayhoe (Eds.), *Connecting people with technology: Issues in professional communication* (pp. 167–175). Amityville, NY: Baywood Publications..

Katz, S. B., & Miller, C. R. (1996). The low-level radioactive waste siting controversy in North Carolina: Toward a rhetorical model of risk communication. In C. Herndl & S. Brown (Eds.), *Green culture: Environmental rhetoric in contemporary America* (pp. 111–140). Madison, WI: University of Wisconsin Press.

Latour, B., & Woolgar, S. (1986). Statement types. *Laboratory life: The social construction of scientific facts*. Princeton, NJ: Princeton University Press.

Lury, C. (1998). *Prosthetic culture: Photography, memory, and identity.* New York: Routledge Publishing.

Marcuse, H. (1964). *One-dimensional man: Studies in the ideology of advanced industrial society.* Boston, MA: Beacon Press.

Mebust, M., & Katz, S. B. (2008). Rhetorical assumptions, rhetorical risks: Communication models in genetic counseling. In B. Heifferon & S. Brown (Eds.), *Rhetoric of healthcare: Essays toward a new disciplinary inquiry* (pp. 91–114). Cresskill, NJ: Hampton Press.

Miller, V. D. (1996). An experimental study of newcomers' information seeking behaviors during organizational entry. *Communication Studies, 47,* 1–24.

Miller, V. D., & Jablin, F. M. (1991). Information seeking during organizational entry: Influences, tactics, and a model of the process. *Academy of Management Review, 16,* 92–120.

Morrison, E. W. (2002). Information seeking within organizations. *Human Communication Research, 28*(2), 229–242.

Moses, M. G., & Katz, S. B. (2006). The invisible ideology of email (a cultural critique). In J. B. Scott, B. Longo, & K. V. Wills (Eds.), *Critical power tools: Technical communication and cultural studies* (pp. 71–105). Albany, NY: State University of New York Press.

Negroponte, N. (1995). *On being digital.* New York: Vintage Books.

Nissenbaum, H., & Price, M. (Eds.) (2004). *Academy and the internet.* New York: Peter Lang Publishing.

Plato (1956). *Phaedrus* (W. C. Helmbold & W. G. Rabinowitz, Trans.). Indianapolis, IN: Bobbs-Merrill.

Pratt, L. (1996). Impression management in organization email communication. Retrieved March 10, 2008 from: http://www.public.asu.edu/~corman/scaorgcomm/pratt.htm.

Pratt, L., Wiseman, R. L., Cody, M. J., & Wendt, P. F. (1999). Interrogative strategies and information exchange in computer-mediated communication. *Communication Quarterly, 47*(1), 46–66.

Rhodes, V. (2008). Temporary organizational change and uncertainty: Applying Uncertainty Reduction Theory and style analyses to email. Unpublished master's thesis. Clemson University.

Smith, M., & Morra, J. (Eds.) (2006). *The prosthetic impulse: From a posthuman present to a biocultural future.* Cambridge, MA: MIT Press.

Stiegler, B. (1998). *Technics and time, I: The fault of Epimetheus* (R. Bearsworth & G. Collins, Trans.). Stanford, CA: Stanford University Press.

Thompson, C. (2006). A head for detail. *Fast Company, 110,* 73–112.

Wellman, B., & Haythornthwaite, C. (Eds.) (2002). *The internet in everyday life.* Malden, MA: Blackwell Publishers Ltd.

Winner, L. (1999). Do artifacts have politics? In D. McKenzie & J. Wacjman (Eds.), *The social shaping of technology* (2nd ed.) (pp. 28–40). London: Open University Press.

Editor and Contributor Biographies

Ann M. Blakeslee is Professor of English and Director of Writing Across the Curriculum at Eastern Michigan University. She has authored two books: *Interacting with Audiences: Social Influences on the Production of Scientific Writing* (Erlbaum, 2001) and with Cathy Fleischer, *Becoming a Writing Researcher* (Erlbaum, 2007). Ann guest edited a special issue of the *Journal of Business and Technical Communication* (July 2007) on writing in the disciplines and she has published on writing in the workplace, research methods, audience, and genre. In 2001, she received the Nell Ann Picket Award for her *Technical Communication Quarterly* article addressing classroom–workplace collaborations. Ann has served on numerous committees for the Association of Teachers of Technical Writing (ATTW), the Society for Technical Communication (STC), the National Council of Teachers of English (NCTE), and the Council for Programs in Technical and Scientific Communication (CPTSC). Before pursuing a career in academia, Ann worked for several years in business-to-business advertising and, since then, she has continued her relationship with industry as a consultant.

Saul Carliner is Associate Professor with the Graduate Program in Educational Technology at Concordia University in Montreal, Quebec. His research focuses on emerging forms of online content for communication and training in the workplace and the management of groups responsible for workplace communication and training. Other research interests include the transfer of research and theory to practice, the design of informal learning, and the training of community leaders. Saul has received research funding from the Social Sciences and Humanities Research Council of Canada, Canadian Council on Learning, Hong Kong University Grants Council, and the Society for Technical Communication (STC). He began his career as a junior technical writer with IBM, and continues to consult in industry, primarily by providing strategic planning services to communications, training, and nonprofit groups. He has authored seven books and numerous articles in peer-reviewed journals and professional magazines. Among them, "Modeling Information for Three-Dimensional Space: Lessons Learned from Museum Exhibit Design" and "Physical,

Cognitive, and Affective: A Three-Part Framework for Information Design" received the 2001 and 2000 Best of Show Awards respectively in the Frank R. Smith Outstanding Article competition. In addition, Saul is a certified training and development professional, a director of the Canadian Society for Training and Development, past research fellow of the American Society for Training and Development, and a fellow and past international president of STC.

Dave Clark is Associate Professor and Coordinator of the Professional Writing Program at the University of Wisconsin-Milwaukee. He is also Chair of the Association of Teachers of Technical Writing (ATTW) Research Committee. Dave's research and teaching focus is on the rhetoric of technology and management; knowledge management, information design, and single sourcing; the ethics of qualitative research; and community engagement. He is working now on a book project that bridges activity theory and the practice of information design in small organizations. Dave has worked in industry for six years as a technical writer, web consultant and developer, and writer/researcher; some Web sites he has designed and maintained have been for the Society for Technical Communication (STC), ATTW, and nonprofits in the Milwaukee area.

R. Stanley Dicks is Associate Professor and Director of the MS in Technical Communication Program and undergraduate minor in Scientific and Technical Communication at North Carolina State University. After starting in academia at Wheeling Jesuit University, he moved to industry, where he spent 17 years as Technical Communicator and Manager of technical communication groups at United Technologies, Burns & Roe, Bell Labs, and Bellcore. His book, *Management Principles and Practices for Technical Communicators* (Allyn & Bacon, 2004), reflects his interest in studying how current management trends affect the work of communicators. He has also published chapters that study interrelationships between industry and academia and the nature of work and of project management in current and future technical communication practice. Stanley has served on several conference committees for ACM SIGDOC, was Reprints Editor and Chief Editor for SIGDOC's *Journal of Computer Documentation*, and is Academic Liaison for the Carolina Chapter of the Society for Technical Communication (STC). While in industry, Stanley received three STC awards for outstanding documents as part of the New York Chapter competition.

William Hart-Davidson is Associate Professor in the Writing, Rhetoric, and American Cultures Department, Co-Director of the Writing in Digital Environments (WIDE) Research Center, and Assistant Director of the Digital Rhetoric & Professional Writing Masters Program at Michigan State University. In 1999–2000, Bill worked at IBM's Silicon Valley Laboratory in the Data Management User Technology division as part of IBM's Faculty Partners Program. Since then, his research interests have focused on intersections of technical communication and human–computer interaction in such areas as visualizing knowledge work processes, information, and user experience design. Through his current work at WIDE, Bill produces writing software that incorporates and extends the range of significance of research in technical and professional writing. Recently, Bill led the development of a suite of web-based writing tools collectively known as the Social Writing Application Platform (SWAP). SWAP is meant to be a foundation for any number of specific writing applications—large or small—that produce intelligible reports of writing activity while providing the basic types of writing functionality that people need.

Steven B. Katz is Roy Pearce Professor of Professional Communication at Clemson University, where he teaches in the MA in Professional Communication Program and the doctoral program in Rhetorics, Communication, and Information Design. He has worked at Rensselaer Polytechnic Institute as an editor for *Urban and Environmental Studies* as well as the Human Resources Office; as a communication consultant for Crop Life Canada and for Crop Life International; and as a researcher examining rhetorical styles and communication models used in biotechnology communication with the public. Steve is author of *The Epistemic Music of Rhetoric* (Southern Illinois University Press, 1996), and with Ann Penrose, *Writing in the Sciences: Exploring Conventions of Scientific Discourse*, 3rd edition (A. B. Longman, 2010). He has published widely on rhetoric and ethics in medical, environmental, and technical communication; the ideology of technology; and identity in cyberspace. He was awarded the Best Article on the Theory of Scientific or Technical Communication Award from the National Council of Teachers of English (NCTE) Committee on Scientific and Technical Communication and this work has been reprinted in *Central Works in Professional Communication* (Oxford University Press, 2004) and elsewhere.

Bernadette Longo is Associate Professor in the Department of Writing Studies at the University of Minnesota. She is author of *Spurious Coin: A History of Science, Management, and Technical Writing* (SUNY Press, 2000) and co-editor of *Critical Power Tools: Technical Communication and Cultural Studies* (SUNY Press, 2006), which won the 2007 Best Edited Collection award from the National Council of Teachers of English (NCTE) Committee on Scientific and Technical Communication. Bernadette has also been a practicing medical writer for thirty years. Her current research, in collaboration with a faculty member in the University of Minnesota Medical School, includes a design analysis of insulin protocols used in hospital critical care units. She is also exploring information design issues relating to mobile technologies and social networking, in collaboration with the founder of First Step Initiative, a nonprofit micro-finance organization working with women entrepreneurs in the Democratic Republic of Congo.

Vicki W. Rhodes is Associate Director of the Center for Developmental Services in Greenville, SC. She has also served as Tourism and Events Manager for the Clemson Area Chamber of Commerce, Director on the YWCA Junior Board, member of the Clemson Area Women in Business, and President and Treasurer of the Association for Women in Communications. Throughout her professional career, she has consulted several small businesses in public relations, marketing, and internal communications, including communication audits and corporate messaging plans. Vicki received a Master of Arts in Professional Communication degree with an emphasis in organizational communication from Clemson University. She was awarded the Society for Technical Communication (STC) Ernie Mazzatenta Scholarship, and has been inducted into numerous honors societies. Vicki plans to continue her research in organizational communication at the doctoral level while pursuing a career in teaching, aiming to help bridge the gap between professional and academic realms.

Paula Rosinski is Associate Professor of Professional Writing and Rhetoric in the Department of English at Elon University, where she also serves as the Writing Center Director. Her research interests include information and digital literacy, digital rhetoric, professional writing and rhetoric, writing program administration, and service-learning. In her work with service-learning, she pairs students with nonprofit educational organizations and small business clients to provide document and information design, Web site development and usability testing. She has published on the organizational and curricular design of professional writing and rhetoric programs and the intersections between human–computer interaction and writing pedagogy. Currently, she is researching the relationship between digital and traditional rhetorical theory.

Michael J. Salvo is Associate Professor in the Rhetoric and Composition Program at Purdue University. As Usability Consultant for Purdue's Online Writing Lab (OWL), Michael has been usability testing and revising OWL's navigation and taxonomy since 2003, and is currently developing user-participatory folksonomy for OWL's millions of users, users who are located in all 50 US states and 150 countries. He is a founding member of Kairos, the longest continuously publishing online journal in new media, rhetoric, and writing; he won the Hugh Burns Award in computers and writing; and with Thomas Rickert, was a recipient of the Ellen Nold Award for research published in *Computers and Composition* and the Kairos Best Webtext Award. Michael's research on usability, assessment, and information architecture has been published in *IEEE Transactions on Professional Communication, Journal of Business and Technical Communication, Kairos, Technical Communication,* and

Technical Communication Quarterly. He also served as 2007 Conference Chair for the Association of Teachers of Technical Writing (ATTW) annual conference.

Rachel Spilka is Associate Professor in the Professional Writing Program at the University of Wisconsin-Milwaukee. She is Editor of *Writing in the Workplace: New Research Perspectives* (Southern Illinois University Press, 1993) and with Barbara Mirel, Co-Editor of *Reshaping Technical Communication: New Directions for the 21st Century* (Erlbaum, 2003); both of these collections received the Best Edited Collection Award from the National Council of Teachers of English (NCTE) Committee on Scientific and Technical Communication. She also won the NCTE Award for Best Article on the Theory of Scientific or Technical Communication, based on her dissertation of engineers writing for multiple audiences in a Fortune 500 corporation. Rachel began her career as a medical writer and over the past thirty years, she has interspersed academic positions with work in industry, including a combined seven years as a technical writer and editor, Senior Information Design Specialist for the American Institutes for Research Information Design Center, and Communications Analyst at RAND Corporation. She has also served as manager of the Society for Technical Communication (STC) Research Grants Committee and Ken Rainey Excellence in Research Award Committee. Rachel's recent research focuses on the continued advancement of research in technical communication, renewed examination of audience, and lack of diversity in academic programs in technical communication.

Barry Thatcher is Associate Professor of rhetoric and professional communication at New Mexico State University. He is also an Adjunct Professor at several Mexican border universities. Barry has taught intercultural professional communication for more than seventeen years, including four years in Ecuador and ten years on the U.S.–Mexico border, and he has published extensively on intercultural professional communication in both English and Spanish. His research interests include intercultural professional communication, U.S.–Mexico border rhetoric, border health and environmental literacy, history of rhetoric in Latin America, second-language writing, and empirical research methods for intercultural contexts. Barry routinely consults with major organizations that deploy new technologies to Mexico and Latin America, including the EPA, US DOT, and private industry.

Author Index

Subject Index